Perth and Kinross

The Big County

D0806727

for Andrew and Connie Duncan

Perth and Kinross

The Big County

JEREMY DUNCAN

JOHN DONALD PUBLISHERS LTD
EDINBURGH

ISBN 0 85976 473 7

British Library Cataloguing in Publication Data.
A catalogue record for this book is available
from the British Library.

PostScript Typesetting & Origination by Brinnoven, Livingston.
Printed & bound in Great Britain by Bell & Bain Ltd, Glasgow.

CONTENTS

Acknowledgements   vii

Introduction   ix

1. Land of the Mountain...   1

2. ...and the Flood   24

3. 1559 And All That   34

4. Groves of Academe   53

5. The Perthshire Working Man   63

6. Perth: The Fairer City   79

7. Strathmore and the Carse of Gowrie   102

8. Strathearn   125

9. Kinross-shire   157

10. Central Perthshire: The Almond and the Braan   180

11. Central Perthshire: Dunkeld to Scone   204

12. Highland Perthshire   224

Select Bibliography   262

Index   267

ACKNOWLEDGEMENTS

This part of the book is the most pleasurable to write. Not only does it mean that the end of a long journey is in sight, but it also provides the opportunity to thank those people who have helped along the way. Among them are the many who have provided information either by letter or over the phone, those to whom I have chatted on my travels throughout Perth and Kinross (and who have perhaps unwittingly contributed to the book), and the true historians of the area, some long dead, whose original research in books and articles I have freely made use of, and to whom I am much indebted.

Thanks are due to various officials of Aberdeenshire Council, Perth and Kinross Council (and in particular the archive, local studies and reference staff of the A K Bell Library in Perth), Scottish Natural Heritage and the Scottish Office. Representatives of several other local and national organisations have also been most helpful.

For permission to take photographs on their property I am grateful to the Ardoch Farming Company, Blair Castle Estate Ltd, the Trustees of the Dupplin Trust, Historic Scotland, the National Trust for Scotland, David Leslie, Sir David Montgomery and the Earl of Mansfield. I am similarly grateful to Dr W H Findlay of Perth, who has kindly allowed me to use some of his high quality photographs, and to Perth and Kinross Libraries and W Davidson and Sons Ltd, who have made their photographic collections available to me.

I should also like to thank Katie Wood for allowing me to make use of a recent article on her favourite places, Stan Keay for uncovering the facts behind the building of the Kinnoull Hill tower, John MacNeill of the National Farmers Union, Robert Mowat of the Royal Commission on the Ancient and Historical Monuments of Scotland and Brendan Murphy for the long conversation about Locus Breadalbane.

Particular thanks are due to the following individuals, experts in their fields, who have read sections of the text and who have made a number of pertinent comments: Derek Hall, Richard Hunter, John Kerr, Patricia Kerr, Stuart McHardy, Adam Malcolm,

Mike Taylor and Nan Walker. It should go without saying, but I shall say it anyway, that the blame for any errors or omissions lies entirely with me.

Warmest thanks are due to my son Adam, for his companionable (and unusual) silence during many a long evening in the study, my daughter Genevieve, for her violin accompaniment from the room below, and my wife, Wendy, not just for her constant support and encouragement but for her sound advice, painstaking proof-reading and incisive use of the blue pencil.

Finally, without my parents, who forsook the ancient, learned and beautiful cities of St Andrews, Edinburgh and Oxford to settle in Perth, the following chapters could not have been written. To them, with love and filial gratitude, this book is dedicated.

J.D.

INTRODUCTION

Katie Wood, television presenter and travel correspondent for a number of newspapers and magazines, has established herself over recent years as Scotland's best known travel expert. When asked to list her personal favourite places in a recent issue of *Scottish Field* she reeled off the not-unexpected holiday destinations of Jamaica, Bermuda and Tuscany, amongst others, and then dropped in Perthshire. This may well have been a surprise to most of her readers and, to be honest, probably to most Perthshire folk as well. But Katie is a widely experienced world traveller and should she should think fit to include Perthshire in the same league as the Caribbean few would be advised to take issue with her.

The weather, of course, is not tropical, the mountains not exactly Himalayan and town life not the Mediterranean carnival of colour, noise and smells which assails the senses. Rather Perthshire, with Kinross-shire, if lacking in superlatives, has a whole range of attractions which in combination can rival anything in the world; take, for example, the contrasting proximity of the breeze-blown heather-clad mountains with the green and leafy tranquillity of the Lowlands; the invigorating freshness of pine-scented woodlands and mountain air; the unspoiled country towns and sometimes sleepy villages; the serenity of the great lochs and the individual character of the many rivers and burns; the flowers, gardens, trees and forests; the castles, stately homes and the attractive vernacular architecture of town and country; mix all these ingredients with a long, fascinating and very visible history, with the arts, folklore and local legend and you have, as the Perthshire Tourist Board rightly says, 'all of Scotland'. All, that is, apart from the less attractive townscapes of the industrialised west for it is true to say that virtually nowhere in Perth and Kinross is there a view which is less than pleasing to the eye. And that, all things considered, is quite a claim.

This book is intended to be of interest and help to residents and visitors alike. It is not, therefore, a simple what-to-see tourist guide although many of the main sights are listed. Neither is it a straightforward history of the area although most of the main historical events are mentioned. I think of it more as a painting of Perth and Kinross in which the myriad splashes of colour, seemingly unconnected, suddenly dissolve into a wholeness which is only seen when the work is finished.

The first five chapters are general in scope, looking at the physical basis of the area, as well as its history and the lives of the inhabitants. The remaining seven look more closely at the component parts of Perth and Kinross, generally taking the form of an armchair tour along the more attractive minor roads, though anyone using this as a car guide would be advised to take a road map as well.

The scope of the book is the present Perth and Kinross Council area. This comprises the whole of the former counties of Perth and Kinross, apart from the large western section of Perthshire which since 1975 has been administered from Stirling. Because of the attendant difficulties of nomenclature and for the sake of convenience and simplicity, I refer to the Perthshire part of the Perth and Kinross Council area as Perthshire. Kinross and its old county have a full chapter of their own, while 'Perth and Kinross' refers to the new council area as a whole. Furthermore, to avoid this jarring phrase 'council area', which the Scottish Office has told me is the correct designation, I use instead the good old-fashioned word 'county'.

Finally that wonderfully named nineteenth century travel writer, the Reverend Chauncey Hare Townshend, drew attention, in his *Descriptive tour in Scotland*, to the dangers of purple prose. To quote him, 'the worst of these grandiose descriptions is that no one after reading them can recognise the objects from which they were drawn'. I have doubtless in places fallen into a similar trap though I have tried to be honest and fair in my opinions and descriptions. If, on the other hand, I have perhaps been too honest then I can only apologise for any offence caused and say that none was ever intended.

CHAPTER 1

LAND OF THE MOUNTAIN...

That venerable newspaper, the *Perthshire Advertiser*, has for many years referred to Perthshire as the Big County. An appropriate enough description judging by any map, yet to infer from this that it is the largest would be wrong. Out of Scotland's 33 counties which existed prior to the reorganisation of local government in the mid-1970s Perthshire, with over 1.5 million acres, occupied only fourth place behind Inverness-shire, Ross and Cromarty, and Argyll. And with a population in 1971 (the last year in which a census of the whole of the former county was taken) of almost 127,000 it is even further down the rankings, in tenth place, behind such counties as Stirlingshire and Fife, both with a fraction of the acreage.

In 1975, after eight centuries of existence, Perthshire became the victim of the political axeman and ceased to function as an administrative unit, surviving only, thanks to the Post Office, as a 'correct postal address'. The old regime of county and town councils, with seemingly little regard for historic institutions, was replaced by those of region and district. A large chunk of south-western Perthshire, including the Trossachs and the towns and villages of Dunblane, Callander, Doune, Aberfoyle, Lochearnhead, Killin, Tyndrum and Crianlarich, was transferred to the new Stirling District, part of Central Region, while the remaining part of Perthshire was linked with Kinross-shire to form Perth and Kinross District, one of the three component parts of Tayside Region. Districts and regions were themselves swept away on their 21st birthday, in 1996, by the new unitary authorities. Perth and Kinross, apart from the small additions of Longforgan and Invergowrie, survived the 1996 reforms almost intact and while these local government changes were not universally welcomed the new council area is at least wholly administered once again from Perth and no longer partially from the rival city of Dundee.

Since reorganisation the population of Perth and Kinross has expanded rapidly, increasing from around 117,000 in 1981 to an estimated total of almost 133,000 in 1995. This is partly due to the area having one of the highest rates of inward migration in Scotland with a large number coming from south of the border. It is also popular with the elderly, having a proportion of retired people which again is well above the Scottish average. This rate of population growth is not only causing problems for the council planners but also for some of the existing residents of Perthshire who are threatened with having 'new villages' built in the middle of their rural communities.

Perthshire, if no longer the Big County in terms of physical size, has nevertheless a big presence, dominating the northern part of central Scotland and requiring almost every visitor to the north to pass across its borders. Culturally strong and economically secure, it has a magnetism of its own which attracts both people and business away from the polarised conurbations of Edinburgh and Glasgow. And with an historical background almost second to none, the county has a heritage to rival any in the country.

But these are just bald facts and broad statements: to understand fully the drama of Perthshire's history and the pageant of its present-day life we must first take a closer look at the stage upon which they are played. For while the landscape may be a picturesque backdrop, it is the underlying geology and geography of the county which has shaped its history and which even today, to a significant degree, colours the attitudes and way of life of the inhabitants. The two most important land features are the Highland-Lowland divide which in population and cultural terms is a north-west south-east split, and the river drainage pattern which generally orientates the county eastwards. We shall look at these both in turn, beginning with the land in this chapter and the Tay in the next.

The Highland Boundary Fault, one of the most significant and well-known geological features of the whole British landmass, transects Scotland from Helensburgh on the Firth of Clyde to Stonehaven in the north-east. This long and straight geological abnormality cuts diagonally across Perthshire between Comrie in upper Strathearn and Alyth in Strathmore. Parallel to this, running from the south-west coast up to Dunbar, is the Southern Upland Fault. Between them lie the Central Lowlands, or, in geological terms, the Midland Valley, an extensive area of lower-lying land which nevertheless boasts several ranges of hills. Although erosion and vegetation have blurred the dividing line between the

Highlands and Lowlands, the boundary is reasonably obvious to anyone with a sensitivity to changing landscape. The A9 Perth to Inverness road is the main route to the north of Scotland and as such is the busiest road in the county to cross the Highland Boundary Fault. In Perthshire, this consists of at least three separate fault lines, all occurring within about two miles of each other. On the A9 northbound the first fault line lies about two miles north of the exit for Bankfoot and the last about two miles short of the Dunkeld and Birnam exit. In this short space the landscape changes dramatically from rolling farmland to wooded mountains, vividly demonstrating the two sides to the county's character. Similarly the traveller heading west on the A85, one of the main east-west routes in north-central Scotland, will notice a distinct change in the landscape in the three miles between the east side of the village of Gilmerton and the western exit road from Crieff.

Such a major geological fault passing through the centre of Perthshire's *terra firma* unfortunately means that certain areas of the county are less *firma* than others. Comrie in particular has suffered from a number of minor earthquakes and has enjoyed the dubious distinction of being the earthquake capital of Britain, although in recent decades the focus of seismic activity has moved elsewhere. Sitting slightly to the north of the Highland Boundary Fault, the local population was regularly reminded of its precarious position by the not infrequent tremors and accompanying rumblings. The year 1789 saw the first attempt at a systematic recording of the dates and severity of the Comrie earthquakes, and indeed it is surprising to read of their frequency with as many as sixty being listed in 1839, including, on 23 October, the most severe ever recorded. Felt over the greater part of Scotland the consequent damage appears to have been remarkably light, although even in Perth, more than twenty miles from the epicentre, the shock wave was sufficiently intense to crack a road surface which later subsided.

Such powerful movements of the soil beneath their feet naturally caused much speculation amongst the inhabitants as to their causes. The Reverend William Mackenzie, writing the New Statistical Account of Comrie in 1838, felt that there was probably 'some connection between the earthquakes and the numerous extinct volcanoes' in the area. Four years later a local shoemaker,

The Earthquake House near Comrie was built in around 1874 so that an early seismometer might be properly housed. For much of the present century the building lay unused until it was restored in 1988 with new equipment supplied by the British Geological Survey.

James Drummond, claimed that earthquakes would never happen in dry conditions or when the winds were blowing from the east or west. Crude musings perhaps, but Drummond and the postmaster, Peter Macfarlane, did actually invent the first instruments for recording and measuring earthquake tremors. A model of one, consisting simply of wooden cylinders, a wooden cross and a tray of sand, is now on display in the Earthquake House, a tiny stone building recently restored which will be of interest to anyone fascinated by seismology. It is only a short detour from the main A85, across the much photographed Bridge of Ross, and well worth a visit, even though the contents may only be viewed through a glass panel placed over the front door. As the vibration from even the gentlest of footsteps within the building can register on the modern seismograph installed inside there is always the possibility, one supposes, that the curiosity of the overweight in Perthshire could cause large-scale panic on the streets of San Francisco!

North of the Highland line the rock of Perthshire is predominantly Dalradian metamorphic, dating in its earliest form from between 600 and 1200 million years. About 400 million years ago the immensely powerful forces of tectonic movement beneath the earth's surface began to push laterally both north-westwards and south-eastwards, folding the rock and creating the mountainous landscape that stretches from Northern Ireland through Scotland to Norway. Originally sedimentary, the rock metamorphosed under this intense heat and pressure into the much harder schists and quartzites which characterise the southern Highlands. Where the geological pressure became too great the rock simply snapped, thus creating not just the well-known fault lines but, as geological maps of the area show, a number of lesser ones as well. Several of the Perthshire lochs lie along these folds and fault lines with lochs Tay and Ericht in particular illustrating the pattern of the folding process.

The Perthshire section of the Midland Valley consists mainly of Old Red Sandstone which is about 350 to 400 million years old. Much younger in age than its northern neighbour, the rock is also softer and remains relatively undeformed either by the meta-morphic processes of heat and stress or by mountain-building movement beneath the surface. Dividing this lower-lying land is a broken ridge of more durable volcanic rock, again broadly parallel to the Highland Boundary Fault, known as the Sidlaws to the north-east of Perth and as the Ochil Hills to the south-west. North of the fault, the narrow glens created by the folding of the rock and to the south the wider straths bounded by the Sidlaws and Ochils define the main areas of habitation in the county.

Although much of the Midland Valley is carboniferous virtually none of this rock lies within the Perthshire boundary. The county is thus scenically fortunate in being free of the coal-scarred landscapes which are so obvious beyond its southern border. There are, however, other minerals beneath the soil which over the years have been targeted by quarriers and miners. A thin bed of slate, close to the Highland Boundary Fault and cutting right across the county, was quarried extensively last century, and during the same period lead mining was the major industry in the area around Tyndrum, now in the Stirling Council area. The Scots have long been aware of the presence of gold beneath their feet, as mediaeval charters indicate, and indeed in recent times it has been found at regular intervals. Each new discovery is usually hailed in the local press as potentially another Klondike, but very few prove to be commercially viable.

The nearest Perthshire has come to a major mining operation was in the mid-1990s when the American-based company MI (Great Britain) Ltd, after eight years of prospecting on the Cluniemore estate near Pitlochry, defined one of the largest barytes fields in Europe. As this mineral is heavily used in the offshore oil industry, there were clearly large profits to be made with the probability of substantial economic benefits for the Highland Perthshire community. But hopes of a new prosperity, however, were dashed when the district council, after much heart-searching, decided to refuse planning permission. The case then went to a lengthy public enquiry which backed the council's stance, and then, in vain, to the Secretary of State for Scotland and the Court of Session. The company even considered an appeal to the House of Lords before finally accepting defeat. What was at stake was not just huge profits and more jobs but the preservation of a lovely landscape and the quality of life in the Pitlochry hinterland. This time ecological principles won over purely industrial but it was a close run thing.

The mountain scenery of Highland Perthshire is undoubtedly one of the county's major tourist attractions, perhaps because it can be appreciated during a comfortable day trip from Perth from the warmth of a family car. Few peaks are very far, at least in north-west Highland terms, from a road or a coffee shop. This relative proximity to civilisation probably also explains why the area is not regarded by Munro-baggers and hill-walkers as being in the same league as the rest of the Scottish Highlands. Nevertheless there is still some fine walking, if not climbing, to be done within the county boundaries.

One of the best known peaks in the whole of Scotland is Schiehallion, a one-word name which, as with Lochnagar, Suilven, and Quinag, seems to ennoble the mountain above 'Ben' status and endow it with an almost human character of its own. The mountain, viewed from the north-west, is virtually conical in shape and in common with many other unusual yet natural features is associated in legend with the supernatural. The name derives from the Gaelic for 'the fairy hill of the Caledonians' and is but one of the many fairy hills which dotted the Scottish landscape in centuries gone by. An unquestioning belief in fairies, even well into the nineteenth century, was an essential part of Gaelic folk culture although they were regarded as mischievous, even frightening, spirits of the underworld rather than the benevolent gossamer-winged beings of Victorian children's literature. As well as living underground and wearing green, these creatures of the night also kidnapped grown adults to work for them and exchanged healthy human babies for weaker look-alikes known as changelings. This belief probably explains the phrase, 'awa wi the fairies'. They were visible to those with second sight and many more could hear them just above the night wind, either singing or playing music. Schiehallion is a useful illustration of the intense relationship, based on fear and respect, which once existed between the Highlander and his surroundings. Incidentally, one of the world's great texts on fairies was written by a Perthshire man, the Rev Robert Kirk of Aberfoyle, whose *Secret common-wealth of elves, fauns and fairies* was published in ca 1691. It was widely believed locally that, as a punishment for revealing hidden knowledge, he was taken by the fairies and one day would return. They are still waiting.

Mythology, however, did not stand in the way of science when in 1774 Nevil Maskelyne, the Astronomer-Royal, employed the symmetry of Schiehallion in his experiments to investigate the weight of the earth. Using one of the fundamental laws of physics, the fact that mass creates its own gravity (a phenomenon known in the eighteenth century as 'the attraction of mountains'), Maskelyne erected weighted plumb-lines to the north and south sides of the mountain and measured the extent of their deflection towards it from the vertical. Professor Charles Hutton, Maskelyne's assistant, was given the job of assessing the volume of the mountain and for this purpose devised a system of marking its shape at different altitudes the whole way round. This appears to have been the first practical use made of contour lines which are now such an essential part of cartography. Both Maskelyne and Hutton are commemorated on a plaque at the foot of the mountain near the car park at the Braes of Foss. An interesting memento of these experiments still survives today in the Clan Donnachaidh Museum at Bruar. To mark the end of his work on Schiehallion Maskelyne held a party in his bothy on the hillside. It was presumably a rowdy farewell as fire broke out and a violin belonging to Duncan

Schiehallion is not the highest mountain in Perth and Kinross but probably the most recognisable. On a hot summer morning it casts its cool dark shadow over the still waters of Loch Rannoch.

Robertson, a local lad who had cooked and cleaned for him, was destroyed. Maskelyne returned to London and from there, as promised, sent him a replacement. The instrument, known today as the Yellow London Lady, is housed in the museum while ownership still remains with the descendants of Duncan Robertson and traditionally passed down the generations to those bearing his name.

On a more mundane level Schiehallion is 3547 feet high and reckoned to be a fairly easy summer afternoon's walk. The only problem for the poorly shod walker is likely to be encountered near the summit where a large boulder field makes rapid progress difficult. The views from the top are well worth the climb, with Loch Rannoch spread out below to the north-west and Loch Tummel to the north-east.

Ben Lawers lies to the south-west and, despite a short-lived attempt in 1878 to take its height over 4000 feet by the construction of a massive cairn, stubbornly remains Scotland's ninth highest mountain at 3984 feet. It is approached initially by a small road which leads from the A827 on the north side of Loch Tay up to the car park beside the National Trust for Scotland visitors' centre. The walk to the top is along clearly marked paths, some noticeably suffering from the effects of over-use, and although lengthy is not particularly arduous. The dedicated Munro-ist will be pleased to learn that on his way to the summit he will also have climbed Beinn Ghlas and, if he plans his route carefully and is energetic enough, will be able to bag others in the immediate vicinity. I would like to report from first-hand experience that the view from the top is stunning but, having only ever arrived there in mist or rain, can only pass on this second-hand comment. To the west of Ben Lawers is the Tarmachan ridge, described as one of the finest short ridge walks in the southern Highlands, which in late 1996 was also purchased by the National Trust for Scotland.

The county's southern-most Munros are Stuc a' Chroin and Ben Vorlich, both situated on the south side of Loch Earn. The latter is the higher at 3231 feet and, even with the help of a well-marked path, can in places be a steep climb, although the effort is amply rewarded by the splendid panorama of the southern Highlands.

Although there may be little in Lowland Perthshire to challenge the serious mountaineer or keen hillwalker, there are still plenty of gentle climbs with fine views, ideal for family excursions. Kinnoull Hill, whose wooded slopes overlook Perth from the east, is a firm favourite with the city's inhabitants, many of whom enjoy long walks along the several miles of laid-out grassy paths and waymarked nature trails. The famous views from the top, towards Ben Ledi in the west, the Lomonds to the south and the Carse of Gowrie to the east, are worthy of a hill much higher than its 729 feet. The dangerous cliffs towering above the Tay to the south side of the summit, better appreciated from the Friarton Bridge or the A90 below, were thought to be so reminiscent of the Rhine by Francis, Lord Gray of Kinfauns that in the early years of the nineteenth century he completed the scene by constructing a small castle-like folly at the top. Kinnoull Hill, gifted to the city in 1924 by Lord Dewar, is usually approached from the car park at the top of Hatton Road although quieter paths can be found by beginning the walk from the Deuchney Wood car park or from Fairmount Road near the entrance to Branklyn Garden.

Dunsinane Hill, eight miles north-east of Perth and lying in the shadow of Black Hill with its distinctive concave slope, is known throughout the English-speaking world, thanks to Shakespeare's

Macbeth. It is pronounced locally as Dunsinnan, with the accent on the penultimate syllable. Here, according to the play if not the history books, the murderer of King Duncan had his castle and met his death in combat with Malcolm Canmore, his victim's son. Although not particularly high the climb is quite steep in places but the well-preserved earthworks at the top and the splendid views over Strathmore make the effort worthwhile.

The present-day landscape of Perthshire was created over many millennia by the surface forces of erosion, together with the more recent work of man, acting on the underlying geological structures of the area. The ice age, which began about a million years ago and which came to an end only within the past 10,000 to 15,000 years, had the greatest effect on the landscape as a whole. In one sense it can be seen as a period marking the end of the geological formation of the area and the start of its natural and human history which has continued uninterrupted to the present. For the ice, which covered the whole country with the exception of the highest mountain peaks, had two important roles to play. Firstly the power of the glaciers was sufficient not just to hollow out countless Highland corries but to gouge deep U-shaped channels out of the rock, forming new valleys and adding greatly to the depth of some of the Perthshire lochs. Aerial photographs of the Highlands portray a landscape which, from this vantage point and thousands of years after the end of the ice age, is still best described as bruised. Secondly, the immense weight and the extremely low temperature of the ice moving over the land destroyed virtually all the existing vegetation of the area, so that when the air temperature began to rise and the ice eventually receded for the last time, the new-shaped land was in a virginal state, ripe for colonisation by plant life and humans from the south.

The county is of particular interest to students of the ice age for two further reasons. Rannoch Moor, which covers part of north-western Perthshire, was one of the few great ice distribution points in Scotland, in effect a huge reservoir of ice. Constantly refilled by falling snow, the ice pushed out in all directions although the main flow, judging by the striations which are still visible on some mountains, is believed to have crossed Scotland in a generally easterly or south-easterly direction. The area also gives its name to the Perth Readvance, a brief reversal during the long period of glacial recession which found ice once again moving eastwards along Strathearn, only coming to a final halt in the vicinity of what is now Scone.

The wind, over millions of years, has played a similar role in shaping the landscape. Almost incredibly, the geological folds in the rock at the summit of Ben Lawers point to that area once having been merely a dip between higher mountains on either side. Far from being an isolated instance, the available evidence strongly suggests that the long-term effects of weathering have reduced the once mighty peaks of virtually all the central and southern Highlands to a reasonably uniform level of between 2000 and 3000 feet. The few exceptions to this rule generally consist of harder types of rock such as the quartzite of Schiehallion. The weathering of the softer Old Red Sandstone of the Midland Valley has resulted in a gentler landscape of more rounded hills.

Towards the end of the ice age, with the level of the ocean being higher and ground level lower (pressed down by the weight of the ice) than they are today, the coast came as far inland as Perth and a channel of sea water reached almost as far as Crieff. The clay soils resulting from this sea water flooding contributed much to the fertility of these riverside areas, to the extent that the Carse of Gowrie in particular is now one of the most agriculturally productive parts of Scotland. In the same way that changing sea levels left their mark on the land, so too did alterations to the courses of the area's rivers. The Earn, for example, may well have originated near the north end of Loch Lomond and have taken a more northerly route than its present course before dipping south-east to emerge at the coast near St Andrews. Even within the past two hundred years a comparison of older county maps with their modern counterparts reveals small but pronounced changes in the courses of some rivers. The Tay in the eighteenth century had taken a meandering loop at the Bloody Inches just upstream from its confluence with the Isla. Nineteenth and twentieth century maps show how the river current began to avoid this detour, allowing the former river bed to become a classic oxbow lake before reverting more recently to marshland. Man too has the ability to change the course of the ancient and natural drainage systems: the construction of the new A9 just to the north of Dunkeld in the mid-1970s necessitated the formation of a new channel for the Tay, removing it to a safe distance from the road's foundations.

PERTH AND KINROSS

The geology of the county naturally has a strong bearing on the type of soil above; indeed it is the Old Red Sandstone which gives the Lowland Perthshire soil its characteristic reddish tinge. This close relationship is continued in the type of vegetation which the soil will support and in the animal life and human activity which in turn is dependent on, or influenced by, the vegetation.

We cannot be sure about the nature of the land at the end of the ice age as all soil changes in substance over the years, depending on the variety of plant life which it has supported. It is also unclear whether during the ice age all vegetation died out or whether small pockets survived. Whichever is the case, and whatever the composition of the post-glacial soil, it seems clear that an increase in the air temperature and the consequent recession of the ice allowed firstly alpine and arctic plants either to follow the ice northwards or simply to multiply more freely where they were. For several reasons, principally those of climate, soil and geology, a remarkable number of alpine plants, some of them unique in this country, have survived and prospered on the slopes of Ben Lawers. The botanical significance of this mountain, the southern side of which was acquired by the National Trust for Scotland in 1950, is such that specialists in British alpines regard it as an essential place to visit. Among the rarer of the plants are the Mountain Bladder-Fern with its triangular-shaped fronds, the hairy and solitary-flowered Alpine Fleabane, and the Lesser Alpine Pearlwort, the last-named growing to a height of no more than one inch and clinging to life only on the highest rocky parts of the mountain.

Following these arctic-alpine species came the moorland plants such as heather, cotton grass and sphagnum moss which are still plentiful in the north of the county. At the top end of the botanical spectrum the hardier trees such as birch, hazel, rowan and pine were the next to arrive, spreading northwards after first crossing into England by way of the neck of land which formerly joined Britain to the European mainland. These types are still a feature of Perthshire's higher ground, while the less hardy varieties such as oak, elm and ash came later still and colonised the lower ground.

Archaeologists, it seems, cannot agree about the extent to which the great Caledonian Forest covered prehistoric Scotland; although it is generally accepted that the high mountains and the wettest areas remained treeless, some think that in total about half the country may have been forested while others argue for a greater or lesser proportion. Whichever is the case we are privileged that remnants of this ancient woodland still survive in Perthshire, most notably on the south side of Loch Rannoch and in the Old Wood of Meggernie in Glen Lyon. Although these areas have been forested for thousands of years, principally with pine and birch, it should be understood that through the natural processes of decay and regeneration the oldest trees are only between two and three hundred years old. What is really important here is not so much the survival of individual trees as the preservation of a whole ecosystem which has not only evolved over the past several thousand years but supports hundreds of different species of plant, animal and insect life. It is a sobering thought that some of the non-native trees such as larch and sitka spruce, two centuries on from their first introduction into Scotland, provide a home for only a tiny fraction of the wildlife to be found in the ancient and native woodland.

The Black Wood of Rannoch, now thankfully under the watchful eye of the Forestry Commission, covers today little more than one square mile, having dwindled over the past century from an area covering five or six. In some ways we are fortunate that the wood survives at all, for in the early 1800s it was sold to an English timber firm which felled a large part of it, and would have removed even more had the difficulties of transporting the timber south not virtually bankrupted the business. This was not before they had constructed a series of canals and locks to enable the trunks to be floated down to the waters of Loch Rannoch and from there, bound into rafts, down the Tummel and Tay to the coast. It has been said that some of these timber rafts were eventually found washed up on the Dutch coast. The remains of the canals, a little known but awe-inspiring piece of industrial archaeology, can still be seen in the hills above the loch.

The coming of agricultural man together with his sheep accounts for the destruction, by the mid-eighteenth century, of more than 80% of the natural Scottish woodland. Forest clearance probably began in the region of 4000 years ago when the earliest farmers cut down trees to make space for growing crops. At the same time their domestic animals, through random grazing on seedling trees, inhibited the regeneration of these woodlands. Such a destructive process, continuing unchecked over many centuries, eventually led the late mediaeval parliaments of Scotland to recognise that the deforestation of the country was becoming a major problem. Replanting was consequently not only encouraged but required by law and it naturally fell to the landowners to bear the brunt of this work. Such a process reached a high point locally in the eighteenth and early nineteenth centuries in the work of the second and fourth Dukes of Atholl, who set about their tasks with such enthusiasm that their present-day descendants can talk of their family trees with quite literally double the pride. The vast Atholl estates include Dunkeld where, in the riverside grounds of the cathedral in 1738, the 2nd Duke planted the five European larch seedlings from which originated all the larches now visible from the A9 north of the town. Indeed, one of the five still stands by the cathedral and is over 100 feet tall. The 4th Duke, during his long tenure of the title, is believed to have planted a staggering 27,000,000 trees over a 15,500 acre area, of which 15,000,000 were believed to be larch.

Just outside Dunkeld and clearly signposted from the A9 is the particularly attractive Hermitage walk. Centred on the classically designed folly overlooking the River Braan the surrounding area was laid out by one of the dukes as a mixture of wild garden and woodland. The gardens have long since reverted to nature although the trees survive, one of which, a Douglas fir now at a height of about 200 feet, is believed to be one of the tallest trees in the United Kingdom. And whilst on the subject of dendrological records, Perthshire can also boast the tallest hedge in the world (at Meikleour), the second oldest tree in Britain, if not Europe (the famous yew at Fortingall seems to have yielded its venerable status to an even older one in Wales) and the widest tree in Britain (at Cluny House Gardens).

Today, centuries on from the days of the great 'planting lairds', the government's policy is still to expand the home forestry industry. Recent attempts to supply a greater proportion of the national demand from within this country have already caused a huge outcry in the north of Scotland where tax incentives for investors coupled with inadequate planning have resulted in large areas of insensitive planting. In 1991 Tayside Regional Council published its proposed strategy for forestry, identifying sizeable expanses of land suitable for this purpose. North of the Highland

Apart from the road markings there is no discernible difference between this recent photo of the Meikleour beech hedge and an engraving of the early 1880s made at the same viewpoint. Then it was described as the most wonderful thing of its kind in existence. Today few drivers, it seems, even bother to glance at it.

Boundary Fault there already exist several large and productive forests, particularly around Loch Rannoch and Aberfeldy, but also, though to a lesser extent, in the north-east of the county. It is gratifying to note that in these northern and western areas the council has recognised that although about half the land is capable of supporting new forestry this would be to the detriment of the local landscape and wildlife. Instead, the preferred areas for new planting lie in Strathmore, particularly around Blairgowrie, and also to the south and east of Crieff.

PERTH AND KINROSS

Perthshire has had a long connection with the science of forestry and indeed with the botanical world in general. Archibald Menzies, born in 1754, was one of the earliest of the local pioneers in this field and, although not a household name, is honoured in the several plants named after him. The 'big pine tree' which he first discovered in California in the early 1790s is now known taxonomically as *pseudotsuga menziesii*, and more commonly as the Douglas fir. He is also credited with introducing into Britain both the Californian redwood and the South American monkey puzzle tree, having first encountered — and kept — the latter's seeds which were served up in Chile as part of a meal. In addition to his botanical achievements he may thus have a claim to be the inventor of the doggy bag as well.

The Douglas fir, of course, is also named after the better known David Douglas who was born in Scone in 1799 and was the first to bring back to this country the seeds of that great tree. Well over 200 other plants were introduced to European soil by Douglas including the sitka spruce, the flowering currant and a host of much loved flowers which, in spite of their foreign provenance, are often considered typical of a British garden. Although not a well-educated man his intense curiosity about the natural world developed into a botanical brilliance which brought him to the attention of, firstly, Professor Sir William Hooker of Glasgow University (and later of Kew Gardens), and, through him, of the Horticultural Society. This august body sent Douglas three times on plant-collecting expeditions to North America where, notwith-standing the genteel image of his commission, he faced death on several occasions and endured almost unbelievable hardships. Douglas met a particularly gruesome end in Hawaii at the age of 34 when he stumbled into a pit already occupied by an enraged bull which, ignorant of his fame, proceeded to trample him to death. Buried in an unmarked grave in Honolulu, there is a fine memorial to him in the churchyard of Scone Old Church, and an unofficial but appropriate one in the shape of the pinetum, planted in 1848, in the grounds of Scone Palace where he first embarked on his botanical career.

Another fine example of horticultural creativity, in many ways the antithesis of the ancient and natural flora of Ben Lawers but like the mountain also under the care of the National Trust for Scotland, is Perth's Branklyn Garden. Begun in 1922 by John and

THE FOLLOWING ARE A FEW OF THE NUMEROUS
TREES, SHRUBS
AND
ORNAMENTAL PLANTS
INTRODUCED BY
DOUGLAS.

TREES

ACER CIRCINATUM.
———— MACROPHYLLUM.
AMELANCHIER FLORIDA.
ARBUTUS PROCERA.
CRATAEGUS DOUGLASII.

PINUS LAMBERTIANA.
———— PONDEROSA.
———— NOBILIS.
———— AMABILIS.
———— MENZIESII.

PINUS DOUGLASII.

SHRUBS.

BERBERIS AQUIFOLIUM.
———— GLUMACEA.
GARRYA ELLIPTICA.

RIBES SANGUINEUM.
———— SPECIOSUM.
RUBUS SPECTABILIS.

GAULTHERIA SHALLON.

ANNUALS, BIENNIALS, AND PERENIALS.

CLARKIA PULCHELLA.
CLINTONIA ELEGANS.
COLLINSIA GRANDIFLORA.

GILLIA TRICOLOR.
NEMOPHILA INSIGNIS.
IPOMOPSIS ELEGANS.

LUPINUS PORYPHYLLUS.
ESCHSCHOLTZIA CALIFORNICA.
DOUGLASIA NIVALIS.
&C., &C.

David Douglas, one of the world's great botanists, is commemorated by a tall memorial erected in 1841 in the grounds of Scone Old Church. A panel on the reverse lists some of the hundreds of plants he discovered.

Dorothy Renton the garden has expanded over the years and now occupies a two acre site on the south-eastern edge of the city. Neither formal nor cottagey, it is quite clearly the personal garden of a couple who took great delight in experimenting with plants and nurturing and displaying them to their best advantage. Trees, shrubs and alpines from all over the world have found a home here with perhaps the most notable being the *meconopsis grandis 'Branklyn'* or the blue Himalayan poppy, whose fame in botanical circles has spread well beyond the confines of Perth. The garden is open to the public between the spring and autumn of each year and is felt to be at its best at the start of the season when the trees are heavy with blossom and the rhododendrons are in full flower. The colouring of the maples in the autumn, however, is an almost equal attraction. All throughout its open period it is a delight to

While a monochrome photograph may not do justice to the colours of Perth's Branklyn Garden it at least conveys a sense of the richness of the plant life. Small alpines, garden flowers, larger shrubs and tall trees crowd together in this two acre paradise.

wander along the narrow grassy paths which wind up and down its gentle slope and to lose oneself amongst the profusion of thousands of plants.

It is fitting that Branklyn Garden should occupy a site very near to the former Perth nurseries which in the later eighteenth and nineteenth centuries enjoyed an international reputation for the quality and range of their stock. James Dickson from the Scottish borders founded the business in 1766 and by the early 1770s was in correspondence with the eminent botanist Carl Linnaeus of Sweden. It was he who sent Dickson some of the first seeds to be introduced to Scotland of the Swedish turnip, better known in England today as the swede and, confusingly, in Scotland as the turnip. The swede/turnip, of course, is traditionally served up as an accompaniment to the haggis at Burns Suppers throughout the world; yet, because of its late introduction into the Scottish diet the question must arise of whether the bard, before his death in 1796, would ever have tasted the vegetable which is always associated with his name. (Having said this, archaeologists have apparently found traces of swede seeds in the excavations of mediaeval Perth, which suggests that the above belief is either completely false or that the vegetable disappeared from Scotland for an unknown period.) Although the nurseries have long since been built over, the name of James Dickson still survives in the plant and garden shop, Dickson and Turnbull, in Perth's Hospital Street.

Worthy of more than just a passing mention, had there been more space, are the Cherrybank Gardens in the grounds of the Bells headquarters in Perth, home to Britain's largest collection of heathers, and the Glendoick Gardens of Peter Cox, a prolific writer and one of the world's leading experts on rhododendrons. Tribute should also be paid to Dr Francis Buchanan White who was one of the founding members of that learned body, the Perthshire Society of Natural Science, and who, together with David Douglas, should be regarded as one of the greatest figures of Perthshire botany. His *Flora of Perthshire*, published posthumously in 1898, is still the standard work on the subject. But let the final illustration of the breadth and range of horticultural activity in Perthshire come from the author of the Old Statistical Account of the parish of Longforgan. Writing in the 1790s, he mentions not only the outdoor cultivation of peaches, nectarines and apricots, but also describes with a certain amount of justifiable pride the construction and function of a steam melon pit. Its purpose being to envelop the whole melon plant in warm steam, the author concludes that 'melons raised in this way are thought to be thinner skinned and rather higher flavoured than those produced in the common way'. Amusing and unusual, yes, but it encapsulates the major role which the people of Perthshire have played in forging new developments in agriculture and horticulture and which nowadays is perhaps too little appreciated.

The variety of vegetation in the county, from turnips and apricots to larch and pine, depends as much on the local climate as on the soil and where the quality of the soil can often be judged by simple observation the same cannot be said of the weather. Apart from broad statements to the effect that the east of Scotland, being in the rain shadow of the mountains, is drier than the west, and that the west through the influence of the Gulf Stream is warmer than the east, the real picture can only be viewed from the vantage point of weather statistics. And these throw up one or two surprising facts. The driest month of the year in much of Lowland Perthshire is actually March, at the tail end of winter and with April showers in prospect, and one of the wettest, at the time we associate with long, hot summer days, is July. The first half of the year is generally drier than the second half with May being the sunniest month. July is the warmest, in spite of the rain, while the autumn usually enjoys slightly higher temperatures than the spring. January is the coldest month as well as a wet and dull one, and not particularly recommended for a fun weekend break.

The principle that the weather usually worsens the further inland from the east one travels unfortunately holds good for Highland Perthshire which receives twice, or in parts thrice, the rainfall of the lower-lying land. The first post-summer snows frequently arrive in September, although there is rarely sufficient depth and coverage for ski-ing before January. By the end of April the winter sports season is over, even though patches of snow can still be seen on the highest peaks during the hottest days of summer.

The fauna of Perthshire is the final link in the chain which binds together the story of the geology, the soil, and the plant and animal life of the county. The back-packer in the wilds of Scotland today has little to fear from the animal kingdom: where a thousand years ago he would have been vulnerable to attacks from wolves and bears, there are now no animals in the country which are by nature aggressive, although he should perhaps be aware of the presence, if not the danger, of adders in some areas. The brown bear, which appears to have been known to the Romans who sent a steady supply of them to fight in the amphitheatres of Rome, probably survived in the Scottish forests until around the ninth or tenth centuries. The once-common wild boar had probably been hunted to extinction by the early 1600s and, judging by the recent protestations about its proposed reintroduction to the Highlands, has not been particularly missed. Some of the most marvellous illustrations of early Scottish wildlife can be found on carved Pictish stones: salmon, eagles and deer, bears, boars and wolves are all instantly recognisable, almost to the extent of being caricatures, and reveal the unsurpassed artistry of Pictish sculptors in early mediaeval Europe.

At about the same period that the Scottish parliament was legislating for the preservation of the nation's woodland it was also promoting the extermination of the wolf. This dangerous animal was a threat to human life and even more so, through the killing of cattle in which a substantial proportion of a farming family's capital was invested, to personal livelihood. One law required householders in any parish where a wolf had been killed to pay the sum of one penny to the wolf slayer, an act which, in spite of several nineteenth century revisions of outdated legislation, managed to remain on the statute books until 1906. Such financial inducements led to a positive approach to wolf hunting (though perhaps not from the wolves' point of view) and there are still traces to be seen in Glen Tilt of the pits in which hunters used to hide in wait of their prey. Although the Lowlands had probably been cleared of wolves by the close of the Middle Ages, they were still such a terrifying menace in the Highlands that travellers' refuges had to be built in the most dangerous areas, some of which at times were almost impassable. This is believed to be the origin of the Spittal of Glenshee, even today an inhospitable enough place to find oneself at nightfall were it not for the hotel, and particularly so 400 years ago with the spine-chilling howling of wolves in the distance.

There has been considerable debate over the years about when and by whom the last wolf in Scotland was killed. Sir Ewen Cameron of Lochiel had a claim to this distinction in 1680 although much depends on the interpretation of the ambiguous phrase, 'the last killed by Sir Ewen Cameron', which was found in a sale catalogue of 1818 and which referred to a stuffed wolf in a glass case. There were later and better documented claims in the eighteenth century when another 'last wolf' was supposed to have perished in Rannoch in 1710 and yet another near Crieff towards the middle of the century. The incident of 1710 is perhaps the least likely story behind the demise of a 'last wolf', although it has lingered long in local legend. It concerned a woman at Mullinavadie (which means 'mill of the wolf') who, on spotting the animal making off with her baby from the kitchen, put an end to his existence by walloping him on the right ear with a wooden potato masher. The poor wolf immediately fell down dead, either from the severity of the blow or, more likely, from sheer surprise at the choice of weapon.

Of the animals which inhabit present-day Perthshire the wildcat, in the assumed absence of the pine marten (which nevertheless has been spotted south-west of Loch Tay in recent years), is now probably the rarest. In 1920 it was already thought to have been extinct in the county for about half a century, but since then has been making a comeback, even in places comparatively close to human habitation such as the Loch of the Lowes near Dunkeld. There are believed to be only about 3000 of the species remaining in Scotland in their pure form, genetically untainted through cross-breeding with feral domestic cats, and almost all of these are to be found to the north of Perth. Foxes, badgers and otters all have a presence in the county but are only occasionally encountered. Several animal species can regularly be seen on woodland walks in Perthshire, including rabbits, hares and both red and grey squirrels. Greys have not yet spread to the north-west of the county (although they have been seen as far north as Pitlochry) and in central areas, such as on Kinnoull Hill, seem to coexist reasonably successfully with reds. Roe deer can often be found close to urban areas and, on the few occasions when they are unaware of the proximity of humans, are always a pleasure to observe. Red deer, on the other hand, are too plentiful in the Highlands and cause much damage to the local vegetation.

Two species of birds are popularly associated with Perthshire, one being the osprey, on account of its much publicised return to breed at the Loch of the Lowes, and the other the grouse, once abundant on the moors of north Perthshire, now expensive on London menus of 12 August, and immortalised in one of Scotland's best known whisky brands. A cousin of the grouse is the capercaillie, a turkey-sized bird which had become extinct in Britain by the 1770s but which was successfully reintroduced to north Perthshire in 1837. Twenty-eight of the birds were given to the Marquis of Breadalbane by a friend who had sent his game-keeper to Sweden to fetch them, and although they are by no means common they have been spotted fairly close to Perth. The Tay estuary is an important feeding and roosting area which in the late summer attracts large numbers of swallows and sand martins. Over 150,000 of them have been seen in the air at one time, a great gathering which has been described in a recent *Perth and Kinross bird report* as 'one of the most spectacular avian displays to be witnessed in the whole of Scotland'. Greylag and pink-footed geese are also seen here in their multitudes, arriving for the winter months and leaving again in the spring.

Wildlife in the Scottish Highlands has never had an easy time of it. Even in the late twentieth century the marketing of a Perthshire estate can still list as one of its attractions the opportunity to 'take the Macnab' — the bagging of a stag, grouse and salmon in one day. Without getting drawn into the morality and benefits of field sports it is clear that, while the demand for good fishing and shooting can inject substantial amounts of cash into the Perthshire economy, overindulgence (particularly by commercial salmon netters) can have an adverse effect on wildlife numbers. In recent years the local press has highlighted the problem of the increasingly erratic quality of salmon catches in Perthshire rivers. If this trend continues then moneyed anglers will go elsewhere and the knock-on effects to the local economy, let alone the local ecosystem, will not go unnoticed. Anyone who doubts the fragility of the relationship between Perthshire man and nature need look no further than J A Harvie-Brown's *A fauna of the Tay basin and Strathmore*. This voluminous survey of Perthshire wildlife, published in 1906, describes the Golden Eagle as 'abundant' and 'greatly on the increase', and yet, within ninety years, is now one of our rarest birds, with only a few pairs remaining in the county. The same author's description of the persecution of the osprey last century would bring tears to the eyes of any ornithologist. The salmon and grouse, the tiny alpines and the wide moorland, the pine-woods and people, are all as much a part of Perthshire as the rivers, mountains and straths. While the latter are relatively un-changing the others to a greater or lesser extent are ultimately dependant on each other. In the years ahead these relationships will need a bit of tender loving care.

CHAPTER 2

...AND THE FLOOD

When water begins to trickle across the floor of the city archives you know you have a problem, and even more so when a breathless fireman, struggling to keep abreast of a situation long out of control, turns up to announce that another four feet of water is on the way at high tide. Thus forewarned a small army of Perth residents, guided by archivists, formed a human chain up the stairs of the Sandeman Library and began the long job of emptying the lower shelves of their irreplaceable contents. This is one small cameo from that memorable Sunday afternoon in January 1993 when, after a week of heavy snow across Perthshire followed by a sudden and rapid thaw, the Tay and its tributaries overflowed their banks and reminded the nation at large just how destructive a river unleashed could be.

The story began on Monday 11 January when, following the Met Office's report of a deep depression heading towards Scotland, Perthshire was enveloped in one of the worst snowstorms in living memory. Most roads were closed and even on the M90 and A9 traffic slithered to an undignified halt. While snow lay thick in the city streets on the Tuesday evening the cast of the annual pantomime at Perth Theatre, normally playing to a packed house, stood on stage and applauded the fifty or so Eskimo-like figures in the audience who nothing daunted had bravely turned up to watch the show. Two days later the temperature started to rise and heavy rain began to fall, a sinister combination which was mirrored in the alarming messages being received at the offices of the Tay River Purification Board from the various river gauging stations throughout the Tay catchment area. On Friday the first reports of flooding came in from several parts of the county, at this stage caused mainly by numerous swollen burns rather than the bigger rivers. In Perth itself, thanks to the Craigie Burn, the South Inch had turned into an enormous pond. On Saturday the air temperature was like spring and meltwater started to pour down even the highest of Perthshire mountains and from there, via the already brimming burns and rivers, into the streets and homes of the lower-lying towns and villages throughout the Perth and Kinross area.

The many people in Perth who had had no need to venture out of the city and who had not tuned into Radio Tay were unaware of the disaster taking place just a few miles away. All this was to change on the morning of Sunday 17 January when they awoke to find the North Inch under water and the Tay beginning to lap over the sandbags along Charlotte Street and trickle down North Port. By mid-afternoon Perth's desperate situation was apparent to most. Cars were almost submerged in Horse Cross and the basement of the Museum and Art Gallery, full of paintings and historic treasures, had been devastated in spite of a feverish rescue operation mounted by museum staff. The flood defences at the North Muirton housing estate had also been breached causing extensive damage to over 1200 houses. By evening the two road bridges and the railway bridge had been closed, with the stability of the Queen's Bridge giving particular cause for concern. Unknown to all but a few, however, the readings from the Ballathie gauging station, just downstream from the confluence of the Tay and the Isla, had peaked at about 6.15 pm and by 7.30 pm the floodwaters at Perth had reached their highest level. Two hours later those at work in the city archives realised that the worst had passed and headed homewards, by whatever route they could find, passing on the way a few hardy souls in canoes paddling along the city streets. After the day's events a sight such as this did not merit a single raised eyebrow.

As the water slowly receded the reckoning began. Many houses were badly damaged, not just in Perth and Bridge of Earn, but right across the district from Aberfeldy, Pitlochry and Alyth to Auchterarder, Bankfoot and Braco. Even Kinross and Milnathort, outwith the Tay catchment area, were affected by floodwater rushing down from the Ochils. Many of those who had left their houses when the water arrived were unable to return for several weeks, and in some cases seven months, owing in part to local tradesmen being unable to cope with the demands made upon them and to the simple reason that waterlogged houses need plenty of time to dry out. The transport infrastructure also suffered: railway embankments were swept away, several bridges were damaged and it was again many months before all the necessary repairs could be carried out. Farmers paid a heavy price, particularly those along the banks of the lower Earn and those near where the Isla and Tay had conspired to create a huge inland lake covering seven square miles of prime agricultural land.

The most enduring cost, however, has been in human terms where the loss of family photographs and other prized possessions, distressing enough, is a small sadness compared with the inescapable feeling of insecurity inside the home. Partly to reassure such people Tayside Regional Council launched the Tayside River Flood Information Line in October 1993 which in just over two years logged more than 14,000 calls. Four years further on the flood line is still heavily used, particularly by the many residents of North Muirton who still suffer from anxiety after even short periods of snow or heavy rain. While these numbers may indicate the wide extent of psychological distress, they do not show the depths of anguish to which some individuals sank. Shortly after the flood had subsided and faced with the heart-breaking job of clearing up, one elderly woman told me that, next to the death of her husband, this had been the worst experience of her life, a sentiment probably shared by hundreds of people across the county.

Over the centuries Perthshire has suffered from a regular surplus of water. The first recorded flood occurred in 1209 and swept away the castle of Perth and drowned a large number of townspeople including the king's son. The flood of 1621 destroyed the Perth Bridge and led the minister of St John's, in a fine example of theological opportunism, to declare to the townspeople that if they should repent of their sins then God would deliver them from the flood. Whether his religious faith was greater than his knowledge of rivers is not made clear but shortly afterwards the flood waters subsided and doubtless on subsequent Sunday mornings they were queueing to get into St John's. A build-up of blocks of ice against the piers of the Perth Bridge, effectively damming the river, caused the greatest flood of all in February 1814 which saw water reaching as far as Newrow and mountains of ice remaining on the Inch until the following summer. The twentieth century, culminating, we all hope, in the flood of 1993 (the second-highest recorded), seems to have had even more than its fair share of similar experiences, as can be seen from the marks on the side of Perth Bridge, near the dry arch, which indicate the levels of many of these floods.

If Perth's major flood prevention scheme goes ahead as planned then the level of the 1993 flood should be the last such disaster to be recorded on the dry arch of Perth Bridge.

The inundation of 1993, therefore, if not the first or worst flood was certainly the last straw. In 1995, after long discussions, in-depth investigations and a mountain of official reports, the local authorities produced a comprehensive plan to protect Perth from any future flooding disaster. A combination of walls, embankments and pumping stations stretching all the way from the Almond to Perth Harbour, and specific measures for the suburbs of Bridgend and Friarton as well as for the Town's Lade and the Craigie Burn will, it is believed, give the city the necessary protection against a repeat of the flood of 1814. Now that the Scottish Office has come up with most of the required funding (the probable cost will be in the region of £20 million, a mere half the estimated cost to the community of the 1993 flood) these measures will usher in one of the biggest changes to Perth in many decades, if not centuries. Two of the major proposals call for a high embankment running the length of the North Inch and a wall to replace the railings along

Tay Street. Perth, it seems, is attempting to turn its back on the very river which has contributed so much, and still does, to its prosperity and attractiveness and in doing so will turn itself into a safer but perhaps less fair city.

What, then, is this river which has so far refused to be tamed? The Tay's vital statistics are impressive. For a start it is the longest river in Scotland, running to around 116 miles from its source near the Argyll border to Tayport in Fife where the estuary becomes the North Sea. The Tay catchment area, covering around 3000 square miles, drains more of Scotland than any other river and at its mouth discharges more water to the sea than any in Britain. This is due to the several major tributaries, some of them lengthy rivers by any standard, and the myriad anonymous burns rushing down many a Perthshire hillside. The Tummel, Garry, Lyon, Isla, Almond, Ericht and Braan have a combined length of over 250 miles while the Earn, the second river of Perthshire, debouches into the Firth of Tay and is therefore considered an independent river in its own right. Whether independent or not each of these rivers, married to the strath or glen which usually bears its name, makes its own unique contribution to the loveliness and diversity of the Perthshire landscape. Strathbraan and Glenalmond, for example, near neighbours on the map, have their own particular characteristics which make them as different to those who know them as the Tay and the Thames.

Trickling down from the high slopes of Ben Lui, a mountain in the far west of old Perthshire, is a little burn which is generally accepted as being the source of the Tay. Under the guise of the Rivers Coninish, Fillan and Dochart this same flow skirts the north side of Ben More, splashes through the much visited Falls of Dochart and enters Loch Tay at Killin. Like a butterfly from a chrysalis, the Tay proper emerges at Kenmore and proceeds gently north-east through the wide Appin of Dull towards Aberfeldy, merging with the Lyon on the way. Beyond Aberfeldy the hills of Strathtay close in and the river becomes more turbulent as it briefly narrows near Grandtully. From this point the Tay turns slowly towards the south-east and then, having been more or less doubled in volume by the Tummel at Logierait, heads virtually due south for Dunkeld and the broad fields of the Lowlands beyond.

But Highland topography plays one last trick. Just before squeezing through the pass at Birnam the Tay suddenly and unexpectedly swings round to the east, a course which it maintains for several miles until, near Meikleour and almost as if regaining its sense of direction, it again loops round to the south-west and heads for Perth. The river around Stanley, where wooded banks rise high on either side and where the popular Campsie Linn beauty spot can be found, is perhaps the most attractive of the Lowland stretches. At Perth, faced with the twin heights of Kinnoull and Moncreiffe, it narrows and once again turns sharply to the east. Finally, as the river broadens into the firth which divides Perthshire and Fife, the great Tay rolls on towards the sea, unimpeded but for mudflats, sandbanks and a narrowing of the firth at Dundee.

The Tay, perhaps now more than ever before, is one of Perthshire's most vital arteries, bringing life to the interior in the form of trade, transport, leisure and tourism. Many people are surprised to find that Perth, an obviously inland town situated 30 miles from the open sea, should have a harbour; not overly busy, perhaps, but a working harbour nonetheless. You will have to look hard to find it signposted from the city and often the first indication of its existence, perhaps seen from the Kinnoull Hill summit, is an ocean-going vessel heading upstream towards Perth, gingerly negotiating the shifting sandbanks and little river islands on the way. These, together with the rise and fall of the tide, are significant hazards for the 200-odd ships which make passage to Perth each year, most of which are strongly advised to use the services of a pilot. Many of these vessels are registered abroad and generally bring in cargoes of animal feedstuff and, less frequently, chemicals and coal. The main export from the harbour is barytes from the Aberfeldy area, bound for the oil companies at Aberdeen, and the occasional load of malting barley.

The Tay was easily navigable as far as Perth in the Middle Ages, a time when transport was easier by water than land, and it is not surprising to find documentary evidence for the harbour as early as 1147. It was situated at the end of the High Street at a point later known as the North Shore, which was still accessible to some shipping as recently as the late eighteenth century. But as the river began to silt up the main harbour had to be moved progressively downstream until it was finally established at its fifth and present location at Friarton in the 1840s. At the end of that decade, however, the railway came to Perthshire and together with the unalleviated effect of silting (which made it difficult for the larger

A Dutch-registered ship unloading at Perth Harbour on a summer morning. The cargo of soda ash was destined for a glass manufacturer in central Scotland.

boats of the time to make the journey as far as Perth) the harbour went into decline. The railway boom lasted in Perth until Dr Beeching waved his axe in the early 1960s since when shipping has been returning in ever greater numbers.

The Tay, of course, is far better known for its salmon which, when freshly caught from the river, is still regarded as a classic delicacy despite the challenge from the more fashionable fish of the 1990s. The 'wild Tay' label continues to sell at a premium as a quick telephone survey at the time of writing revealed. Shops in Perth in early 1997 were charging up to £4.00 per pound while the staff of the fish counter at Harrods were quoting figures of around £20.00. And what of the poor angler who has spent all day up to his chest in icy waters and still pays for the privilege? He might be lucky enough to sell his catch to a local hotel and even luckier to get as much as £2.00 per pound.

The Tay salmon fishing season, for rod and line, runs from 15 January to 15 October each year and is opened with a little ceremony at Kenmore. A small crowd, led by a piper, wends its way through the village and down to the river where the first boat of the new season is hanselled by a sprinkling of whisky across the bow. And with a wee drop down the throats of the occupants

A fisherman on the Tay at Perth displaying his latest catch to two admiring children (© Dr W H Findlay).

the first anglers of the new year, fortified as much against the cost of hiring a salmon beat as against the winter weather, take to the water and wait for the first tug on the line.

The economics of salmon fishing, for what — to the outsider — is essentially a sport involving a glorified stick, line and hook, are astonishing. The Tay between Kenmore and Perth is divided on both sides into a number of beats, each covering a few miles of river bank and each stretch containing several salmon pools with evocative names such as Honey Hole, Tail of Horsey, Mouse Trap and The Minister. Such is the demand for fishing on what is reckoned to be one of the great salmon rivers of Europe that in 1993 the Lower Scone beat, on one of the best stretches of the whole river, could be advertised for sale at an asking price of almost £7 million. The Dalguise beat, which lies upstream of the highly regarded Meikleour to Scone section, was offered for sale in the same year at £800,000. Daily charges and catch statistics for Dalguise are available in published sources and allow some interesting calculations to be made. With a maximum of six rods at an average of around £50 per day the potential daily takings for the owners of the beat are £300 or, over the nine months of the season (excluding Sundays), a hefty £70,000. Divide this sum by the average catch over the season of 100 salmon and you have a price of £700 on the head of each one. It would be cheaper, easier and probably quicker to sit in the comfort of the local hotel and have Harrods send up a fish by chauffeur-driven Rolls-Royce.

A very few stretches of the river are owned by angling clubs and together with the council-owned section through Perth can be enjoyed for a reasonable daily fee. But the fact that most of the Tay salmon fishings are in private hands and can cost up to £150 a day at the height of the spring and autumn runs, coupled with the recent regulation of public freshwater fishing which had hitherto been regarded as an historic and traditional right, causes much resentment among certain sections of the local angling community who feel that they have been prised and priced out of an ancient and much loved sport. The root cause of this ill-feeling was the Freshwater and Salmon Fisheries (Scotland) Act of 1976 which was designed to conserve fish stocks and at the same time increase access to fishing waters but which, according to SCAPA (Scottish Campaign for Public Angling), has effectively made river angling the preserve of the wealthy. SCAPA and locally the Tay Access Group are both pressing hard for the public ownership of fishing rights under a proposed Scottish Anglers' Trust and a radical reform of the complicated laws which surround this seemingly peaceful and innocuous sport. Whilst SCAPA and TAG may stay on the right side of the law the many poachers of Perthshire do not. Their activities have been described in the local press as nothing less than organised and occasionally violent crime. The days of 'one for the pot', to which many a sympathetic magistrate would have turned a blind eye, are apparently over.

It is perhaps ironic for the moneyed male devotees of salmon fishing that the heaviest recorded rod-caught salmon was hooked by a woman on one of the less popular beats. Georgina Ballantine lived in the old ferryman's house beside the new Caputh Bridge and on 7 October 1922 caught her monster fish after an exhausting two hour struggle, helped by the advice, boating skills and physical strength of her father who was in the boat with her. It weighed 64 pounds, was 4' 6" in length and lives on in the original plaster cast, privately owned, and in the resin copy on display in Perth Museum. There is a growing belief in the fishing fraternity that women tend to catch more and bigger salmon than men, to the extent, in fact, that a whole book has recently been devoted to this theory. The proffered but still untested explanation is that male salmon, who have an acute sense of smell, detect pheromones on the bait previously handled by a female and are attracted to it. So that's the answer, ladies. Hold the hook in your hand for a moment (for extra-large fish, spray it with your favourite perfume), then cast your line and watch the salmon fighting to be the first into your fish kettle!

The value of the Tay lies in much more than mere harbour dues or fishing revenues. As residents and visitors appreciate, if only passively, it is the rivers and lochs which make Perthshire the beautiful county it undoubtedly is. The hills and mountains have their own special attractiveness but they cannot compete for grandeur, height and wild remoteness with the ranges further north. Ben Lawers, to the north of Loch Tay, has the height to be one of Scotland's great mountains but lacks the noble cragginess to justify inclusion in the ranks of the truly picturesque, while those to the south have been described somewhat disrespectfully, but with a certain amount of truth, as 'pudding-like uplands'. What transforms this otherwise unspectacular region into an area of outstanding natural beauty is the long stretch of water in the middle. And that is how the hills and mountains of Perthshire should be regarded — as settings for the jewels of the county, the lochs and rivers, whether they be dull and tarnished under a heavy leaden sky or shining bright under a summer sun.

CHAPTER 3
1559 AND ALL THAT

The history of Perthshire begins with a canoe and in its wake comes a whole flotilla of unanswered questions. What induced the last owner to abandon it by the river's edge 8000 years ago in what is now the Friarton suburb of Perth? Where had he come from and where was he going? Had his people decided to venture further into the thick forest in search of better hunting? Had the hollowed out Scots pine simply rolled over in choppy waters and drowned him? Or had the poor occupant literally found himself up a creek without a paddle? All we know is that it belonged, probably, to one of the earliest inhabitants of the area and is not only one of the very few Mesolithic remains discovered in Perthshire but one of the oldest logboats ever found in Europe.

The Mesolithic hunter-gatherers had yielded by the fourth millennium to the Neolithic farming folk who were more advanced in every way. For example, they were traders; one of Perthshire's earliest 'factories', at Creag na Caillich, just to the north of Killin, produced axe heads which have been found along the east coast of Britain and as far away as the Thames valley. They were also the first to undertake the process of forest clearance to create space for rudimentary agriculture, barley being the main crop during this period. From the middle of the third millennium they were joined by the Beaker people (so called from the pottery they left behind) who crossed the North Sea from the Low Countries and settled in eastern Scotland. They were the first people in this area to be able to work with copper, gold and latterly bronze. Around the middle of the first millennium the more aggressive Celtic peoples crossed over from Europe, a migration which coincided with the construction of defensive structures such as hillforts, of which the one at Barry Hill near Alyth is an excellent example.

Perthshire is rich in archaeological remains from the pre-Roman era. Standing stones abound in the countryside, either in the midst of fields, carefully avoided by tractor and plough, on lonely bare hillsides or hidden in deep woodland. Stone circles are less common, though one easily accessible example can be found in

The recently completed crannog at the east end of Loch Tay is already a popular tourist attraction and educational facility. Having used only ancient construction techniques and natural building materials found locally it was only right that the crannog should have been officially opened by the cutting of a handmade nettle rope!

the middle of the village of Scone where the housing development at Greystanes surrounds it on three sides. Such a juxtaposition of ancient and modern is unsettling and one cannot help thinking that stone circles are better appreciated in open country where the silence is allowed to speak. Two unusual types of ancient building, not unique to Perthshire but found in considerable numbers here, are crannogs and souterrains, the latter being underground stone chambers, probably for storing agricultural produce, and which date from around the first century AD.

Crannogs date back to the middle of the first millennium and are therefore broadly contemporaneous with the Perthshire hill forts, both owing their existence to the tribal wars of those less peaceful times. They were built in lochs, near to the shore but far enough out for comparative safety, and consisted of a dwelling, resting on a wooden platform, which in turn was supported by poles, some 25 to 30 feet in length, driven into the bed of the loch. These man-made islands were connected to the shore by way of a short timber causeway. In recent years several have been discovered in Loch Tay where, beneath the surface, they have been remarkably well preserved by the cold and peaty water.

The water has also preserved much organic material deriving from the crannog dwellers and has allowed archaeologists to build up a detailed picture of the way of life in prehistoric Perthshire 2500 years ago. Raspberry, bramble and wild cherry seeds have been found in the Oakbank crannog near Fearnan, along with a large amount of wood chips (from the original construction process) and remains of cattle, sheep and goats. Artefacts have included coarse pottery, a wooden plate, a stone hammer and parts of a bucket. Based on these recent discoveries a team from the Scottish Trust for Underwater Archaeology has completed a meticulous reconstruction of a crannog using as far as possible the methods and materials of the original builders. It stands adjacent to the Croft-na-Caber watersports complex at the eastern end of Loch Tay and is intended to be both an educational and tourist attraction.

There is undoubtedly strength in adversity as the Romans, the next wave of invaders, found to their cost. Their push into Scotland under Agricola in around AD 79 and again in around AD 143 under Antonine helped to weld the diverse native tribes into a strong defensive force which was later to develop into the Pictish nation. That Scotland was never completely conquered by the Romans is due to a number of factors, the principal one probably being the crossing of the Danube by the Dacians in around AD 85. To meet this threat, a British-based legion was sent to eastern Europe, a logistical decision which certainly saved the north European frontier but which ultimately meant that there were insufficient troops left in Britain to complete the conquest of the mainland. Central Perthshire therefore remained for brief periods the front line of one of the world's great empires, a distinction which deserves to be better known. Perthshire may thus not have the beautiful mosaic floors and associated domestic paraphernalia of civilised Roman life which can be found further south but does have a considerable number of Roman military remains, from small watch towers to a great legionary fortress.

The earthworks surrounding the Roman fort at Ardoch in the south-west of Perthshire have been described authoritatively as some of the most impressive remains of the entire Roman Empire. Standing here, faced with several rows of defensive trenches and

The Roman fort at Ardoch with its remarkably well-preserved defensive ditches. Try an attack on the fort by running down, then clambering up, the steep slopes three or four times and discover how effective this seemingly simple measure must have been. An active learning technique much favoured by local Latin teachers!

the overwhelming size of the fort, makes one appreciate the sheer invincibility of Roman military might. From Ardoch the Romans advanced along Strathearn and Strathmore, positioning a fort at the entrance to every major Highland glen and at every significant waterway. Thus the fort at Dalginross, near Comrie, blocked the Earn valley, while the one at Fendoch did the same for the Sma Glen. Other forts were built at Strageath on the Earn, at the confluence of the Tay and the Almond just to the north of Perth (the so-called Bertha, a name which dates from only the fourteenth century), and at Cardean on the Isla. Between Strageath and Bertha, along the length of the Gask Ridge, were built a string of small watch towers or signal stations and the remains of several, with the aid of the appropriate guide books and Ordnance Survey maps, can still be seen.

The central point on Agricola's front line was the legionary fortress at Inchtuthil, built to house upwards of 5,500 soldiers plus all their support personnel, and designed to dominate the important Tay valley route to and from the Highlands. There has been much debate about whether the Highland line forts were intended for defensive or offensive operations, but the situation of Inchtuthil, built on the *north* bank of the Tay and at about the same time as the Roman victory at Mons Graupius (wherever that was) in AD 83, surely suggests that the forts were intended as springboards for a future final assault on the Highlands. Within three or four years, however, as a consequence of the Dacian threat, the fortress at Inchtuthil, even before it had been finished, was carefully and completely demolished, and within a further twenty years the Romans had withdrawn to the Tyne-Solway line.

In around AD 143, in a twenty year campaign, the Romans again pushed north into Scotland, building the Antonine Wall and reoccupying the forts at Ardoch, Strageath and Bertha. The construction in around 212 of the major fort at Carpow, near Abernethy, marked their final, serious, attempt at establishing superiority over the Caledonian tribes.

The Picts, who evolved from the pre-Roman tribes of Scotland and who can thus probably be equated with the above-mentioned Caledonians, are first named as such in a Roman source of 297. These people, about whom so little of substance is actually known, held sway in eastern and northern Scotland for the next six centuries. That formidable geographical barrier, the Mounth, which extends westwards across Scotland from south Aberdeenshire, effectively divided the northern Picts from their southern brothers, the latter, in Perthshire, Angus and Fife, occupying what were known as the provinces of Fortriu, in the west, and Fotla in the east. The boundaries of Fortriu are not clear as this one name has been applied in its most limited sense to the areas of Menteith and Strathearn, and in wider senses to the territory of the southern Picts and even to Pictland in its entirety. Fotla was subdivided into the smaller, northern, district of Atholl, possibly bounded on the south by the Tay and the Isla, and the southern district of Gowrie. Menteith, Strathearn and Atholl were later to evolve into the great earldoms of mediaeval Perthshire. The chief settlements in these provinces were Dunkeld in the Atholl district and possibly either Scone or the fort on Dunsinane in Gowrie. It is also possible that Forteviot enjoyed pre-eminence in Fortriu but this can only be speculation.

St Columba, regarded as the apostle to the Picts, is recorded as having travelled up the Great Glen to the court of Brude, king of the northern Picts, and preaching the gospel in front of him. While he may not have been immediately successful it nevertheless seems that most of Pictland was converted by the end of the sixth century. Much of the credit for this great work must go to the many Irish missionaries who crisscrossed the land with their Christian message and whose names are still commemorated in place names and in old church dedications throughout Perthshire and elsewhere. Saints Brendan and Finan, for example, are both remembered in Glen Lyon, as is St Modwenna in Longforgan, St Madoc in St Madoes, St Maelrubha in Amulree and St Moluag in Alyth. The legend that St Ninian visited the east of the country in the fifth century is one possible explanation for Abernethy church's claim to a remarkably early foundation date of 457.

This is not the place, intriguing though it may be, to discuss the current debate about matrilinear succession and the possible non-Indo-European origins of the Pictish language. Suffice it to say that these Dark Age inhabitants of eastern Scotland left the world a remarkably rich heritage of stone carvings, that they allowed Christianity to take root in the east and that following the Battle of Dunnichen in 685 they drove the Angles back south of the Forth, thus preserving what later became the distinctive differences between the English and Scottish peoples. For what are sometimes regarded in Anglo-centric history books as mere savages, we owe them a lot.

The Vikings were the next people to have exerted their influence over the Perthshire area. Not through direct invasion, however, though the east coast was not immune to their murderous raids (the Picts of Fortriu suffered a devastating defeat at the hands of the Vikings in 839) but through their terrorisation of the kingdom of the Scots in Argyll. This was a continual process which gradually forced the Scots to move away from the coastal areas and look for safety towards the Pictish lands in the east. There are signs that the Picts and Scots had been establishing closer relations by the early eighth century and Kenneth MacAlpin was by no means the first Scot to rule over the Picts. He was, however, the first actually to unite the two peoples, quite possibly by conquest though this is not certain, and is therefore regarded as the father of the Scottish nation. His new kingdom, governed from Forteviot and known as Alba, was nevertheless small and extended to probably little more than the Perthshire, Angus and Fife of today.

The Dupplin Cross near Forteviot, having enjoyed a commanding position high above Strathearn for well over a thousand years, may shortly be moving to a new home. Whether it be in Edinburgh or somewhere a little nearer home it will almost certainly be sheltered accommodation. It was possibly erected by Kenneth MacAlpin to mark the union of the Pictish and Scottish kingdoms.

The Vikings were the dominant power around the coasts, Scotland north of the Mounth was practically an independent kingdom under the mormaers of Moray, and the Britons of Strathclyde and the Angles of Northumbria still ruled south of the Forth-Clyde line. Perthshire was truly Scotland's cradle.

By the early tenth century the seat of secular power had been moved to Scone and that of ecclesiastical authority to St Andrews. Within another hundred years Malcolm II had pushed back the southern border to roughly its present position, although it took a great deal longer for his royal descendants to achieve any real political control over the northern half of the kingdom. Hand in hand with territorial expansion went the need to keep a firm grip on distended royal authority and this was achieved in a number of ways.

Firstly, Edgar, son of Malcolm Canmore and St Margaret, having claimed his throne with English help, brought with him a number of Anglo-Norman followers and endowed them with large estates and positions of power. The Perthshire families of Hay, Menzies and Oliphant are all Norman in origin and would, in simple terms, have maintained law and order on the king's behalf in their territories. Secondly, David I began the policy of creating royal burghs in which he granted trading rights and other privileges to the burgesses in return for a share of their revenues. Perth was one of the earliest royal burghs in Scotland, probably receiving its charter in around 1125, and was joined by 1246 by Auchterarder, the only other mediaeval royal burgh in the county. Culross, an isolated pocket of Perthshire on the banks of the Forth (which was transferred to Fife in 1891), achieved the same status in 1592 and Dunkeld in 1704. Burghs of barony, with limited rights, were also established during the same period. Thirdly, David also created the office of sheriff, another English import, through which in practice was administered justice, law and order in areas not under the direct control of the chief landowners and burghs. Perth was the seat of a sheriff by the mid twelfth century whose authority extended to more or less the present boundaries of Perthshire. Auchterarder and Scone were both briefly sheriffdoms before being absorbed into that of Perth. And fourthly, the twelfth century also saw the introduction of a number of monastic orders into Scotland whose presence was as much a force for spiritual good as secular. Before the founding of the universities in the fifteenth century the great abbeys of Coupar Angus, Inchaffray and Scone, together with the almost mythical educational centre at Dull, would have acted as havens of advanced learning while the first named, under Cistercian rule, was equally well known for its land improvements.

It can be seen, therefore, that Perthshire, with authority and trade centred on Perth, was already becoming a territorial entity. It stayed this way, virtually intact, for more than eight hundred years until the sweeping local government reforms of the 1970s abolished, at least as administrative units, the county and its burghs. Such ancient territories, however, could not be so easily erased from the memory as they could from the map; there was an outcry in 1996 when in the wake of the latest round of local authority changes it was proposed that the former Stirling District, which from 1975 had included a sizeable chunk of south-western Perthshire, should be formally renamed Stirlingshire. The good councillors of Stirling had clearly underestimated the continuing strength of loyalty to the centuries-old concept of Perthshire and eventually had to back down.

Perth in the Middle Ages had developed into a town of economic importance, heavily dependent on the produce of its hinterland, on its local merchants and craftsmen and on its overseas trading links. With its fine town kirk and surrounding monasteries it was also a religious centre of some significance and it was therefore quite natural that the kings of mediaeval Scotland should have considered it as one of their chief towns. Whether or not it could ever have been regarded as the capital of Scotland, however, is a question which continues to intrigue many people. The main point to remember is that the concept of a national capital would have been incomprehensible in the later Middle Ages when it was accepted and expected that the king and his entourage should travel around the country, holding court in a number of important towns. Even so, judging by the dates and places of issue of royal charters, the bulk of royal administration and business seems to have been carried out in Perth (or Scone) until at least the middle of the fourteenth century, and in this sense Perth could be regarded — anachronistically — as Scotland's capital. After this time a greater proportion of charters were issued from Edinburgh and by the time of the murder of James I in 1437 at Perth's Blackfriars monastery (the royal residence in Perth following the destruction of the castle in 1209), and perhaps even partly because of it, Edinburgh was well on the way to becoming the capital of the nation in the modern sense.

The regicide of 1437 was one of the most notorious events ever to have occurred within (or correctly speaking, just outside) the city. James I was a forceful monarch and in the course of stamping his authority on the kingdom had alienated a number of his nobles, one such being Robert Stewart of Atholl, grandson of the Earl of Atholl. Using his position as head of the king's household he quietly prepared the scene for the assassination by tampering with the locks in the royal apartments, dismissing the guards and arranging for planks to be laid across the surrounding moat. Just before the king retired to bed, clad in his nightshirt and furry slippers, a number of well-armed men, perhaps as many as 300, burst into the Blackfriars house. The king, with no obvious means of escape, managed to prise up a floorboard and drop into a tunnel below. Unfortunately, fed up with losing tennis balls into the same tunnel, he himself had ordered the only egress to be blocked up shortly beforehand. He was trapped and it was only a matter of time before he was discovered and brutally hacked to death. A possibly fanciful, and certainly later, addition to the story concerned one of the ladies of the court, Catherine Douglas, who, realising that the doors could not be locked, bravely used her arm to bar the door. The legend of Kate Barlass, from whom the Barlas family claim descent, was born the moment her arm was cruelly broken.

In the later Middle Ages the Lowlands and the Highlands began socially and culturally to drift apart, divided as much by language as by the geographical barrier of the high mountains. Scots had been established as the language of the early burghs and by around 1400 had become the language of the whole of Lowland Scotland, spread because of the simple and basic need in a commercial world to communicate. The Gaelic-speaking Highlanders, on the other hand, were settling into an almost self-sufficient lifestyle, and on the occasions when they required food or animals from the Lowlands they came south without any of the social niceties and took it. Lowlanders regarded themselves as peaceful and cultured and saw the Highlanders as little more than thieving, feuding barbarians. From across the Highland line Lowlanders were viewed as cowardly, weak and contemptible. Towns such as Dunkeld were essentially frontier outposts on the very edges of civilisation, a view doubtless shared by both sides.

At the end of the mediaeval period we can imagine Perth as a great town, still enjoying its wealth, privilege and royal patronage, but no longer the seat of political power. But instead of enjoying a peaceful retirement in the sun, the storm clouds were gathering on the horizon. The Reformation, whose destructive power was first unleashed in Perth in 1559, marks the beginning of two centuries of dreadful turbulence in which political and religious tensions, natural disasters and civil war, combined to make this period the lowest in the town's history.

The old religious establishment was swept away by a violent mob which, having heard John Knox's sermon in St John's Kirk in May 1559, rampaged through the town damaging beyond repair almost all the city's churches, chapels and neighbouring monasteries. From this time Perth's protestant (and later presbyterian) sympathies were never in doubt and in 1640, at a time when the beleaguered Charles I was intent on imposing the Prayer Book on Scotland,

Perth was staunchly behind the Covenanting movement. The Battle of Tibbermore in 1644 was nevertheless a defeat for the Covenanters at the hands of Marquis of Montrose and serves as a reminder that many of the gentry of rural and Highland Perthshire remained loyal to the Roman Catholic or Episcopal faith.

In 1603, shortly after the Gowrie House conspiracy, James VI acceded to the English throne and thereafter royalty rarely came to Perth, another contributory factor in the declining fortunes of the town at this time. Half a century later, following the execution of Charles I and the coronation of the exiled Charles II at Scone, the town was occupied by Cromwell's troops who were stationed in the massive citadel on the South Inch. The construction of this deeply hated stronghold entailed the demolition of many of Perth's buildings and the lifting of good grazing turf from the Inches, again causing further hardship to the inhabitants. And if such tumultuous events were not enough Perth had to endure a number of natural disasters, including the devastating plague of the mid-1640s, which killed possibly as much as half of the city's population, the severe famine of the 1690s and a series of hard winters in the early 1700s. The destruction by flood of the Perth Bridge in 1621 and the gradual silting of the Tay posed a serious threat to Perth's status as a trading town. The city only emerged from this long catalogue of problems and setbacks in the mid-eighteenth century.

The Glorious Revolution of 1688, in which the Roman Catholic James VII and II was forced to abandon his throne to his protestant daughter Mary and her husband William of Orange, led directly to more than half a century of Jacobite unrest and triggered the final round of battles and skirmishes on Perthshire soil. The first of these took place in 1689 when John Graham of Claverhouse, Viscount Dundee, raised the standard of King James and having captured Blair Castle, the strategically important seat of the Marquis of Atholl, began to advance on the Lowlands. The government army meanwhile was heading north to retake the castle and the two sides met, almost by chance, at the pass of Killiecrankie where the opening battle of the Jacobite campaigns was fought and where Dundee was shot at the very moment of his victory. The Jacobite army moved south under a new commander but was soundly defeated at Dunkeld the following month in a military action which also resulted in the near destruction of the ancient cathedral city.

At about 9.00 in the evening on 28 January 1716, in a bitter frost, the Jacobite troops under the command of Lord George Murray put the village of Dunning to the torch. Only a few houses escaped and several inhabitants died from shock and exposure. The Dunning Thorn was planted to commemorate this inhuman act of war.

The 1715 uprising owed much to the unpopular Act of Union of 1707 and to the replacement of the House of Stuart, with its ancient ties to Scotland, by that of Hanover. With much of Scotland as a consequence now for the Jacobite cause the reason for its failure is reckoned to have been the military ineptitude of its leader, the Earl of Mar. The short-lived adventure was checked at the Battle of Sheriffmuir, near Dunblane, which although indecisive was a strategic defeat for the Jacobites. Mar withdrew along Strathearn and, in order to deny the government forces both food and shelter during this particularly harsh January of 1716, burnt the towns and villages of Blackford, Auchterarder, Crieff, Muthill and Dunning along the way. Eventually, realising that he could no longer hold his base at Perth, he fled the country by ship from Montrose in the company of the Old Pretender, James, who had briefly set up court at Scone. One practical benefit from this disastrous affair was the construction of a network of military roads which were designed to allow the government forces to move quickly around the Highlands should another rebellion ever happen again. The present A9 follows the line of one of these roads where previously the more direct Minigaig route took the traveller high over the mountains between Blair Atholl and Kingussie.

The '45 has been so steeped in romance that even from a perspective of two centuries historians can still vehemently disagree about whether Culloden was good or bad for Scotland. The main events are of course well known and although few of them took place within the Perthshire boundary, the Jacobite passage southwards through the county was a time of consolidation and preparation. On what has been described as a walk to Edinburgh the Young Pretender's army stopped off at Blair Castle where the exiled Jacobite Duke William, having been out in the '15 and consequently deprived of his right to inherit the Atholl title and estates, entered his ancestral home. His younger brother, the lawful Duke James and a Hanoverian supporter, did not stay to welcome him. From Atholl the army moved south to Perth where the magistrates, and probably many of the townspeople too, had little love for Prince Charles Edward and his unruly Highlanders. Nevertheless, in an eight day period of recruiting and drilling, the third brother of the House of Atholl, Lord George Murray, rallied to the cause and together with James Drummond, the Jacobite Duke of Perth, provided the military leadership for a campaign which was surely lost before it had even begun.

The repressive measures taken by the government after Culloden were designed as much to punish the Highlands, irrespective of the political leanings of the various clans, as to prevent the possibility of yet another uprising. Rebel estates were forfeited, including those of the Duke of Perth and the aged arch-Jacobite Robertson of Struan, the powers of all the great landowners were reduced, the bearing of arms was forbidden and the bagpipes and Highland dress were outlawed. A legal document of the time records the somewhat pathetic petition of an elderly man in Killin who, having been caught wearing the kilt by a military patrol and then jailed, requested to be released because his goats were running wild and he had no-one to look after them. He should perhaps have circumvented the law, as others did, by loosely stitching the kilt in the middle. The Gaelic poet Duncan Ban Macintyre, who had connections with west Perthshire, penned a *Song to the Breeches* of which this in translation is the first stanza:

O the light grey breeches
cast a gloom on us this year!
'Tis a thing not seen on us before,
one we dislike to keep on us;
and had we all been loyal
to the king who appealed to us,
we had not been seen till doomsday
submitting to this garment.

This was one of the poet's earliest works and he was happily around to celebrate in a much lighter mood the repeal of the hated Act and the return of the tartan in 1782.

The draconian actions of the London government served only to hasten, rather than initiate, the end of Highland isolation. From the beginning of the eighteenth century the Gaelic-speaking frontier, which had been more or less stable for about 300 years, began again to recede. This was due to a number of factors, among them the large number of English language schools set up in Highland parishes through the missionary zeal of the SSPCK (the Society in Scotland for Propagating Christian Knowledge) and the gentry's increasing preoccupation with English ideas of improvement. Furthermore, the gradual move away from the self-sufficient Highland economy to one founded on more commercial principles, stimulated by landowners who were looking for better returns on their money, naturally resulted in more contact with the Lowlands. By the end of the eighteenth century Gaelic Scotland had been tamed: the language was increasingly on the wane, the landlord-tenant relationship had taken over from the old clan-based system of land tenure, and the traditional dress of the Highlands was shortly to reappear as a virtual pastiche on the corpulent figure of George IV. On the other hand, the literature and culture of the Highlands had achieved a new respectability thanks mainly to James 'Ossian' Macpherson whose writings had become the focus of much interest and debate in the cultural circles of western Europe. This, perhaps more than anything, encouraged the beginnings of the Scottish tourist industry which is now the mainstay of the Perthshire and Highland economies.

The second half of the eighteenth century witnessed almost as much of a change in Lowland Perthshire as was taking place north of the Highland line. The Agricultural Revolution is the umbrella term for the tremendous improvements in farming practice which

The Round House is now home to the Fergusson Gallery but was originally designed by Adam Anderson as the Perth waterworks. The column beside it, topped by the classical urn, was actually the chimney for the steam pump, the mechanical process being alluded to in the Latin quotation above the door: Aquam igne et aqua haurio — I draw water by fire and water. This was chalked on the wall by Anderson himself only a few days before he died.

saw, for example, the introduction of new crops such as potatoes and turnips, the adoption of the principles of crop rotation, the drainage of land (particularly in the Carse of Gowrie), and the move towards enclosures and the enlargement of farms. While this resulted in a considerable increase in the wealth and standard of living of farmers it also signified the end of rural life for many agricultural labourers who were forced off the land and either into the towns in search of work or into the emigrant ships in the hope of a better life overseas. This was exacerbated in the early nineteenth century by the clearances in parts of Rannoch, Breadalbane and Atholl when people were evicted from their homes to make way for sheep. These major rural changes were reflected in rapid urban growth throughout the Lowlands and in many a town, Perth included, there developed a thriving community of Gaelic-speaking Highlanders.

The demise of Jacobitism also marked the end of Perth's two centuries of troubles. Agricultural improvements and the strength of the county's linen industry were important factors in the new prosperity and outward optimism of the city, which were expressed in the construction of the new Perth Bridge of 1771 and in the Georgian suburbs to the north and south. As the better off moved out to these desirable properties the poorer families crammed into the town centre in ever increasing numbers. Social improvements to minimise disease were thus of prime importance and resulted in the provision of a healthy water supply by the early 1830s and by 1838, following a devastating cholera epidemic which claimed around 10,000 Scottish lives, the opening of the Perth Infirmary. Most of the larger towns in the county followed Perth's lead during the course of the nineteenth century. The Victorian era, as has been described elsewhere, witnessed a further expansion of the town, the diversification of local industries and social legislation to provide for the poor and to formalise the educational structure of the nation.

The main events of twentieth century history left their mark on the county. Suffragettes were active in the area and reached new heights of protest in February 1914 by successfully burning down two large country houses. The authorities retaliated with particularly harsh treatment at Perth Prison where the rough force feeding of suffragettes was notorious. The industrial unrest of Red Clydeside during World War I spread in a much diluted form to Pullars, the county's largest individual employer. By 1917 labour relations at the Perth dye-works had deteriorated to such an extent that on one occasion a crowd of 2000 angry workers besieged the factory gates and had to be dispersed by a detachment of mounted police. This, perhaps more than anything, persuaded the family to sell the company the following year. In May 1926 many local employees with varying degrees of enthusiasm were drawn into the General Strike as the shutting down of the railways had an immediate effect on tourism and business.

PERTH AND KINROSS

With Perth being the home of the Black Watch and Perthshire the main recruiting territory, the two world wars exacted a high cost from local families. The regiment, as part of the Highland Division, served in Flanders and the Middle East during the first war and suffered around 28,000 casualties including 8000 men dead. There was relief but little joy at the war's end and within a few years most towns and villages had the names of their lost sons inscribed on newly erected war memorials. The Second World War ended rather too abruptly for many local men of the 51st Highland Division when they were captured by Rommel at St Valery-en-Caux in Normandy in June 1940. Whiling away their time in a German prisoner of war camp, some of the officers devised a new Scottish dance which is known today as the Reel of the 51st Highland Division and which, the details having been posted back to Scotland, was actually performed in their home country long before the originators were freed. Later in the war the reformed 51st pursued Rommel across the deserts of North Africa and were given the honour of liberating St Valery in 1944. In May 1995 Perth hosted one of the biggest and best-attended celebrations in the country to mark the 50th anniversary of the end of the war, though locally there was some disquiet when it became apparent that no-one had ever thought to compile a complete list of Perthshire's war dead.

The main conflicts in Perthshire today are fought by proponents of the various political parties, either through the letters columns of the local press or through the ballot box. Perthshire has the air of a prosperous Conservative stronghold which indeed it generally has been in recent decades. The Scottish National Party, however, has long contended that there is a solid bedrock of nationalist support beneath the Tory topsoil and vindicated the claim by winning the 1995 Perth and Kinross by-election, overturning the late Sir Nicholas Fairbairn's slender majority. In the 1997 general election the SNP held onto the new Perth seat and swept the long-sitting Tory member from North Tayside. The Labour Party is also active locally but enjoys little success outside Perth city.

Perth and Kinross have had more than their fair share of parliamentary by-elections, having undergone three in about 60 years, two of which hit the national headlines. The first of these occurred in 1938 and centred on Katharine, Duchess of Atholl, who was Scotland's first woman MP and the first Conservative woman to hold ministerial office. One of a small group of parliamentary anti-appeasers she found herself, in the wake of Chamberlain's Munich Agreement with Hitler, totally at odds with her constituency association and with the mood of the party as a whole. Having been de-selected by her association she resigned her seat and prepared to fight as an independent. With the central pillar of the government's foreign policy in danger of collapse, the Tory party machine leafleted every household in the constituency and sent in an army of MPs, speaking out for appeasement and depicting the 'Red Duchess' as little less than a warmonger. It must have been hard on polling day to have voted against 'peace in our time', yet the fact that she came within 1400 votes of inflicting a humiliating defeat on Chamberlain testifies as much to her personal following as to her powers of persuasion and her politics of principle. It was rumoured, probably with justification, that Hitler himself regarded the election result as an indication of Britain's reluctance to fight. It is tempting to speculate that if the result had been different he might have thought twice about invading Czechoslovakia three months later.

The events surrounding the Kinross and West Perthshire by-election of 1963 again caught the attention of the nation. The death of the sitting MP coincided with the decision of the ailing Harold Macmillan to resign the premiership and the subsequent 'emerging' of the 14th Earl of Home as his successor. On 18 October Home was invited to form a government and on the 19th the Conservative candidate, George Younger (later Margaret Thatcher's defence secretary) was publicly offering his congratulations to the new premier and privately expressing his relief that his adoption process had been concluded before Home's need to find a Commons seat had become apparent. Three days later, however, and doubtless after intense pressure, Younger stood down and Home became the official candidate. The next day he resigned his peerage and in doing so created a situation unparalleled in modern times whereby the Prime Minister, albeit briefly, had neither a seat in the House of Commons nor in the House of Lords.

Perthshire at the end of the twentieth century enjoys a self confidence based on its scenic attractions, distinguished history and sound economic base. The future, however, is impossible to predict: while it seems that agriculture and tourism will sustain the economy for many years to come there are nagging doubts about the future of the whisky industry and about the continuing loyalty of the General Accident to Perth. Politically no-one can discount the possibility that Scotland will one day gain full independence. If this should happen — and the general benefits or otherwise will long be argued — Perthshire would at least regain its central position within the nation and with it might come, perhaps, a claim based on historical precedent that Perth should be the national capital. And why not? Perthshire's future may yet prove to be as lively as its past.

CHAPTER 4
GROVES OF ACADEME

The great 'what-ifs' of history are endlessly fascinating. What if, for example, the Romans had had an industrial revolution, Napoleon had won at Waterloo or Hitler had been born a girl? Just to add to the fun of speculation, what if Pope Martin V, back in 1426, had agreed to the request of Scotland's James I that the new university at St Andrews be translated to Perth? Instead of developing relatively slowly under the bishops and archbishops of St Andrews at the very edge of eastern Scotland, the University of Perth, situated in one of the kingdom's chief towns and enjoying a large measure of royal patronage, might well have expanded rapidly. There would in all probability have been a King's College which in turn might have stimulated the powerful families and wealthy bishops of the nation to endow colleges of their own. It has even been suggested that, had the move taken place, there would have been no need for any other Scottish university, and the possibility then arises that Perth, with a concentration of educated administrators, might conceivably have blossomed into the modern capital of Scotland, instead of Edinburgh. A present-day Perth, with mediaeval quadrangles, a richness of libraries and great civic buildings, with students, tourists and begowned academics, was perhaps only a papal decision away.

On two subsequent occasions Perth again came very close to becoming a university town. The first was in the late 1690s when the staff and students at St Andrews were enduring such poor living conditions that they themselves made approaches to the Perth magistrates with a view to the university being translated thirty miles westwards to the Fair City. Judging by the following extract from the university's list of reasons the proposed move was perfectly understandable: 'This place being now only a village, where most part farmers dwell, the whole streets are filled with Dunghills, which are exceedingly noisome and ready to infect the air, especially at this season when the herring gutts are exposed in them...'

Another paragraph in the same document describes an incident in 1690 when some of the townspeople 'chased the Students into

53

the Colledges and broght their cannons to the very gates to throw down the Colledge...'. The relative tranquillity of Perth and its status and central location within the kingdom must have been powerful incentives for the authorities at St Andrews. Yet, following the sudden and unexpected healing of the town-gown rift, they proved to be insufficiently attractive to allow the translation to take place. Although there is no surviving record of how the negotiations were wound up, the proposals appear to have been quietly dropped by both sides. Almost 300 years later, in the 1960s, Perth was one of the front runners (competing with Ayr, Dumfries, Falkirk, Inverness and Stirling) in discussions about a possible fifth university for Scotland. The decision eventually went in favour of Stirling which was the first such complex to be purpose-built in Scotland since Edinburgh's foundation in the sixteenth century.

The growth of distance learning in recent years, pioneered most notably by the Open University, has led to the proposed University of the Highlands and Islands. This embryo network of colleges in the north and west of Scotland, with the backing of National Lottery funding as well as a number of organisations for economic development, may well be awarding its first degrees before the end of the century. As Perth College marks the southern outpost of this educational confederation, which stretches as far as Shetland in the north and Skye in the west, the city may yet realise its long-held dream of achieving — if only to a limited extent — university status. Should the scheme be successful then the first MA degrees in rock music performance may not be long in coming. Perth College hit the headlines a few years ago by establishing the first 'academic' course in this subject in Britain, attracting students from all over the country.

If at the moment the county cannot boast a university it at least has a highly regarded research establishment. This is the Scottish Crop Research Institute at Invergowrie, close to the centre of Dundee but still properly in Perth and Kinross, and whose lengthy staff list reads like a Who's Who of horticulture. It developed from a scientific inquiry into the failure of the raspberry crop in the Blairgowrie area in the 1930s and 1940s and is still primarily concerned with local produce such as soft fruit and potatoes. As well as researching crop diseases the institute also develops new varieties of fruit and vegetable. One particularly popular product is the tayberry, a hybrid of the raspberry and blackberry which is reckoned to be bigger and tastier than both.

One of Perthshire's best known educational institutions closed in 1996 after 60 years of service to the aviation industry. Perth Aerodrome, situated about 400 feet above sea level on a site to the north of Scone, was the setting for a flying school which has trained many of the world's commercial airline pilots. Opened in 1936, the aerodrome initially had the dual functions of providing flying training to RAF and associated personnel, and, through the company North Eastern Airways, of operating regular passenger services between Perth and cities such as Aberdeen, Newcastle, Leeds and London. One of the early recruits in the later 1930s was former Perth Academy pupil, Neil Cameron, who rose to become Chief of the Defence Staff, Marshall of the Royal Air Force and later still, Lord Cameron of Balhousie. Towards the end of the 1950s the training role of the aerodrome shifted from military to civil aviation while the teaching programme expanded to embrace both aeronautical engineering and English language. The latter might have seemed an odd adjunct to a flying school but, with many foreign students under training and the fact that English is the international language of the air, it was indeed an essential part. The aerodrome was owned and operated latterly by Air Service Training Ltd, a division of Bristows, the helicopter manufacturers. In a sense, the rotor blade had turned full circle as a prototype of the Kay Gyroplane, a forerunner of the modern helicopter, was built by David Kay at Perth and tested at the aerodrome in the 1930s. The soft drone in the skies above Perth and Scone, which was such a familiar noise to the residents, will not disappear altogether as the Scottish Aero Club still operates from the aerodrome and still offers flying lessons, but no longer to jumbo jet standard.

School education has had a long and distinguished history in Perth. The Grammar School, which evolved into the present day Perth Academy, is first mentioned in a charter of 1150 and may owe its origins, as do the great universities of Oxford and Cambridge, to that spirit of intellectual regeneration known as the Twelfth Century Renaissance. The school has occupied a number of locations in the course of its development, ranging from Speygate and St Ann's Lane (where a commemorative plaque can be seen) in the town centre to Rose Terrace and Viewlands, which at the time of building were both greenfield sites on the edge of town.

In 1807 the two main schools in Perth, the Grammar School and the Academy, were brought together under the roof of this splendid building in Rose Terrace, now known as the Old Academy. Here, 'the ancient office of Teacher of Music…is at present [1849] occupied by Mr David Peacock, a gentleman of acknowledged talent and of long experience'. So says the author of Perth: its annals and its archives, *one Mr David Peacock.*

The Old Academy building, designed by Robert Reid and completed in 1807, is perhaps the finest example of late Georgian architecture in the city. Its quiet repose, overlooking the North Inch and the River Tay beyond, was rudely interrupted in 1989 when a development company tackled the problem of the building's dry rot by ripping out the celebrated ornate plasterwork from the famous Octagonal Room. The developers, incurring by such drastic action the wrath of Perth Civic Trust, the district council and the local newspaper too, have since restored the room to its original state, but even during its reconstruction the bare shell of this former school assembly hall stood out as a remarkably fine piece of architecture. The main part of the building, having remained empty for a number of years following the departure of the library service's headquarters, has also been successfully renovated and now houses, amongst others, the local registrar's office.

The wide frontage of the present Academy complex at Viewlands, with its central clocktower and large grassy area in front, seems to echo its predecessor on Rose Terrace. The school, sitting high above Perth amidst its acres of playing fields, was opened in 1932 and until the later 1960s, when comprehensive education was introduced, was reckoned to be the strongest academically in the area. In recent years, however, Perth High School has mounted a strong challenge for that accolade and, as if to demonstrate in a physical sense the perceived but arguable reversal of roles, now occupies a modern building looking down over the Academy to the town below. Perth has two other senior secondary schools, the resurrected Perth Grammar and the Roman Catholic St Columba's.

As befits a long established and highly regarded school a number of distinguished people have passed through the Grammar School/Academy doors. One such, probably, was James Crichton, better known as the Admirable Crichton (not to be confused with the character in Barrie's play of the same name), who was born in 1560, the son of the Lord Advocate of the time. He mastered, it is said, no fewer than twelve languages, disputed successfully with the most learned European scholars of the day, and was a poet and musician of some note. Not content with being an academic polyglot this remarkable man also found time to serve in the French army and become an expert swordsman. At the age of about 25 he was treacherously killed in Italy by his pupil, the son of the Duke of Mantua, having more than earned his somewhat understated epithet.

Another former pupil with a tenuous French connection was Sir Patrick Geddes who was born in 1854 and who later came to be known as the 'father of town planning'. Although hardly a household name, it has been argued that through his pioneering work on planning and sociology he should be regarded as one of the most influential figures of the nineteenth and twentieth centuries. Such a statement, which would place him on a par with Marx and Darwin, may not be too wide of the mark; his theories are still quietly influencing our lives, even if not as blatantly controversial as those of communism and evolution. He ended his varied career at Montpellier in south-west France, where he died in 1932. More than sixty years later the Geddes Society is investigating ways of commemorating the man in his home town.

Controversial though Darwin's theory may have been when it first appeared in print in 1859, it stirred not theological outrage but a sense of indignant injustice in the heart of Patrick Matthew, an elderly gentleman who owned the small estate of Gourdiehill in the Carse of Gowrie. Matthew was born in 1790 and, after schooling at Perth and an undistinguished career at Edinburgh University, succeeded to his estate at a comparatively young age. The ensuing years were devoted to farming and forestry, the latter an awakening interest which came to fruition in the publication in 1831 of his *Naval Timber and Arboriculture*. One of the appendices to this work, based on his close observation of nature, was no less than a succinct exposition of the theory of evolution by natural selection. While evolutionary theory alone was not new, the suggested process of natural selection undoubtedly was. Almost thirty years later, having read a review of *The Origin of Species*, Matthew wrote to Darwin to remind him that he had already arrived at, and published, the same conclusions. Darwin then replied with the following remarkable statement: 'I freely acknowledge that Mr Matthew has anticipated by many years the explanation which I have offered of the origin of species under the name of natural selection'. Although Matthew and Darwin corresponded over the years they never actually met, and indeed one gets the distinct impression from some of the published letters that the by now world-famous Darwin was disconcerted, if not embarrassed, by his rival's undeniable assertion to be the first published enunciator of the theory of evolution by natural selection. Patrick Matthew clearly did not appreciate at the time the full enormity of the ideas he was propounding. Had he published them more widely and pressed for recognition earlier, he, rather than Darwin, might well have been celebrated as one of the towering figures of the nineteenth century.

Two years behind Patrick Geddes at the Academy was William Archer, a Perth-born lad whose family connections with Norway allowed him to spend much time in that country. At the age of 17 he first read the works of Henrik Ibsen and was so captivated by Norway's greatest playwright that he is now remembered primarily as the translator into English of his plays. Archer was also a leading drama critic and in his time one of the big names in the world of British theatre. It is time, perhaps, that Perth took steps to honour yet another of her almost forgotten sons.

The Scottish education system has had an enviable reputation for several centuries and to this day remains proudly independent of its southern neighbour. While the burgh schools, such as the

Grammar School at Perth, enjoyed a long history as centres of academic excellence, the parish schools, which flourished in the eighteenth and nineteenth centuries, provided the foundations for the educational structure of the nation as a whole. These were complemented, amongst others, by schools established and supported by the Society in Scotland for Propagating Christian Knowledge, an organisation which originated in 1709 and which by 1781 was funding 180 schools and educating around 7000 children, chiefly in the Highlands and Islands.

The Old Statistical Accounts of the northern Perthshire parishes give interesting details of the types of schooling available in the 1790s and illustrate the value which families in these remote but once populous areas placed on education. In Fortingall, for example, there was one parish school and four others run by the SSPCK. The writer adds that some parents, 'who are distant from these, and the parish school, pay for a boy to teach their children to read and write.' There were apparently six of these 'private' schools in the parish, making a total of eleven altogether. Contrary to what might be assumed, some of these local schools provided a very high standard of education, equipping their most able pupils to proceed direct to the universities.

These days the Perthshire glens are sadly depopulated and, with the provision of schooling now a function of the local authority, the concern formerly shown by charities such as the SSPCK has long since dwindled. Education chiefs now have to confront alone the problem of catering for the needs of a comparatively small but widespread population and consequently face accusations of either financial overstretching or unfairness to small communities. Hard decisions regularly have to be taken and regularly result in howls of protest, some of which may win a stay of execution or a reprieve but rarely a full pardon. In recent years, following a logistical review, Pitlochry High School has been demoted in status and Alyth High School has been closed, leaving Blairgowrie High as the only full six-year secondary school in north-east Perthshire.

One particularly difficult decision concerned Georgetown Primary, a small, single-teacher school beside Loch Rannoch in one of the remotest parts of the Scottish mainland. Partly through the intervention in 1988 of the well-known conservationist, David Bellamy, a project on trees and tree-planting resulted in the creation of a twinning link with a school on Rarotonga, part of the Cook Islands, in the South Pacific. The school was featured on the children's television programme *Blue Peter* and, perhaps as a consequence of all the publicity, succeeded in raising sufficient funds to enable the head teacher and four pupils to visit Rarotonga in 1993 on an educational exchange. But even an excellent and high-profile school such as this could not escape the cuts in local authority spending. In the summer of 1994, Tayside Region's Education Department, amid vociferous but ultimately fruitless protest, closed the school for the last time.

Breadalbane Academy, which can trace its roots back at least as far as the early nineteenth century, is situated in Aberfeldy and acts as the main secondary school for the north-west of the county. Its huge catchment area, which ranges from Dunkeld, only fifteen miles north of Perth, to the furthest reaches of Rannoch, close to the Argyll and Inverness-shire border, necessitates the provision of weekly boarding facilities for some of the more distant pupils. A vivid illustration of the distances involved is provided by the timetable for the school bus which, during the 1994–95 session, had to leave Bridge of Gaur at 6.55 am on a Monday morning in order to reach Aberfeldy in time for the first class. With a school population of less than 600, about half the number at any of the big Perth schools, Breadalbane has nevertheless enjoyed a sound academic reputation; indeed, it has been known to attract boarders from England and overseas, though what these pupils would have made of the Gaelic classes is anyone's guess.

Perthshire is often regarded as being an anachronistically feudal county, where vast tracts of land are owned by the local aristocracy and where the gentry and county families still dominate the social scene. This may partly account for the siting of so many independent schools in the area; apart from the urban concentrations in Edinburgh and Glasgow no rural Scottish county has a greater number than Perthshire. Although many of the pupils at the boarding establishments come from beyond the generally accepted local catchment areas, a considerable proportion still hails from the home territory.

A short article in the *Perthshire Courier* of October 1841, drawing attention to the 'intended Puseyite University at Perth', must have raised as many eye-brows then as it does today. This, in fact, is one of the earliest written references to Perthshire's

The wide frontage of Glenalmond College viewed from Front Avenue. Such was the youthful enthusiasm behind the school's foundation that at the 50th anniversary celebrations in 1891 the guest list could boast not only the very first pupil (a distinction hard won by erroneously turning up a day early) but one of the founders (Gladstone) and the first Warden.

oldest and best known public school, Glenalmond College, or, to use its pre-1983 name, Trinity College, Glenalmond. Whereas the guiding spirit of the new foundation was the blossoming Oxford Movement, the driving force behind it was the future Prime Minister, William Ewart Gladstone who, with a small group of like-minded friends, sought to revive the fortunes of the Episcopal Church in Scotland. Originally conceived as an Anglican theological college as well as a school, Glenalmond performed its dual roles from 1847, when the first students were admitted, to 1876 when, following a major fire, the theological students departed permanently for Edinburgh. The college has nevertheless maintained its close links with the Scottish Episcopal Church, with daily chapel services at the centre of school life and a number of bishops on the governing body. The main building has an impressive frontage behind which is a cloistered quadrangle worthy of any Oxbridge college. The grounds extend to around 250 acres and stretch out on either side of Front Avenue, the long and winding approach to the school, and down to the banks of the River Almond behind. All the teaching and some of the ancillary staff live on campus, a necessary arrangement as the college on occasions can find itself cut off from the outside world by the snow of its own little microclimate.

Glenalmond's chief rival on the playing field is undoubtedly Strathallan, a fully co-educational boarding and day school which, despite its comparatively recent foundation date of 1912, has become one of the biggest independent schools in Perthshire. Although reasonably close to Strathallan Castle near Auchterarder the name of the school is explained by its original eight year sojourn at Bridge of Allan in Stirlingshire; it moved in 1920 to Freeland House at Forgandenny, about seven miles south-west of Perth, retaining the old name. Nearby lies Kilgraston, a Roman Catholic (though not exclusively) school for girls which moved to its present site at Bridge of Earn in 1930, ten years after its first beginnings in Edinburgh. The main school building, a superb example of Georgian elegance, was for many years the home of one of the Grant families of Strathspey. Morrison's Academy, the largest of the county's independent schools, is situated in Crieff, while Rannoch School braves the less hospitable climate further to the north, beside the loch of the same name. The strong emphasis on community service at Rannoch, based on the Gordonstoun ethos, has led to the school's fire service being fully recognised as an auxiliary branch of the Tayside Fire Brigade.

Private and state sector schools co-exist peaceably, although a certain amount of rivalry is inevitable. They meet together on the sports fields but also in other activities such as debating. The motion for one particularly lively inter-school debate early in 1995 was that private schools should be abolished; to the credit of all the budding young parliamentarians, it was conducted in a spirit of great good humour with half the children being in the unenviable position of having to argue the case against systems of education from which they themselves were benefiting. To report that the motion was defeated testifies as much to the debating skills of local schoolchildren as to their commendably fair-minded approach to life.

CHAPTER 5

THE PERTHSHIRE WORKING MAN

'**P**it yer coat on, wumman, A'm aff tae the pub', said the Perthshire farmer to his goodwife. 'Why, that's braw, Jimmy,' said Jessie, 'an are ye takin me too?' 'You?' came the reply. 'Nae wey. A'm turnin the heatin aff'. On men such as Jimmy has the economic wellbeing of Perthshire long depended; farmers, of necessity careful with their money, who know only too well the hard living off the land, the unforgiving weather and the capriciousness of the market place. In the days before the Agricultural and Industrial revolutions probably the majority of country dwellers would have been tied to the land, either as farmers or as agricultural labourers. Nowadays, as a result of increasing efficiency and mechanisation, only 7% of the county's workforce is engaged in this industry, but they still make an impressive contribution to the Perthshire GDP.

The varied topography of the county is reflected in the variety of agricultural enterprise. The Lowland fields abound with cereals, (wheat, barley and oats), root crops (virus-free seed potatoes), soft fruit and oil seed rape; on marginal land and in the hills and mountains the emphasis is on livestock production. In total about 85% of Perthshire land is devoted to agriculture of some sort.

It is the commercial soft fruit industry, however, which, thanks to the nature of the soil and climate around the Blairgowrie area, has enjoyed a growing international reputation. Within hours of being picked many of these strawberries and raspberries, reckoned to be amongst the most flavoursome in the world, will be found on the shelves of some of England's favourite supermarkets and in the hospitality tents of Wimbledon and Henley. Undoubtedly the best way to enjoy this succulent fruit is to buy a freshly-picked punnet from a wayside stall and eat them immediately. What really brings out the flavour is not sugar, cream or even pepper but the rumours of 'a pound a berry' at Wimbledon. A century on from the first tentative attempts at commercial berry production some of the local farmers are now adopting the latest agricultural technologies to remain at the industry's cutting edge, and forging

Strawberry growing in the 1990s. This innovative system, incorporating techniques pioneered overseas, was introduced at Scones Lethendy farm in 1992. The use of polythene tunnels has extended the strawberry season by almost three months. Such is the competition in the soft fruit industry that photography inside the tunnels was forbidden.

business alliances across the globe in the ceaseless quest to find new markets. Technology and wheeler-dealering apart, the growers still depend on an army of berry pickers, ranging from local school-children, keen to supplement their pocket money, to travellers and the unemployed from Scotland's inner cities. Until recent years the back-breaking work of the potato harvest also depended to a great extent on the physical strength and willingness of Perthshire school-children, who were rewarded with a fortnight's autumnal 'potato holiday'.

Perthshire has for centuries been a focal point within Scotland for the sale of cattle. By the mid-1600s, due to the expanding cattle trade with England, there was a clear need for a central market where buyers and sellers could meet and do business. In 1672, James, Earl of Perth, won the right to hold an annual fair at Crieff, a town ideally situated on the edge of the Highlands and at the end of the network of drove roads which funnelled cattle into it from all parts of northern Scotland. By 1700 Crieff was hosting the largest cattle tryst in Scotland and in its heyday around 30,000 beasts were changing hands during the week-long fair. The town retained its pre-eminence until after the 1745 uprising when English dealers, instead of waiting for the Highland drovers to deliver their purchases, began to play a more active role in the business process and pressed for a more convenient location for their transactions. Thus by 1770 Crieff had given way to Falkirk as Scotland's chief cattle town.

In less than a century, however, Falkirk too had lost its prime position, being unable to compete with new methods of animal transportation and with the new development of selling animals by auction. This latter innovation was pioneered in the 1860s by the Perth firm of Macdonald and McCallum, which later became Macdonald Fraser and in 1962, United Auctions. Until early 1990 the Perth auction mart consisted of a huge agglomeration of animal pens centred round the railway line immediately to the north of the Glasgow Road. It has since moved to the brand new Perth Agricultural Centre at East Huntingtower while a Safeway super-market occupies the original Caledonian Road site, still selling beef, but nowadays prepacked and no longer on the hoof.

Thanks to United Auctions, Perth has a worldwide reputation for its bull sales which are now held biannually in February and October. Buyers come from all over the world and regularly part with sums measured in several thousands of pounds, making the Perth event one of the biggest sales of pedigree stock in the world. The record price for a beast stands at 60,000 guineas, paid in 1963 for an Aberdeen-Angus, Lindertis Evulse. As the *Guinness Book of Records* rather unkindly points out, it was later found to be infertile 'thus becoming the world's most expensive piece of beef'.

Life as an agricultural worker is not one of today's easy options and was distinctly less so in years gone by. Even in the early decades of this present century the hours were long, the work physically hard, the pay poor and the accommodation basic. It was quite usual then for the younger workers to live communally in bothies where the bare essentials of a bed, a fire and the wherewithal to cook the morning porridge were the only comforts provided. Typically the lads would be wakened at 5.30 am six days a week and would be expected to clean and feed the horses and muck out the stables before any thought of their own breakfast. Ahead lay perhaps ten hours of work in the fields or around the farm with the prospect of a day off only on Sunday. A hard life indeed but probably healthier than one spent in the city.

There were one or two high points in the year when farm workers were allowed time off to attend a local fair of which there were once several in various parts of the county. The Lustylaw Market near Glenfarg, the Hallow Fair in Aberfeldy, the Smiddyhaugh Fair in Dunning and the St Sars (to Lowlanders) or St Kessocks Fair (to Highlanders) at Comrie, to mention just a few, probably all have their origins in the mists of unrecorded time. The biggest fair was Perth's Midsummer Market which would have been attended by thousands of people trekking in by road from all over the county and arriving by steamer from Fife and Dundee. This was the great annual celebration of Perthshire agriculture and commerce where animals were bought and sold, where butter and cheese by the cartload exchanged hands, where the town's artisans displayed their wares and where stalls lined both sides of the High Street between St Paul's Church and the Skinnergate. The streets would have been bursting with life, the noise deafening and the smell of food, sweets, sweat and animals on a hot day probably quite overpowering. Children would stare wide-eyed at the amount of sugary delicacies for sale, from candy walking sticks to aniseed balls, unworldly young men from the country would part with their hard-earned cash to the smooth-talking tricksters (who would sell, for example, machines which appeared to be able to print ten-shilling notes) and then take their revenge in scrapping with the townies, others would be hoping to arrange new employment on a different farm, while the old men would doubtless be shaking their heads and bemoaning the changes from the days of their own youth.

The Little Dunning Market (the name derives rather tortuously from St Dennis and has nothing to do with the village of Dunning) took place in Perth every October and became the county's main one for feeing, a Scots term for the hiring of agricultural workers. On this particular day many of the farmers and farm workers from around Perth would congregate towards the foot of the High Street, the former trying to hire new men for another year or half-year as cheaply as possible and the latter looking for the best conditions and pay and nearly always being disappointed. The agreement when made was sealed with arles, a one-off payment by the employer which committed the employee to turning up at the farm and staying the agreed period of time. It was not a day for the faint-hearted. Some of the less scrupulous workers would enter into several agreements and disappear into pubs to drink the arles while some farmers would only hire workers at the very end of the day when the latter were so desperate for any employment that they were past haggling over pay and conditions. This may seem like a picture from centuries ago but in fact took place as recently as the 1920s, after which time the city to a certain extent, and possibly to its detriment, turned its back on the ancient links with the Perthshire farming community.

The rivers of Perthshire, like the soil, have been harvested for centuries. The Tay has long been feted across the nation for the quality of its salmon, although for the local population this king of fish was regarded as rather ordinary fare. Indeed sometimes too ordinary as farm labourers in centuries gone by would insist, in what passed for a contract of employment, that they be fed on salmon no more than three or four times a week. But away from the riverside there was a steady demand for salmon from all over the country and beyond, and in the early years of last century steamers would transport the fish, packed in ice, to the markets of London and further afield to France, Italy, Spain and on one occasion even North America. In 1835 a grand total of 250 tons of fish left Perth in this way. The well-known company Mac Fisheries set up shop in Perth in 1919 and by the following year had acquired, according to their publicity, 'complete control over the supply of Tay salmon'. All salmon commercially caught on the Tay were either sent to a refrigerated collection point at Perth Station or collected from the river netting stations by the company's own steamer, before being sent off on overnight trains to all corners of Britain. The boast was that a salmon caught in the Tay at 8.00 pm could be on sale in a Mac Fisheries shop in London by the following morning. Mac Fisheries left Perth in 1978 but a year or two before they closed I spent a few weeks during the summer as a van driver for the Perth branch and as such was regularly sent to bring fish into the High Street shop from various points on the Tay. Judging by the many admiring glances the passing public clearly assumed I had caught these massive salmon myself and who was I, whose tally to date is but one six-inch trout, to shatter their illusions?

To find an account of the salmon fishing industry, historic or recent, which does not complain about declining fish stocks is

A statuesque group of salmon netters in the pale light of winter, fishing the cold waters of the Tay at Seggieden. This ancient skill will soon disappear from the Tay, leaving the river to a happy band of leisure anglers (© Dr W H Findlay).

rare indeed. In a situation where a finite number of fish are heading upstream along a relatively narrow waterway the net fishermen near the mouth of the river are clearly in the most advantageous position. Certainly last century those in the upper reaches would regularly lay the blame for poor catches on their counterparts lower down. In the course of the present century, however, net fishing has been driven steadily downstream; whereas in 1935 there were around 100 netting stations strung out between Campsie Linn near Stanley and the river estuary there are now none upstream of Perth and it looks as if this ancient occupation, known to have been practised by the monks of Coupar Angus as early as the thirteenth century, is set to disappear from the river altogether. The death knell is being sounded by leisure anglers, some of whom pay thousands of pounds for the privilege of fishing the famous Tay beats and who in such circumstances might feel cheated at a miserably small catch. Behind them is the Tay Foundation, an organisation which is actively raising funds to buy out the last of the netters in the Tay estuary, although how they intend to deal with the sudden increase in the seal population, also in the estuary and having a similarly adverse effect on salmon numbers, remains to be seen. Writing them a cheque may not be quite so easy.

While the price of Tay salmon in the shops of Perth may rekindle your taste for the humble haddock, the Perthshire rivers yield an even more expensive commodity, the freshwater pearl. One of the last of the dwindling band of Scottish pearl fishers is Bill Abernethy who lives near Coupar Angus and who is best-known for finding one of the most magnificent examples ever seen of river pearls. The Abernethy Pearl, known informally as Little Willie, was found in the Tay in 1967 and where the average pearl weighs in at around 10 grains and exceptional ones at 20, this hit the headlines at an astonishing 33. It is now owned by Cairncross, the Perth jewellers, and although they decline publicly to state its official value it has been estimated in recent years to be worth around £70,000. Sadly the discovery probably did more damage than good to the ancient art. A swarm of amateurs descended on the Tay and, instead of carefully prising open mussel shells to examine the contents without killing the creature inside, usually broke their way in and made sure that no pearl would ever grow there again. This, coupled with the effects of minor river pollution, has resulted in a significant and steady decline in the number of pearls found. Bill Abernethy may, perhaps, still be patrolling the chill waters of Scotland, peering at the river bottom through his viewing glass, or he may have retired. Certainly at the time of writing the Cairncross staff had not seen him for a long time. Wherever he is and whatever he is doing, the days of the professional pearl fisher are surely numbered.

After agriculture the manufacture of linen was Scotland's main industry, flourishing in the eighteenth century in the eastern counties of Fife, Angus and Perthshire, and in the west in Lanark and Renfrewshire. By around 1800, however, the cotton industry had taken a firm hold in the west and was rapidly extending its tendrils across the central belt. This left Perth in the happy position of being, in the early nineteenth century, one of the most important textile towns in Scotland. By thus remaining open to influences from Glasgow's cotton industry and Dundee's tradition of linen weaving, Perth became both the main cotton town in the east and, partly because of the quality of the waters of the Tay and Almond, the country's largest linen-bleaching centre. With a foot firmly based in both camps the area should have been well-placed to survive the vagaries of business fortune, but nevertheless was unable to withstand the huge financial crash of 1810. This was caused by the French blockade against British exports, which closed most of the sixty-odd textile firms in Perth, many of them permanently. The industry revived to a limited extent and even flourished until the middle of the century, after which the closely related process of textile dyeing helped to carry the prosperity of the city well into the 1900s.

It was during the difficult times of the 1810s that Robert Pullar set up in business in Perth, trading in the locally made waxed ginghams which, when made into umbrellas, kept most of Britain dry during this period. In 1823, perhaps in response to the contemporary fashion for brighter colours, he set up his son, John, in a small dye works. The business prospered and by 1866 had also diversified into dry-cleaning. Within a century of its modest beginnings John Pullar and Sons was the largest employer in the city and reckoned to be the largest and best-known cleaning and dyeing works in the world. No job was too big for the company and there was nothing, it seemed, which they could not clean or dye. In the 1890s, for example, ostrich feather fans could be cleaned from between 3/6 and 18/6 and Persian carpets from around 3/- per square yard. These *fin de siecle* years were probably the company's finest. In 1918, having been beset by industrial relations problems, the family lost control of the company and a gradual decline set in. Now a subsidiary of the Johnson Group, it still has a presence in Perth although the Pullars name is set to disappear in the very near future.

With agencies in every town and reasonable-sized village, Pullars of Perth put the city on the map as effectively as Scott's novel had done some decades earlier. It was a hard act to follow but the whisky industry rose to the challenge and has ever since kept Perth's name quite literally on the lips of the world. The first native of the county to make his fortune from an alcoholic beverage was George Sandeman who gave his name not to a whisky but to a brand of that most English of drinks, port. George, belonging to one of Perthshire's more notable families, left Perth in 1790, at the age of 25, to set up in the wine trade in London. He rented a cellar there, filling it with imported sherry and port from Spain and Portugal, and conducted his business from the fashionable coffee shops of the capital. The facts speak for themselves: within two years he had sold over 100,000 bottles of sherry throughout the country and his business not only survived but flourished throughout the French wars, which threatened much of the trade and commerce of western Europe until 1815. Today, over two hundred years on from the bold beginnings of that enterprise, the name Sandeman is still almost synonymous with port.

Thomas Sandeman, a relative of George, was the founder of one of Perth's best-known companies. In 1825 he set up shop in the town's Kirkgate selling beer, whisky and wine. Twelve years later he passed his thriving business on to a new owner who shortly afterwards took on a travelling salesman, one Arthur Bell. By 1851 Bell had been taken on as a full partner and was experimenting with the art of whisky blending, a technique which, by marrying a variety of malt and grain whiskies, achieved a popular and reasonably consistent balance between the depth of character of the former and the smoothness of the latter. Jack House, in his history of the company, states that Arthur Bell was understandably secretive about the ingredients of his blends but once confided that 'the best is made in Banffshire's Glenlivet district, and the other is Pitlochry and Stirlingshire whiskies.'

Before he died Bell made good use of the rapidly developing railway system to sell his product in all parts of Britain. It was his son, however, Arthur Kinmond Bell, who was to expand the business overseas and make the brand name famous the world over. Even so, in his native town, 'A.K.' is remembered primarily as one of Perth's greatest philanthropists. He built, for example, the red-stone housing estate of Gannochy on the north-eastern edge of the city, not for his employees as is commonly believed, but for a large number of unemployed local railwaymen. This was admired by Neville Chamberlain as the finest housing scheme he had seen. In 1937, in the closing years of his life, 'A.K.' set up the Gannochy Trust, which ever since has contributed vast sums of money to local worthy causes, such as Bell's Sports Centre, Perth Theatre, the A K Bell Library, and various university buildings throughout Scotland. Today Bells operates from a comparatively new headquarters at Cherrybank though it is no longer independent. It was taken over by Guinness in 1985 after a viciously fought corporate battle which resulted in the downfall and subsequent jailing of the Guinness chairman, Ernest Saunders.

While the original Arthur Bell was still an itinerant salesman, John Dewar, a crofter's son from near Aberfeldy, had started up in business as a wine and spirit merchant in the High Street, not far from the Kirkgate. Even from these earliest days the histories of Dewars and Bells have proved to be remarkably similar, with both companies owing their success to the popularity of their blends and to dynamic worldwide sales drives. Earlier this century the respective chairmen showered Perth with their benevolence and in recent years both firms have come under the umbrella of Guinness plc. From today's viewpoint it is easier to see them as brothers rather than rivals. Or at least it would have been, had the parent company not decided to end the long Dewar connection with Perth by closing the Inveralmond bottling plant in 1994. At the time of closure it was estimated that over 1.5 billion bottles had been sent out from the factory in its 32 years of existence.

The firm of Matthew Gloag and Son, producers of The Famous Grouse, is the third in the triumvirate of Perth whisky firms. It too dates from the early nineteenth century, is now owned by Highland Distilleries and has recently moved from its cramped headquarters in Kinnoull Street to a brand new building at Walnut Grove.

The big three blenders of Bells, Dewars and Gloags have dominated the Perthshire whisky scene to such an extent that the county's distillers are frequently overlooked. There are now admittedly few of them, but in the early years of last century there were a great many more, most of them attached to farms where a still was the easiest way of converting a field of barley or some such cereal into ready cash. Edradour, a cluster of white-painted cottages nestling in the hills above Pitlochry, enjoys the distinction of being the smallest distillery in Scotland, while the Glenturret Distillery, just outside Crieff and dating from 1775, claims to be the oldest surviving producer of single Highland malt. One employee of this latter enterprise is featured in the *Guinness Book of Records*: this is Towser, the company cat, who in her 24 year-long residence in the still house caught a grand total of 28,899 mice. While she has been rightly celebrated, few if any have queried the not inconsiderable rodent problem the distillery must have had. Judging from her photographs Towser, with her alley cat name and killer reputation, was not the bruiser puss one might have imagined. On the contrary she was a model of feline elegance and pulchritude — and there must be a moral there somewhere!

The warehouses of the Glenturret Distillery, close to the town of Crieff, occupy a pleasant setting beside the River Turret. Crieff was long famed for the quality of its whisky until most of the local distilleries suddenly went bankrupt in the late 1830s. The Hosh distillery, as this was formerly known, is one of the few which survived.

For those who prefer their drinks a little less strong Britain's most popular mineral water comes from the Strathearn village of Blackford. Highland Spring Ltd was founded in 1979 and, following an investment of over £30 million, boasts one of the most advanced natural mineral water plants in Europe, challenging companies of the stature of Evian and Perrier. Britain's largest producer, its bottles are opened every day in almost 40 countries around the world and can be found on the refreshment trolleys of all British Airways jets. The quality of the product is guaranteed by the strictly controlled use of the designation 'natural spring water'; around 2000 acres of land above the water source are kept permanently free from pesticides, fertilisers and animal waste, allowing uncontaminated rainwater to filter through several hundred feet of mineral-bearing rock, a process which is believed to take around 30 years. Pure, refreshing and healthy, the nation clearly regards it as a drink well worth waiting for.

To say that Perth also provides the tumblers from which to drink its own whisky would have been the perfect way to introduce another important home industry. Alas for the literary art of linking paragraphs, the North British Glassworks, founded by John Moncrieff in 1865, specialised only in industrial glass and supplied at one time many of the world's steam boilers and railway engines with the small but essential pieces of equipment which allowed operators to monitor the water levels in their boilers. The company also employed a few specialists in hand-made glass and in 1922 took on the Barcelona-born Salvador Ysart who with his sons produced over a long period some of the most sought-after pieces of twentieth century art glass. Monart glass (the name comes from MONcrieff and YsART) was made by the Ysarts in a corner of the Perth factory between 1924 and 1961 and is characterised by its free-blown designs, vibrant colours and swirling decoration. In 1946, leaving son Paul behind as the sole maker of Monart, Salvador and his sons, Vincent and Augustine, left Moncrieff's to set up their own business producing Vasart glass (from the initial letters of the three founders), an almost equally highly regarded product characterised by the same swirling decorations but by rather more muted colours and moulded shapes. In 1963 they were commissioned to make a large number of lighting globes for 10, 11 and 12 Downing Street although these have since been removed. In spite of this official recognition, production of both Monart and Vasart ceased in the 1960s and the family spread out into other parts of the country, taking their skills with them. Paul, having developed an interest in paper-weights, moved to Wick to work for Caithness Glass while Vincent became works manager of Strathearn Glass (the successor to Vasart Glass) in Crieff. A further spin-off from this latter business took shape in 1968 when Stuart Drysdale left the management and set up Perthshire Paperweights. In recent years the company started by John Moncrieff has had an unsettled history. After a succession of take-overs and a management buy-out the firm closed its doors for the last time in 1996. It is appropriate, however, that Caithness Glass, one of the best-known British glass companies, should have a presence in Perth in the form of a factory and a popular visitor centre.

In 1885, twenty years after John Moncrieff founded his company, another enterprise started in a small way at 44 Tay Street. What developed into the General Accident Fire and Life Assurance Corporation, now one of the world's leading insurance companies, was begun simply as a local response to the Employers' Liability

Act of 1880 by which workmen, injured in the course of their employment, were legally entitled to compensation. Two years later the very young Francis Norie-Miller was appointed as manager and quickly embarked on a programme of rapid expansion. A network of agents was created throughout the country and by the early years of the present century the company was also operating overseas. The GA, as it is known locally, was the first company to offer burglary insurance and one of the earliest to provide motor cover. By the turn of the century the company had outgrown its offices and had built a prestigious new headquarters on the southern corner of Tay Street and High Street. In 1983, again faced with problems of space, this building was sold to Perth and Kinross District Council, and the insurance giant moved to its new world headquarters at Pitheavlis, beside the new Bells building, on the western outskirts of the city. With over £5 billion being received annually in premium payments and pre-tax profits approaching £450 million it is not difficult to comprehend the importance of the GA to the Perthshire economy. The company has also contributed generously to local worthy causes, with the Norie-Miller Riverside Walk, pleasantly laid out gardens on the east bank of the Tay between the Perth and Queen's bridges, being a prime example.

While legislation of 1880 led to the founding of the GA, exactly a century later the Transport Act of 1980 led immediately to the foundation of Stagecoach, yet another world-class business organisation with its home in Perth. One function of this Act was to deregulate the British bus and coach industry and within days of it coming into force, in October 1980, enterprising Perth nurse Ann Gloag had launched a cheap and cheerful overnight coach service between Dundee and London. She was joined shortly afterwards in the business by her accountant brother Brian Souter and together, with their policy of combining low fares with luxury coaches, quickly established a leading position in the Scottish public transport network. In 1987, with its acquisition of Hampshire Bus and Pilgrim Coaches, Stagecoach began to expand over the border, a process which has since led to business interests in Africa, Asia and Europe. The Stock Exchange, when the company was floated in 1993, valued it at £134 million, and turned Souter and Gloag overnight into the wealthiest residents of Perthshire. This remarkable success story is well-illustrated by the statistics:

between 1980 and 1995 the company went from owning 2 buses to 7,300 (a remarkable expansion which has been credited with keeping the home bus building industry solvent during the days of recession) and from employing a staff of 3 to one of 19,700. But Stagecoach was not to be content with just buses and coaches. Before the privatisation of British Rail had been discussed in any depth the company had dabbled, unsuccessfully, in rail transport. Undeterred, it returned with greater vigour to the same theme in early 1996 and made a successful bid for the franchise for South-West Trains. Stagecoach is still a young company, lean and particularly hungry, and many Perthshire folk will watch its progress over the next few years with considerable curiosity.

At the end of the twentieth century, however, it is tourism which accounts for almost a quarter of all economic activity in the area and which pumps well over £200 million annually into the local economy. Compare this figure with the 1947 equivalent of £679,000 and the rapidity of growth becomes apparent. The success of this industry is due firstly to the many undoubted attractions of Perthshire, and secondly to the hard work of the Perthshire Tourist Board which has promoted the county across the globe.

Tourism is not in fact new to the area; in the early nineteenth century a series of guides to Perth was published, quite clearly written for the benefit of visitors to the town, and in 1836 the following lines appeared in the *Perthshire Constitutional*:

> A great many strangers [are] visiting Perth on pleasure tours...
> On the other hand, many of our citizens are, as is their custom,
> setting out to seabathing quarters, exchanging this scene, in the
> very luxuriance of its beauty, for the pleasures of a barren coast
> and the chilly breeze.

Some, if not many, of these 'strangers' will have ventured to the town as a direct result of reading Scott's *The fair maid of Perth*, in which he wrote, in the well-known opening paragraph:

> Among all the provinces in Scotland, if an intelligent stranger
> were asked to describe the most varied and the most beautiful,
> it is probable he would name the county of Perth.

A finer endorsement from one of Britain's most popular writers could hardly have been imagined. Tourism took off in a big way, helped in no small measure by Victoria's high esteem for the

The statue of Sir Walter Scott now stands at the end of King Street beside the South Inch. This pre-1878 photo shows him in the original location at the foot of the High Street. Despite a grandiose public subscription scheme, the Town Council eventually bought the statue from a local sculptor, when he was in financial difficulties, for a knock-down price of £10.00. Scott's famous creation, the Fair Maid, occupies the High Street instead, seated on her bench outside the Tourist Information Centre (Courtesy of Perth & Kinross Libraries).

Highlands, and indeed it would not be too wide of the mark to state that some towns and villages owe their very existence to the nineteenth century tourist industry.

Perth silversmiths, Perth as a railway centre and even the production of rat poison all merit rather more than just a passing mention. But this chapter cannot conclude without a lengthier reference to one of Perth's most notable but long-forgotten industries. Thanks in particular to three generations of the Morison family, the city had developed by the end of the eighteenth century into the main centre of book production in Scotland outside Edinburgh and Glasgow. Indeed, according to one source, no other British publishing company produced as many books annually between the years 1780 and 1800 as did Morisons, and it may have been this level of success which prompted the firm in 1796 to embark on its hitherto most ambitious undertaking. This was the publication in monthly parts of the *Encyclopaedia Perthensis*, which was conceived as a rival to the Edinburgh-published *Encyclopaedia Britannica*. Vigorous advertising accompanied the publication, including claims that it contained as much information as its rival and at half the price, and later that it contained 40,000 articles not found in any other encyclopaedia. The set was completed with the publication of the 23rd volume in the early months of 1806 and stands as one of the greatest but least known achievements of the city in the Age of Enlightenment. Crawford Smith, the biographer of Perth historians, described the encyclopaedia as 'perhaps the most wonderful which has ever been produced and published in a provincial town…an extraordinary production for the time', and it is indeed hard to quarrel with that. Unfortunately the effort took its toll on the company. A footnote to the preface of the 1806 publication, *Memorabilia of the city of Perth*, apologised for the fact that the book had had to be printed in Edinburgh and gave the explanation that the Perth presses had been fully occupied in printing the encyclopaedia. The company had clearly over-stretched itself and never regained its pre-eminence in the printing world. William Morison, the grandson of the founder and the overseer of the project, had also pushed himself too hard and died in July 1806, not long after correcting the final page of proofs. It is an intriguing prospect, however, that had things turned out differently the 15th edition of *Perthensis*, rather than *Britannica*, might now be enjoying pride of place on library shelves throughout the world.

CHAPTER 6

PERTH: THE FAIRER CITY

Had Moultrie Kelsall announced his intention to visit Perth on 31 May 1951 he would doubtless have been met by the Scottish equivalent of a lynch mob. His 'crime', committed the night before during a nationwide BBC radio broadcast, had been that of being too honest in his opinion of the Fair City. Where were the historic buildings, he wondered, and why were the new ones in such poor taste? Echoing his disappointment in the town was the local resident and novelist, Olive Dougan, who was described anonymously in the programme as a 'Welsh woman', but who had the courage to put her name to her views and repeat them in the columns of the *Perthshire Advertiser* shortly afterwards. She argued with passion the case for the conservation of the old city and the need for a greater tourist awareness. Almost half a century later these words of Kelsall and Dougan would be regarded as prophetic, yet at the time they prompted one listener, in a letter to the same newspaper, to describe the broadcast as 'one of the worst things that has happened to Perth within this century'.

More recently the *Spectator* columnist, Roy Kerridge, wrote about the town in that magazine in 1985 and his comments in contrast were generally warm, even affectionate, though not entirely without criticism. 'A clean, gracious city, with few modern additions, Perth resembles Bath, Cheltenham and the better parts of Brighton...' sums up his views on the city's architecture. He was more wary of the townspeople, however, and saw them as 'gentle [and] well-mannered...by day' but 'brawling and dangerous at night when the pubs turn out'. His landlady, clearly not a unionist, was quoted as saying 'A wee bomb wud dae England the most guid, Ah'm thinking — not to hurt a'body, of course'. Kerridge thus neatly illustrates attitudes which are still prevalent today: the ladies of Perth do dress up to go shopping, central Perth is best avoided at closing time, and nationalist sentiments are strong in the area. This was Kerridge's third visit to Perth and although he saw in it a certain quaintness — he claims to have overheard housewives discussing Christian doctrine and quoting

Stevenson and Congreve in the streets — he also displayed a deep regard and fondness for the town which stemmed from his first visit in 1965. On that occasion he 'stood entranced on Perth Bridge in the half light of evening', gazing across to the beautiful Tay Street frontage where 'the civic buildings of Perth, their Gothic contours bathed in orange lamplight, seemed wonderfully strange.' He concluded with a wish that he should be able to return before too long.

Kelsall and Kerridge, each with different and essentially independent impressions of Perth. Had they been looking at the same town from opposing viewpoints or had the town really changed so radically in 34 years? The answer, I suspect, comprises a good measure of each. Kelsall made the mistake of looking for signs of its mediaeval greatness, of which few survive, and went away disappointed. Kerridge, on the other hand, took it at its face value, fell in love and vowed to return. He was also writing at a time when great civic improvements were underway and may have picked up the growing sense of confidence that was beginning to permeate the town.

This reawakened civic pride coincided with a tidal wave of change which hit Perth in the 1980s, washing away the accumulated shabbiness of earlier decades and refreshing and revitalising the civic leaders. A remarkable number of new projects were pushed through, though not totally without opposition. New public buildings appeared, streets were pedestrianised, slum areas rebuilt and tourism and new businesses encouraged. Anyone wishing to discover the modern spirit of Perth should begin by investigating this new vibrancy.

Take, for example, the very centre of the city, the ancient High Street, where the width of the some of the shop fronts is still determined by the size of the original twelfth century burgage plots (which were parcels of land granted to burgesses by the king in return for performing certain civic duties). It was naturally never envisaged at that time that the street would have to cope with the stranglehold of twentieth century two-way traffic with the towns-people being squeezed into the narrow pavements on either side. A one-way system was introduced in the 1950s followed by full pedestrianisation (between Kinnoull Street and Skinnergate) by early 1990. Instead of being a noisy, fume-filled hazard to be endured, the High Street has once again been repossessed by those for whom it was originally meant. Attractively laid out with trees, benches, hanging baskets and street sculpture, and with entertainment provided by fiddlers, flautists, pipers and accordionists, it is a lively place to stroll on a sunny Saturday morning.

Most High Street shoppers are probably unaware of the location of the old town centre which is marked by a small stone slab, incised with a cross, set into the edge of the pedestrianised area. This indicates the site of the old market cross of Perth which stood where the High Street bisected the important mediaeval thoroughfare between the church and the castle along Kirkgate and Skinnergate. In 1765, when it began to impede the flow of traffic, the cross was sold by public auction for a little over £5 and eventually, I believe, found its way into a garden in Caithness.

Two of Perth's greatest literary figures are commemorated in modern sculptures in the High Street. The two men linked by a chromium ring (opposite Woolworths), inspired by the poem 'Nae day sae dark' by the Perth poet William Soutar, is a thought-provoking piece and a fine example of how good public art can be. Soutar was born in Perth in 1898 and in his early years was skilled both athletically and academically. Had he not been struck down by a crippling spinal disease at the time of his graduation he could well have reached the top of whatever profession he chose. At the age of 32 he was forced to retire to bed where he remained, in a book-lined room overlooking his father's garden, until his death fourteen years later. In this period he produced some of his finest work and was visited by many of the leading Scottish poets of the twentieth century, amongst whom he is now rightly numbered. His vast collection of books, embracing a wide range of subjects, is shelved in Perth's A K Bell Library while his former Wilson Street home now provides accommodation for the library service's writer-in-residence.

At the eastern end of the pedestrianised area a statue of the Fair Maid of Perth, sitting on one of the new benches with a book on her lap, has caused many a smile of amusement and now probably appears in countless family photographs across the globe. This is actually a second, more robust, casting of the statue as the first one did not stand up well to vandalism, while the scrawling of 'Kama Sutra' across the cover of her book was felt to be projecting the wrong image. She should really be considered as a memorial to the famous novel by Sir Walter Scott which, following its publication in 1828, flung Perth into prominence throughout nineteenth century Europe. Sadly there is no evidence to suggest that the Fair Maid is anything other than a fictional character.

The St John's Centre, a £20 million shopping mall opened in 1987, runs between the High Street and South Street, and despite the initial opposition appears to have integrated successfully with the main city centre shops. The first of the two main objections to its construction was that it required the disappearance of Meal Vennel, which up until the end of last century was one of the main thoroughfares between the High Street and South Street. Had the vennel not been a city centre eyesore, consisting of a run-down primary school on one side and goods entrances for the earlier 1960s shopping centre on the other, then this might have been a strong argument against the proposed development. As it is, few now mourn the vennel although, almost by way of apology, the rear entrances to two of the mall shops carry plaques to remind customers of the line of the historic street. The second point raised was that the planned shopping mall was in essence no different from any other in the country and that by such creeping development Perth was gradually losing its individuality. Again this might have been a valid point had the character of the city's main streets been under threat. But, apart from the blocking up of Meal Vennel, there has been little change to the frontages of the High Street and South Street, with most of the construction work going on behind, on the site of the outdated St Johns Square.

One of the boldest proposals in recent decades concerning the city centre was the topic of recent fierce debate. Having been invited by the Millennium Commission to submit requests for the funding of a civic project to mark the new millennium, Perth and Kinross District Council in conjunction with a firm of Glasgow architects drew up ambitious plans for the demolition of the City Hall and the redevelopment of Horse Cross. The present City Hall has served Perth since 1911 and with all respect to its architects and present day devotees is not a building of particular beauty or merit; indeed, it could be said that the *putti* on the facade look utterly out of place. Neither is it functional for late twentieth century needs: environmental health regulations have effectively ruled out any further use of the building's kitchens and, as better halls continue to be built elsewhere, big-name conferences, such as the Scottish Conservatives, have moved to other venues. The

In spite of its growing list of problems the City Hall is close to the hearts of many people in Perth. As home to the local music festival and as a popular venue for concerts, coffee mornings and charity events it is one of the cornerstones of life in the Fair City.

building of a brand new City Hall and conference centre at Horse Cross, loosely connected to the Museum and Art Gallery, would have allowed the site of the old hall to be turned into a central civic space of lawns and flowers. The planners and their supporters further argued that St John's Kirk, hitherto hemmed in, would have been allowed to breathe more freely, and that the Horse Cross area would have become far more attractive than the car park and the Pullar's Building presently permit. It seems, however, with the weight of public opinion apparently being against any development and with the bid for lottery funding having been rejected, that this forward-looking project will advance no further.

Leisure and cultural facilities in the town have been improved beyond recognition in this same short period. Perth's professional football team, St Johnstone, had been playing at Muirton Park, their Dunkeld Road ground, since the mid-1920s. Originally designed to hold 30,000 spectators, the effects of wear, tear and age, coupled with stiffer safety regulations, reduced its maximum capacity at one brief period to a mere 2,500. Fortunately, Muirton Park had been built on the then outskirts of Perth which, as the town expanded, was gradually turning into an inner city site and therefore of growing interest to developers. The club was eventually made an offer which it could hardly refuse when the supermarket chain, Asda, offered to buy Muirton and in return build a brand new covered stadium seating over 10,000 spectators on a field off the Crieff Road, once again at the edge of the city. The new site was donated by a local farmer Bruce McDiarmid after whom the new ground is named. Fans must have had mixed feelings about leaving Muirton Park, a ground hallowed, for example, by the unforgettable 3–0 victory over S V Hamburg in 1971 in the club's only foray so far into European football. On the other hand the memory of ignominious defeats such as the 1–9 thrashing at the hands of Rangers in the early 1960s was probably best erased by the move to a new ground. Opened at the start of the 1989–90 season, this first state-of-the-art, all-seater football stadium in the country is now the envy of many top clubs across the land. Saints did well in the period immediately following the move, perhaps inspired by their new surroundings, and having then survived a few mediocre seasons are once again rising through the ranks of Scottish professional football.

If spectators, seated and sheltered, can now watch football in comfort, it is only fair that the sporting participants of the city should be equally well catered for. The Perth Leisure Pool in Glover Street was opened in 1988 and replaced the old Swimming Baths on the Dunkeld Road (on the site now occupied by the Royal Bank of Scotland) that had served the townspeople well for about a century. The Children's Pool, the little-used Soldiers' Pool and the popular and comparatively recent 'Big Pool' will linger long in the local memory. So will the primitive changing cubicles and the icy draughts which used to freeze the dripping body, not just while queueing for towels and clothes but, worst of all, while actually waiting for the attendant to turn up to hand them over. The new pool is blissfully warm and caters equally well for the small child, the leisure swimmer and the serious sportsman. The extras, in the form of flumes, water cannon and Jacuzzis, as well as outdoor swimming, the health suite and the cafe, have helped to make this facility one of the most popular in the area, to the extent, in fact, that in terms of numbers through the turnstile it is one of the most frequently visited attractions in Scotland.

Beside the Leisure Pool are the Dewar's Rinks, named after the well known whisky company whose huge, cuboid, redbrick building, one of the great Perth landmarks, used to occupy the site. It was opened in 1990, replacing the former ice rink on the Dunkeld Road, and is now used primarily for curling. Major competitions are regularly held here, including Scottish and European championships and in 1995 the World Junior Curling Championships. Perthshire's long enjoyment of curling came to fruition in Canada in 1991 when the Scottish team, consisting entirely of local curlers, won the world championship.

The centre for most participative sport in Perth, however, is to be found beside the North Inch. Bell's Sports Centre for almost thirty years has played its part in the lives of the city's youth, providing access to a wide variety of sports, ranging from indoor tennis and trampolining to martial arts and fencing. Its playing area, beneath the distinctive domed roof (the largest in Britain), has been extended on several occasions, the most recent being when the centre linked up with the neighbouring pavilion of the Perthshire Rugby and Cricket Club to form the Gannochy Trust Sports Complex. Unfortunately a question mark hangs over the future of the buildings as they were badly damaged by the floods of 1990 and 1993 and there may well be some truth in the rumours that insurance companies are becoming wary about providing further cover.

The Museum and Art Gallery is centrally situated at the end of George Street and is instantly recognisable by the classical portico sheltering the figure of Thomas Hay Marshall. The building was extended in the 1930s to cope with a collection which is numbered amongst the finest outside the capitals and largest cities. Its interior has been revamped in recent years: gone are the stuffed lions and walruses in glass cases, to be replaced with colourful and stimulating displays, more concerned with the natural and human history of the local area. A popular extension of the museum service is the Fergusson Gallery which occupies the former city waterworks on the corner of Tay Street and Marshall Place. The successful attempt to bring to the city the works of the Scottish colourist, J.D. Fergusson, in the face of strong bids from other parts of the country, was regarded as a considerable coup for Perth and bolsters its reputation as a major centre of the arts in Scotland. The gallery has curatorial oversight for around 6000 separate items, including 200 oil paintings, with an estimated total value of £30 million. It was opened in March 1992 and by December of that year, in record time, had won the Scottish Museum of the Year award.

The fine red stone Sandeman Library in Kinnoull Street served the Perth public well for almost a century before being replaced in 1994 by the A K Bell Library (above) in York Place. With its array of modern equipment and extras in the form of an archive repository, theatre, shop, exhibition area and cafe it is the envy of many library authorities across the country. The front porch originally formed part of the Perth Infirmary built in 1836.

The most recent public building to be completed is the A K Bell Library which, along with Bell's Sports Centre, was heavily subsidised by the Gannochy Trust. The decision to move out of the more central but smaller and considerably outdated Sandeman Library, amid a certain amount of local protest, has been vindicated by the tremendous popularity of the new building and its ultra-modern facilities. Professor Archibald Sandeman, whose munificence provided the city for almost a century with a valuable educational and recreational resource, would probably fail to recognise the oak from which his acorn grew. The new library was officially opened in 1995 and has been described as the finest of its size in Britain.

The main cultural event in Perth is the annual Festival of the Arts which celebrated its 25th anniversary in 1997 and which for a while rejoiced in its reputation as Scotland's second festival. The idea for such an event had been triggered by Conrad Wilson, music critic of the *Scotsman*, who in 1970 described Perth as 'an ideal festival city without a festival'. Following a promising feasibility study the first festival was launched in April 1972 with appearances by Scottish Opera, the Scottish National Orchestra and the late renowned pianist John Ogdon. Now held in late May of each year there are events, almost always of a high standard, to suit all tastes. The only part of the festival, it seems, in which quality is a secondary consideration is the popular Art Mart where artists and craftsmen of varying abilities display their works along the Tay Street railings. To counterbalance the spring festival the three professional orchestras of Scotland have recently joined together to produce a well-attended series of concerts throughout the winter.

The festival revolves around Perth Theatre which for many decades has been the bedrock of the arts in Perth, providing good quality drama throughout the year. Perth audiences, while not fickle, demand high standards and tend to give most support to productions they know they will enjoy. This was as true last century as it is today. In 1831, for example, the virtuoso violinist Paganini, whose visit was described in the press as 'the greatest event in the musical history of Perth', played to a packed house in the Theatre Royal (presently functioning as a restaurant on the corner of Atholl Street and Kinnoull Street) where the normal prices for tickets were trebled. Yet a mere seven years later the theatre was described as 'seldom open and thinly attended'. The present theatre in the High Street was opened in 1900 and underwent a major refurbishment in 1980–81. Its reputation today as the most successful theatre in Scotland, borne out by the outstandingly popular subscription system, is largely due to the late Joan Knight, artistic director between 1968 and 1993, who was much loved by Perth audiences and who staged as her finale the still remembered production of *Shadowlands* with Tom Fleming.

While the blossoming of the arts and of new public buildings has helped to foster a positive impression of the town, the authorities have not been slow in tackling the various blemishes. Perth's reputation as the Fair City has for many years masked the fact that the 1930s council housing in the former Hunter Crescent area ranked amongst the worst in Scotland. The local press would regularly feature problems such as chronic damp, rat infestation, and discarded syringes in children's play areas. The houses themselves were frequently boarded up, the exterior walls covered in graffiti and in places showing signs of deliberate fire damage. Every major city in Scotland will have experienced these problems. The turning point came in 1985 with the publication of a report commissioned by the Scottish Development Agency which led in 1989 to the launch of a £19.5 million redevelopment of the area. The finished result has been a triumph of cooperation between the Scottish Office, local authorities, private enterprise and the tenants themselves, although the new name, Fairfield, perhaps the only matter in which tenant consultation was overlooked, has not been universally popular.

The *Perthshire Advertiser* was also in at the beginning of another remarkably successful attempt at improving the city's image. In March 1989 they ran a story headlined 'Foul City!' which featured certain comments made by an American television director to the effect that he had decided against filming on the North Inch because of the unacceptable amount of dog excrement. Quite what relationship exists between this complaint and flowers (apart from fertilizer) is unclear, but it prompted the chairman of the Perthshire Chamber of Commerce to form the Perth in Bloom committee the following year. Other groups sprang up in the county, such as Comrie in Colour and Crieff in Leaf, all of which in 1993 came under the umbrella of the Take a Pride in Perthshire campaign. Perth in Bloom, however, has been the most successful. By organising hanging baskets along the length of the city's main streets, persuading local businesses to sponsor flower beds, and encouraging householders to keep their gardens tidy, they have transformed the face of the city by a huge injection of colour and beauty. The district council's Leisure and Recreation Department also did splendid work in the creation of new gardens, such as those at Rodney at the east end of the Queen's Bridge, and the careful maintenance of others throughout the town. The rewards from such efforts started to flow in quickly. Perth won the large town category of Beautiful Scotland in Bloom every year between 1992 and 1995 (and again in 1997), and the overall championship between 1993 and 1995. As winner of the large town category in the Britain in Bloom contest in 1993 (and again in 1995), Perth was nominated as the sole British representative in the European competition, the Entente Florale of 1994, picking up third prize overall and a special award for community involvement. Not bad for a town dismissed as the foul city only five years earlier.

Perhaps the highest accolade to come Perth's way, and not just Perth itself but the whole of Perth and Kinross District, was its top position in a survey conducted by the Glasgow Quality of Life Group. Jointly funded by the universities of Glasgow and Strathclyde the 1990 report, following an investigation of 145 non-metropolitan district councils throughout the country, concluded that Perth and Kinross District offered the best quality of life to its inhabitants. Several factors were taken into consideration and when the responses from the public were analysed it revealed that the district scored the highest ranking overall for its educational facilities and was near the top for health services, housing, transport infrastructure, cost of living and proximity to pleasant scenery. On the other hand it was given a low ranking for climate, wage levels and, surprisingly, sports facilities, all factors which apparently do not significantly affect general feelings of well-being. While many in the district were perfectly aware of the advantages of living in this part of the United Kingdom, they must have been a little surprised to find it rated well ahead of many hugely popular places south of the border such as Stratford upon Avon, Cambridge and Torbay. Honesty demands that I report the fall to an overall tenth place in the latest report of 1997 (fifth place amongst the 24–44 age group but not even in the top fifteen for the over-65s), and while the only major change to the council area has been the incorporation of Longforgan and Invergowrie, it would be invidious to suggest that this has anything to do with the supposed decline in quality of life!

Late twentieth century Perth is undoubtedly flourishing. This is not to say, however, that Moultrie Kelsall, for all his unpopularity, got it wrong in 1951. He merely voiced what many visitors to Perth, then and now, must think. Where were the reminders of its leading position in the mediaeval kingdom? Where were the carefully preserved buildings; the parliament house, the monasteries, the town houses, the castle and the city walls? The truth, sadly, is that almost all the glories of mediaeval Perth lie beneath the present-day streets and buildings, and the blame for this, in the main, can be assigned to external forces and not the popular butt of such criticism, the Town Council.

Take the castle, for instance. It stood on a low-lying piece of ground, roughly where the museum now stands. Most likely built on top of a high mound of earth, it was nevertheless unable to withstand the flood of 1209 and was swept away, along with many other buildings and their inhabitants. Sources indicate that one of the king's sons also perished as did, very nearly, the king himself. Another major flood in 1621 ended the brief existence of the newly built and 'stately' bridge over the Tay.

The history of the city walls, of which there have been several, is reminiscent of a game of musical chairs. In 1296 Perth fell into the hands of Edward I of England and in order to defend his prize he replaced the original defences, perhaps consisting of little more than a wooden palisade, with what was probably the first stone wall around the town. Robert the Bruce repossessed the town in 1313 and, in case it should yet again fall into enemy hands, immediately had the walls knocked down. They were rebuilt under the brief and chequered rule of Edward Balliol and once again levelled as soon as he had left the area. In 1336, by order of Edward III of England, the walls were rebuilt for the last time and remained standing for as long as Perth was content to stay within its mediaeval bounds. From the later eighteenth century, however, the town began to expand in all directions and the walls were demolished at around this time, never to rise again. The rubble wall to be found along one side of Albert Close (off George Street) was believed to be the only surviving section of the city wall but this is now considered unlikely. Certainly it follows the line which the wall would have taken but its construction does not match the fourteenth century description of 'squared stone'.

Two cataclysmic events, almost a century apart, destroyed many of the mediaeval stone buildings. The spark which ignited the Reformation firestorm is generally attributed to a sermon preached by John Knox in St John's Kirk in 1559. Drunk on his words, Knox's audience first attacked the altars within the church and then overflowed into the streets to devastate St Ann's Chapel, Loretto Chapel, amongst others, and the four great monasteries surrounding the town, the Greyfriars, the Blackfriars, the Whitefriars and the Charterhouse. Ironically, the town kirk, where it all began, was the only such building to remain structurally intact after the terrible events of that day. Ironically too, the Charterhouse haunted St John's for the next two hundred years as its gateway, the only major part of any monastic building to survive, was rebuilt as one of the church's doorways and, according to one source, was even regarded as the church's most beautiful feature.

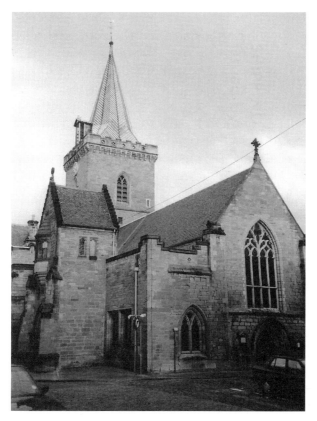

St John's Kirk in Perth is one of the great mediaeval burgh churches of Scotland. John Knox preached here in May 1559 and in doing so prompted the violent start to the Scottish Reformation.

In 1651 Oliver Cromwell was in Scotland in pursuit of Charles II. In August of that year he negotiated the surrender of Perth and had one of his five great citadels built on the South Inch, in the vicinity of what is now the Marshall Place-Edinburgh Road junction. The builders were ruthless in their quest for stone and proceeded to demolish several fine buildings, including the original King James VI Hospital (at the east end of the High Street) and 140 houses. Into this huge fort also went garden walls, gravestones from the cemetery, the remains of the short-lived bridge of 1617 and even the town cross. The presence of the citadel was universally reviled in the town and it is no surprise to find that after the Restoration of 1660 attempts were immediately made to demolish the structure. It was refortified briefly by the Jacobites in 1715 and

1745 which explains why, at the end of the eighteenth century, the outline was still clearly visible and was shown on contemporary maps of the town. But memories live longer, and even after three centuries, when considering names for a new block of flats being built partly on the site, that of Cromwell was dismissed without a second thought.

To say that St John's Kirk is the sole survivor of mediaeval Perth is not completely accurate as the building has been restored so many times that little remains of the original stonework. It was founded by David I in the mid-1120s and retained its probable modest proportions until the mid-fifteenth century when civic pride demanded that a town of the stature of Perth should have a correspondingly impressive church at its centre. The main reconstruction was complete by the early sixteenth century and by all accounts was richly decorated inside. This fine church, for the remaining few decades before the Reformation, sat enthroned in the centre of the town, enjoying the obeisances of the neighbouring monasteries and chapels, and regulating with its bells the daily routines of the magistrates and townspeople.

In the eighteenth century, to cope with the pastoral care of a growing population, the church was physically subdivided by new internal walls into three separate and self contained sections, each with a minister in charge. Hence the rather unimaginative names of the new parishes — East, West and Middle. Further reconstruction work was carried out during the next century, followed by the great restoration programme of the 1920s. The work, intended as a memorial to the Perthshire dead of World War I, was entrusted to Sir Robert Lorimer and resulted in the dividing walls being removed and the church once again becoming a single unified building. The sensitivity with which this massive work was tackled can be appreciated by simply wandering around the interior and listening, in the recesses of the stone arches, to the echoes of a mediaeval world, long since departed.

With a collection of 63 bells, arguably the finest in Scotland, St John's is a campanologists' dream. Eight of them, in fact, date from pre-Reformation times, a figure unequalled by any other church in Britain. The oldest bell, the 'Ave Maria', was probably cast in the early 1300s, and was joined by the 'Agnus Dei' in around 1400, this possibly being the old curfew bell which rang out over the town at 8.00 every evening. Included in the figure of 63 are the

35 bells which form the second largest carillon in Scotland and one of only fourteen in the whole British Isles. All but one were cast in 1934, the other being the Johannes Baptista, the old Preaching Bell, which dates from 1506, weighs almost one and a half tons and which has been described authoritatively as 'one of the finest pre-Reformation bells in existence'. The carillon is still played regularly in spite of the recently heard comment that there are more trained astronauts in the world than trained carillonneurs. To get round this little difficulty the carillon can be played automatically with the help of pianola-style paper rolls, supplied with the original order of 1934 and still going strong. The repertoire includes several well known tunes, such as *The vicar of Bray* and *Charlie is my darling*, some of which used to waft pleasantly over the town in the middle of the day. In 1994 the district council, using money from the Perth Common Good Fund, decided to offer an honorarium in return for regular performances to a top carillonneur who had settled in the town. Thus it was that the rather more mellifluous sounds of a second John Knox, for that really was his name, were broadcast from St John's over the streets of the city.

While the kirk may be Perth's only remaining mediaeval building, other clues to the town's ancient past are still visible, although their interpretation requires great care. For example, the broadly geometric layout of the streets of the central area, as can be seen from any street plan, gave rise to the long held view that the city had been a Roman foundation and perhaps originally a Roman camp. But in spite of the wealth of Roman remains surrounding the town no Roman structure has yet been discovered within the historic centre. It is true that a prehistoric midden and wattle house were found on the corner of the High Street and Tay Street in 1956 but no evidence exists to suggest that the town has been continuously inhabited for much more than, say, 900 years. Perth almost certainly postdates the Roman occupation by several centuries, owing its origins both to the proximity of royal Scone and its prime location on the developing trade and communication network of eastern Scotland.

Perth's central area, thankfully, is not an absolutely rigid network of parallel and perpendicular streets. The northwards curve at the bottom of the High Street, when considered in isolation, is curious; but looked at in conjunction with Hospital Street, with which it is more or less aligned, and we begin to see, perhaps, the line of an ancient pre-urban road, one which may have brought the early traveller from the south to a crossing point over the Tay. While certain facts about the development of the early town can be deduced from the layout of the old streets, the street names themselves provide valuable clues to the occupations of the mediaeval burgh. Those of the little lanes and vennels which thread their way through the centre add particular splashes of colour to the otherwise drab uniformity of names such as High Street, South Street, George Street and Princes Street, all of which can be found in many other towns throughout Scotland. Such gems as Cow Vennel, Flesher's Vennel, Horner's Lane and Skinnergate all suggest a certain occupational dependence on our bovine friends, while Baxter's Vennel, Ropemaker's Close and several others, some now disappeared, bear witness to thriving mediaeval commerce. Vennels, incidentally, are simply narrow town lanes and are found in several other Scottish towns.

Before moving on to more recent developments, tribute should be made to the late Dr Margaret Stewart, a highly respected archaeologist and a lover of the city. She was one of the founder members of the Perth Civic Trust in 1967 and five years later was behind the formation of the Perth Archaeological Survey. At around this time she wrote and published (in partnership with Lisbeth Thoms) an influential booklet, *It will soon be too late,* which drew attention to the fact that almost nothing at that time was known of the archaeology of mediaeval Perth. This state of affairs was quickly remedied. Plans were drawn up for the systematic archaeological investigation of the town, the Urban Archaeology Unit was founded in 1978 under the auspices of the Society of Antiquaries of Scotland, and in 1982 this developed into the Perth-based Scottish Urban Archaeological Trust. The extent and speed of the progress made can be gauged from R.M. Spearman's comment in *The Scottish medieval town* (1988), that Perth 'has been the subject of some of the most detailed and extensive urban excavations in Scotland'. All thanks to Margaret Stewart's combination of foresight and forcefulness.

The 1600s and early 1700s were bad times for the city. The Scottish parliament, until it enacted its own final dissolution in 1707, was firmly settled in Edinburgh. Kings were rarely seen in Scotland, never mind Perth, and when Charles II made his brief appearance in 1651 he brought Cromwell and his strong-arm tactics in his wake. Even the university authorities at St Andrews, desperate to escape the appalling squalor of the town, drew back from making that final decision in the 1690s to relocate to Perth.

At around the middle of the eighteenth century, however, the town finally turned its back on distant memories of former greatness, knocked down the old walls and, under the leadership of a small circle of eminent families, embraced the Age of Enlightenment with enthusiasm. Thomas Hay Marshall belonged to one such family and is generally credited with the building of Perth's New Town, although the plans were originally drawn up, and the land acquired, by his father-in-law Thomas Anderson. Expansion to the north and south was the main feature of these first successful attempts at town planning. Atholl Place, Atholl Crescent and Rose Terrace, all facing the North Inch, are excellent examples of Scottish Georgian architecture, as is Marshall Place overlooking the South Inch. Streets on a smaller scale were built behind these grand frontages; in particular, the area bounded by Marshall Place, Canal Street, Princes Street and King Street has a marvellous collection of small town houses which, though so close to the city centre, enjoy the peace and quietness of an almost forgotten suburb.

One of the great achievements of this era was the construction of the Perth Bridge, which was begun in 1766 and completed five years later at a cost of just over £26,000. Communications with the north-east of the country were instantly improved as Perth, until the rail bridges were built between Dundee and Fife in the later nineteenth century, was still the great crossing point of the lower Tay. Its effects were felt locally too, first of all by the thirty or so ferrymen who would have become immediately redundant, and secondly by the residents of Bridgend, a hitherto run-down hamlet at the east end of the bridge, which suddenly blossomed into a thriving village with many new houses. (Two hundred years later, however, some of these houses, particularly in Commercial Street, had deteriorated to such an extent that the council purchased them, brought in the bulldozers, and in their place built the imaginative new Commercial Street development. It was completed in 1978 and won a host of national and international awards and, perhaps most prestigious of all, was featured on a 31p postage stamp in 1984.) The bridge was designed by the renowned engineer, John Smeaton (who built a very similar one

Perth Bridge and the New Town in the early 1840s, viewed from the garden of Rosebank on the lower slopes of Kinnoull Hill. Note the clothes stretched out to bleach on the North Inch, the Britannia-less Academy building and at the left the little bridge over the Town Lade (© Dr W H Findlay).

over the Tweed at Coldstream), and was immediately hailed by Thomas Pennant as 'the most beautiful structure of the kind in North Britain'. His only criticism was that it was too narrow. It was widened in 1869, but once again struggles to cope with the demands of late twentieth century traffic. As the bridge steadily gets older the people of Perth are perhaps beginning to realise once again what a treasure they have in their midst. It is now featured, along with St John's Kirk, on the 'Welcome to Perth' signs at the outskirts of the city and for the past few years has been the subject of excellent floodlighting.

The Victorian era witnessed eastwards and westwards development. Fine mansions began to spread up the lower slopes of Kinnoull Hill from the riverside village of Bridgend. In one of these, Bowerswell, lived the solicitor George Gray whose daughter, Effie, married firstly the art critic John Ruskin (who also had Perth connections) and secondly, following the annulment of the marriage, the painter Sir John Everett Millais. The Millais family then moved into nearby Annat Lodge where 'Autumn Leaves' was painted. (Sir John was particularly fond of Perth and once claimed

*The classically-inspired County Buildings were erected in around 1819
on the site of the old Gowrie House. The Sheriff Court now occupies the
building and every two months or so the High Court returns to try those
accused of more serious crime.*

that the view northwards from Perth Bridge was 'much better than
the Riviera') On the other side of town similar houses stretched
out in a ribbon development along the Glasgow Road while
smaller ones clustered together to form Craigie. The present
century saw the arrival of the big housing schemes: Muirton,
Letham, Tulloch and North Muirton consist in the main of local
authority housing while those at Oakbank, upper Kinnoull and
most recently the Western Edge are owner-occupied.

The splendid domestic architecture of the Georgian and Victorian
periods provides a dignified setting for several contemporary
public buildings of an equally high standard. The neo-classical
court building, standing sentinel at the southern corner of Tay
Street and South Street, was built in around 1819 and provides an
imposing entrance into the city centre from the Queen's Bridge.
Unfortunately its grandeur is overshadowed by the ghost of the
historic Gowrie House which stood on the same spot and which,
as the setting for the infamous conspiracy of 1600, would have
had tales of mystery and intrigue to tell. The whole length of Tay
Street, in fact, is built in a wide range of architectural styles and
deserves more than a passing glance. Wander along by the river
and take time to admire the classic restraint of the Perthshire

Advertiser offices, the soaring Gothic of the St Matthew's spire (known as the Whisky Steeple), the Renaissance-style former bank (currently a nightclub) and, on either side of the High Street corner, the old and new Council Chambers. These were all begun, and all but one completed, in the second half of the nineteenth century when Tay Street itself was created from the gardens which used to lead down to the river from houses in Watergate.

Although no other street in Perth can match Tay Street for impressive and varied architecture, there are many individual buildings of note dotted around the town. One of the best known Perth landmarks, St Paul's Church at the west end of the High Street, is itself of no particular architectural merit (apart from the huge domed ceiling), but if it were ever to be pulled down, as indeed is now being discussed, the character of the street over which it presides will be changed for ever. Having lain empty for several years, and with various conversion plans having come to naught, the gradual deterioration of the fabric means that its time is running out.

The Fair Maid's House was home to a highly successful and popular craft shop until an unfortunate dispute with the district council resulted in it going out of business. This was supposedly the home of Catherine Glover, the fourteenth century heroine of Sir Walter Scott's famous novel. Although Catherine herself is almost certainly a fictional character there is a Glover connection with the building: in 1629 the Glover Incorporation of Perth, one of the nine Incorporated Trades (akin to a trade union), purchased the property and used it as a meeting room for over 150 years. Their motto, 'Grace and Peace', is carved in Gothic lettering above the door. The building was heavily restored in 1893–94 and little of the original structure now remains. Almost next door is the distinctive three-arched town house, or at least its surviving front portion, of Lord John Murray which dates from the eighteenth century. Lord John was a son of the 1st Duke of Atholl whose family was tragically riven by divided political loyalties. He was a staunch Whig at a time when two of his half-brothers risked everything on the Jacobite cause. They lost, and he served as the MP for Perthshire between 1734 and 1761.

For a more detailed impression of the wealth of architectural activity in Georgian and Victorian Perth the following are also well worth a visit: the Bank of Scotland premises in St John Street with its stunning Renaissance-style ceiling, St Ninian's Cathedral in Atholl Street, the first cathedral to be built in Britain since the Reformation (apart from the rebuilding of St Paul's in London), Balhousie Castle by the North Inch, the home of the Black Watch, the church of St Leonard's in the Fields by the South Inch, and the King James VI Hospital in Hospital Street.

The first half and more of the present century found Perth drifting into complacency, oblivious to the gradual decay of its public buildings and seemingly unconcerned by the relentless erosion of the historic centre and with it the essential character of the city. This is not to say that no real progress in town development was made as the Victoria Bridge (replaced by the present Queen's Bridge in 1960) and the new City Hall, as well as King Edward Street and the museum extension, all saw the light of day during this period. But the fact that the Perth Town Council as recently as the mid-1960s could permit both the construction of the tasteless Woolworths building at the heart of the High Street and the demolition of the Earl of Kinnoull's town house, an early seventeenth century building in the Watergate, simply beggars belief. It was this careless attitude to the heritage of Perth which so forcibly struck Moultrie Kelsall in 1951 and which persisted until the Perth Civic Trust was founded. In recent years, of course, parts of old Perth have gone a similar way, not least of them the old Parliament Close now beneath Marks and Spencer, but at least their cases are argued at length before the demolition teams move in.

The two public parks, the North and South Inches, are as much a part of Perth as the best-loved buildings and indeed it would be true to say that over the years the townspeople have been more protective towards them than they ever were towards their architectural heritage. The Inches are low lying expanses of parkland near the river and, as the name derives from the Gaelic for a small island, it seems reasonable to assume that the Tay once flowed on both sides. They were apparently given to the town of Perth by Robert II in 1377, although there is an age-old tradition that they originally belonged to the powerful Mercer family who gifted them to the city in exchange for the right of burial in St John's Kirk. As an old rhymer put it:

> Folk say the Mercers tried the town to cheat
> When for two inches they did win six feet.

While no documentary evidence exists to verify this story, other than a charter which shows that they perhaps owned a small corner of the North Inch, the Mercers certainly do have a vault in St John's.

Today the Inches are green and leafy havens on the edge of a busy city centre where residents and workers can stroll, jog or cycle, play golf, rugby, cricket or petanque, or simply just lie in the sun with a Marks and Spencer sandwich and the daily paper. On occasions they can enjoy a feast of international cricket when the Scottish team struggles to keep its end up against the mighty Australians or West Indians. The South Inch offers a wide range of facilities for children including putting, crazy golf, trampolines, and a popular boating pond.

Last century the people of the city might have watched the horse racing around the North Inch, or hung out their washing to dry, or even allowed their cattle to graze on a sward less closely cropped than today. Before that, however, some of the activities seen on the Inches were less peaceful. The South Inch, for example, was one of the places in town where archery practice was held. It was also the site chosen for Cromwell's hated citadel. On the North Inch Bonnie Prince Charlie paraded his troops in September 1745 before heading southwards, and the following year a large number of soldiers belonging to the Prince of Hesse-Cassel, the Duke of Cumberland's brother-in-law, encamped there and stayed for several years. On 18 July 1623 three local women were led out to a hollow at the north end of the North Inch and there strangled and burnt at the stake for the crime of witchcraft.

Undoubtedly the most famous event to be witnessed on the North Inch was the Battle of the Clans in 1396. Although a detailed fictional account of this forms the finale to Scott's *The fair maid of Perth,* what really brings the event to life is a brief entry in the *Exchequer rolls of Scotland* which records the cost of erecting barriers around the combat area for 'sexaginta personarum pugnancium in Insula de Perth'. The two warring factions, clans Kay (or Quhele) and Chattan, having been unable to settle a long-standing feud by any other means, agreed to end the matter once and for all by fighting it out, thirty a side (perhaps according to some chivalrous code), in front of the king. Scott's account is wonderfully bloodthirsty and ends with the sole survivor from Clan Kay swimming the Tay to escape from the local hero, Hal o the Wynd, who had been drafted into the Clan Chattan side at the last minute to even the numbers. Around twelve of the sixty are believed to have survived the day as did, apparently, the bagpipes played by the mortally wounded Clan Chattan piper. Part of this relic, the Black Chanter, is now in the possession of Clan Macpherson and can be seen in the clan museum at Newtonmore. Supremely romantic though the story is, it nevertheless reveals the vastly different culture of the Highland clans and how little power the Scottish kings had to intervene in their affairs.

Perhaps the only proper 'inch' still surviving in Perth is Moncreiffe Island, a large and low-lying river island which, with its attractive woods and fine views of Kinnoull Hill, has been designated an Area of Great Landscape Value. Access is via the railway bridge which also carries a narrow footpath between Tay Street and Barnhill. The northern tip of the island, under the auspices of the Perth Working Men's Gardens Association, was divided into allotments in 1896 and these are still going strong in spite of the ravages of flooding in 1990 and 1993. In 1897 the King James VI Golf Club moved from its North Inch course and took up residence on the remainder of the island where the legendary Tom Morris had laid out a brand new course. The club dates only from 1858, the name having been chosen to commemorate the belief that James VI himself played golf on the Perth inches.

Perth is a complex town. Forward-looking yet still proud of its early history. Old, but with few ancient buildings. Scottish, yet with many English voices heard in the streets. Comfortably off in spite of the drunks lying on the city benches. Cultural, but at times with unimpressive box office figures. Good for shopping but dreadful for parking a car. But most of all Perth is a real working town with a good mix of age ranges and where commerce, industry, tourism, sport and the arts all coexist successfully. With a population of around 42,000 it is not too big to be impersonal and not too small for privacy. Those who visit Perth, be they tourists, residents, businessmen or even *Spectator* columnists, will today find a confident, forward-looking city, ready to be one of the bright spots on the map of 21st-century Scotland. And were Mr Kelsall able to return, he might manage more of a smile.

CHAPTER 7

STRATHMORE AND THE CARSE OF GOWRIE

Strathmore, the 'great valley', has an undefined length for the simple reason that the term means different things to different people. Some consider that it cuts right across Scotland, following the Highland Boundary Fault from Stonehaven to central Dumbarton-shire and including large parts of Stirlingshire, Strathallan and Strathearn. Others, including the cartographers of the Ordnance Survey, limit its extent to the area roughly between Perth and Brechin. Geologically, the former are probably correct while topographically the latter offer a more sensible definition. The sides of the strath are formed by the Highland foothills to the north and the Sidlaws to the south, the distance between the two, as far as Perthshire is concerned, being in the region of six miles.

A long and wide valley like Strathmore might be expected to have a notable river flowing through it, and in this respect the Isla is something of a disappointment. It is a short river, 47 miles in length, which meanders slowly through the western end of the strath, picking up the Dean Water near Meigle and the Ericht near Coupar Angus before joining the Tay south of Meikleour. Further upstream and across the county boundary, however, it has a different character, that of a Highland burn hurrying south between the heights of Glenisla from its source on the Aberdeenshire border. At Reekie Linn, north of Alyth but still in Angus, it becomes briefly one of the finest waterfalls of eastern Scotland with a combined drop, when in spate, of almost 80 feet. As the Isla approaches the Lowlands it bends to the south-east to avoid both the Hill of Alyth and Barry Hill and then, bursting into the openness of the strath, turns sharply south-west and adopts a more restrained nature, better suited to the gentility of the Lowland countryside.

Comparatively small though the Perthshire section of Strathmore may be, it nevertheless includes three of the larger towns in the county, the ABC triangle of Alyth, Blairgowrie and Coupar Angus, together with several sites of historic interest, and some of the most fertile agricultural land in Scotland. Scenically, from the valley floor, it lacks variety. A drive around Strathmore, avoiding the busy main roads, will take you into a lattice work of long and straight side roads, almost devoid of traffic, past field after field of growing corn. There are trees dotted around the landscape but at this level few actual woods; they can be found instead growing up the sides of the valley, particularly on the Sidlaws where the deep dark green of the conifers acts as a frame for the softer colours of lower-lying farm land. The landscape of Strathmore, and indeed its sheer size, have to be seen from above to be appreciated properly. If climbing a hill is not possible, then the higher roads along the edges of the strath will do almost as well in providing splendid views over what has been called the queen of Scottish valleys. Certainly, from this vantage point, the full meaning of 'the great valley' becomes abundantly clear.

The evidence of place-names and surviving carved stones shows that Strathmore was one of the Pictish heartlands. As a farming people they would have gravitated towards the rich soil of the area where they could support themselves by tending cattle and growing barley. This, of course, is not the image that comes over to the general public; several of the better known Pictish stones depict spear-carrying soldiers on horseback, an image reinforced by dim recollections of warlike Picts from school Latin lessons. A good artistic tradition, however, needs time to develop and for this reason alone it seems unlikely that all the Picts were fighting all the time.

One of the best collections anywhere of Pictish carved stones, or indeed of European Dark Age sculpture, is now in the care of Historic Scotland and housed in a small museum at Meigle, a village near the county boundary with Angus. It is well worth a visit, if only to become close physically to some of the few surviving remains of the indigenous people of Scotland. The carvings are remarkably naturalistic and tell us a lot about Pictish dress, horses and weaponry. Their purity of line and sense of artistry, rather than craftsmanship, are also noteworthy. Quite what the carvings mean, however, is a very different matter. While battle scenes could probably be taken at face value, what are we supposed to make of the mysterious Z and V rods, and of the mirror and comb symbols? One recent suggestion is that they represent different Pictish families and that their various combinations indicate marriage alliances. What, also, can be deduced from carvings of creatures such as sea horses which rarely if ever are found in the waters of the North Sea? The marked resurgence of Pictish studies in recent decades may yet provide a solution to some of these intriguing problems.

The most interesting stone in the museum is also one of the largest, that listed as Stone 2. The front shows a typical cross with various carvings around it. The back depicts, amongst others, a centaur, an angel, a dragon seizing a bull by the nose and a cleverly executed group of three horsemen riding abreast. The main scene, showing a central figure surrounded by four broad-shouldered animals, is generally taken nowadays as illustrating the story of Daniel in the lions' den. This is a comparatively recent interpretation as the stone was traditionally regarded as the gravestone of King Arthur's wife, Guinevere or Queen Vanora, whose death is illustrated by the central carving. The story, which was mentioned by Boece as long ago as the early sixteenth century, tells of how she was captured during a battle between Arthur and the united forces of the Scots and Picts and was held prisoner in the Pictish fort on nearby Barry Hill. During her captivity, to quote the author of the Old Statistical Account of Meigle, she 'held an unlawful correspondence with Mordred, a Pictish king' which so incensed Arthur that after they had been reunited he had her put to death by being torn to pieces by wild animals.

While few nowadays would place much credence on the writings of Boece, some brave souls still go against the flow of expert opinion and continue to argue the case for locating the Arthurian cycle in Scotland. They point out that the first known reference to Arthur appears in *Gododdin*, a late sixth or early seventh century poem which was written in Scotland, albeit in a Brythonic language, and it has further been suggested with some justification that the Arthurian names of Lyonesse and Tristan should be equated respectively with Lothian and the Pictish king Drust. Not far from Meigle there was even a Stone of Arthur, reputedly 15 feet high and weighing 100 tons, which was apparently deliberately shattered by explosion to provide building material for the nearby farm of Arthurbank. Until evidence is found to the contrary, the fascinating possibility remains that the mound in Meigle churchyard, from where Stone 2 was removed, really might be one of the most historically significant graves in the whole of Britain.

Apart from its museum Meigle has nothing to lift itself above the level of an ordinary eastern Scottish village. So when wandering

This mound in Meigle churchyard is traditionally the spot where Queen Guinevere, wife of King Arthur, lies buried. Certainly she keeps a royal distance between herself and her neighbours. Her gravestone, the famous Stone 2, can be seen in the nearby Meigle Museum. There used to be a tradition amongst the young women of the village that walking across the mound would lead to a childless marriage.

around the churchyard the casual visitor may be more than a little surprised to find the grave of so eminent a personage as a British prime minister. Sir Henry Campbell-Bannerman was a Glaswegian who held the Stirling Burghs seat in Parliament for 40 years. A member of Gladstone's government for several years he finally entered the Cabinet in 1886 as secretary of state for war. He became leader of the Liberal Party in 1899 and prime minister at the end of 1905. Ill health made his tenure short and he died in April 1908, shortly after his wife. His connection with Meigle dated from 1885 when he purchased the Belmont Castle estate on the southern edge of the village. The castle itself had been badly damaged by fire the previous year and the new owner spared no energy or expense in its restoration and enlargement, spending, it is said, no less than £10,000 on the stables alone. The villagers were obviously proud of their famous new resident, so much so, in fact, that when he became prime minister the local football team hauled his carriage from the estate gateway to his front door and then divided the rope they had used between them as souvenirs of the great day. The following year, during the general election, the post office remained open till 1.00 am for several days to allow news of the constituency results to reach him as soon as possible. Belmont was eventually gifted to the city of Dundee as a home for disabled soldiers and now functions as a Church of Scotland eventide home.

The small town of Alyth lies four miles north-east of Meigle on the southern edge of the Highlands at an altitude of around 300 feet. Historic, and with an attractive centre, it was once a destination popular with many Dundee holiday-makers. 'Bracing', however, which used to appear in the town's holiday brochures of several decades ago, is a word which no longer pulls in the tourists who now, it seems, have deserted Alyth for the warmer climes of the Algarve. The town consequently gives the impression of having been stuck in a 1950s time warp. Far from being shabby or run-down, Alyth is simply old-fashioned in a particularly pleasing way, and where some of the shops have changed little in recent decades their staff have at least retained an old-fashioned courtesy for their customers.

The town spreads out from the Market Square, an unremarkable centre but for the Alyth Burn which flows through the middle. One of several which rush down from Highland Perthshire, the burn is really a small river by the time it reaches Alyth. A touch of old world charm is provided by the several little footbridges over it of which the earliest surviving, and the most picturesque, is a bulky two-arched structure known as the Auld Brig. Most authorities tend to place its origins in the sixteenth century. It seems that packhorses made much use of this narrow crossing which may explain why it was originally built without the parapets. Weaving was one of the main industries of the town and it is not difficult to imagine laden horses struggling up the slope of the bridge, piled high with the latest products of the town's looms, and trying hard not to put a hoof too far to the right or left.

The old parish church, now ruined, was dedicated to St Moluag, a sixth century Irish saint who based himself at Lismore and who is primarily associated with the west of Scotland. Whether or not Moluag himself ever visited Alyth is unknown but the indications are that the ecclesiastical history of the town probably began at

The solid structure of the Auld Brig is one Alyth's most attractive features.

around that time. The site of the north wall of the church is now dominated by three large arches, a memorial to an unsuccessful post-Reformation attempt to increase the size of the town kirk. The congregation, perhaps dispirited by this ever present reminder of failure, had to wait a long time for their larger premises which finally materialised in 1839. It must have been worth the wait because at the time the new parish church was described as the largest in Strathmore and the tower and spire as the finest north of the Forth. More recently, it has been considered 'the most dramatic and successful example of nineteenth century church architecture in Tayside'. Built with red sandstone taken from the quarry in the Den of Alyth, as indeed is much of the town, it can almost glow in the warm light of the setting sun.

In their burial plot in the churchyard lie some of the Ramsays of Bamff, an ancient and distinguished Perthshire family who, over the years, have been one of the town's main benefactors. The progenitor of the family fortunes was Neis de Ramsay, physician to Alexander II, who by 'cutting a hair-ball from the King's heart' and thus saving his life (the king survived a further 17 years making this, so it is said, the first successful abdominal operation ever recorded), was rewarded in 1232 with the grant of what is now the Bamff estate. Of the several eminent members of this family, pride of place must go to Katharine, daughter of the tenth Baronet, who married the 8th Duke of Atholl and became a highly respected politician, musician and writer.

Stretching out to the west of the town is the Den of Alyth, a deep and wooded valley which, because of the richness of the woodland habitat and the number of plants rare in the locality, has been declared a Site of Special Scientific Interest. It was gifted to the town in 1923 and is still a popular place amongst the townspeople for a walk and a picnic. In contrast, the Forest of Alyth, to the north and north-west of the town, is a large and barren area which, together with the adjoining Forest of Clunie, was one of the most important royal forests in thirteenth century Scotland. The lack of trees, which one would normally expect to find on land so designated, is explained by the fact that these early 'forests' were essentially hunting reserves and therefore not necessarily wooded.

Blairgowrie and Rattray, with a population of almost 8000, is Perthshire's second town. It developed on the edge of the Highland Boundary Fault, a frontier settlement occupying the strategic position at the end of the pass by which the River Ericht enters the Lowlands. The web of roads which today radiates from the town testifies to its important position within central Scotland. From here you can travel north to the ski slopes of Glenshee and further on to Deeside, north-east to Aberdeen, south-east to Dundee, south to Perth and west to Dunkeld.

Since 1928, Blairgowrie and its neighbour across the Ericht, Rattray, have been joined as one town, with Blairgowrie and Rattray being the official name although, naturally enough and no doubt to the chagrin of Rattray folk, the latter name has fallen into disuse in everyday speech. This union has happily turned the Wellmeadow, a triangular area of grass and trees once on the edge of Blairgowrie proper and formerly used for grazing, fairs and markets, into the centre of the enlarged town. The tall war memorial now acts as the centrepiece of this popular little park and around it lie flower beds and well tended lawns. The town's main streets either border the Wellmeadow or lead into it and with their good range of local and specialist shops attract sufficient numbers to ensure that Blairgowrie has the pleasant feel of a self-contained and bustling country town.

Both Blairgowrie and Rattray are built on the sides of hills, a feature which greatly adds to the character of the joint town and makes possible the sometimes unexpected views over Strathmore or of the wooded hills behind Rattray. Through the middle flows the Ericht, which in the summer is generally shallow and, unusually for a Highland stream, fairly slow-moving. The lovely River Ericht Walk follows the lightly wooded banks upstream from the bridge and is one of the several attractions which have made Blairgowrie one of the busiest tourist towns in the county.

The population of Blairgowrie in the eighteenth century numbered only around 400 and judging by the following contemporary description was a poor, neglected backwater of Perthshire:

> There were only four slated houses in Blairgowrie;...then it had one minister and one dominie [schoolmaster]; it had a brewer and a few drinkers; a baker who lived a hungry life; a butcher, small of paunch, who seldom killed a beast; a miller not much troubled with dust; a smith with too many irons in the fire; a cloth merchant who generally wore a very seedy coat, and came to serve his customers after dark...; a barber nicknamed Skin-em-alive...; there were some laws but no lawyers to teach them; broken bones and various diseases, but no doctor...; we had no banks and little money...; we had no brokers and nothing to pawn; the town's bellman used to perambulate the town with his bell and intimate to the inhabitants that 'good beef at fourpence a-pound is on sale at John Lowrie's — the Bailie's ta'en ae leg, an the minister anither, but gif nae ither person taks a third leg the ox will no be killed.'

The characteristic dryness of Scots humour was alive and well two hundred years ago, even if the poor old ox wasn't.

In the nineteenth century the population of Blairgowrie expanded exponentially, increasing tenfold to around 4000 by its end. This dramatic growth was caused mainly by the mechanisation of the town's textile industry, during which the new spinning mills along the banks of the Ericht, 12 in total, put an end to traditional hand loom weaving in cottages. These mills were fully occupied with flax spinning until mid-century when the first cartload of jute, straight from the docks at Dundee, was brought to the town. James Grimond, a member of one of the several families behind the industrialisation of Blairgowrie, was the first to experiment success-fully with jute, which then became the town's principal manufacture.

One of James' descendants, Jo Grimond, served as leader of the Liberal Party between 1956 and 1967.

The textile industry reached its peak in the last years of the nineteenth century and then went into slow decline. By 1963 only four of the twelve mills were still working and in 1979 the last one, Keathbank (originally spelt as Keithbank), closed its doors and in doing so ended a significant chapter in the history of the town. Keathbank, however, was not to go into retirement. It now functions as a museum, housing one of the largest working water wheels in the country together with some of the mill's early steam-powered equipment and, perhaps incongruously, a heraldry centre where heraldic carvers and painters can be seen at work. Children, on the other hand, may prefer to busy themselves with one of the largest model railways in Britain.

Providence saw to it that the soft fruit industry should fill the employment gap created by the gradual silencing of the mills. Blairgowrie had long enjoyed a reputation for the high quality of its strawberries but, just at the time when the civic leaders were honouring the plant by having strawberry leaves incorporated into the new town seal, the growers were realising that it had no commercial future. Instead, at the suggestion of a local solicitor, James Mackenzie Hodge, the focus switched to raspberries, which were first grown commercially at the end of the 1890s. This industry developed so quickly that within a few years the local workforce was unable to cope with the sheer volume of fruit being harvested and had to rely on outside help. Two distinct groups, the poor from the slums of Glasgow and the travelling people from all over Scotland, thus began the tradition of flocking to Blairgowrie for eight or nine weeks in the summer to pick the fruit. Living in hastily erected shanty towns, they swelled the town's population and, with their horse dealing, drunkenness and fighting, turned Blairgowrie, as the writer Roger Leitch put it, into 'Perthshire's answer to Dodge City'. Each summer extra police had to be drafted into the town and the local magistrates were kept busy with a variety of petty offences.

The travellers, who regarded 'the berries' as the social event of the year, kept themselves apart from the other pickers, not from any sense of inferiority but on the contrary because they regarded the town dwellers as unclean. In the post-war decades the travellers of Scotland have been the focus of much research, pioneered

Raspberry picking at Essendy, near Blairgowrie, in the early years of this century. To quote from a source of 1921, 'the pickers in normal years were…a respectable class — waitresses, servants, shop assistants, factory girls, and industrial school children'. 'The tramp' was not at all welcome. (Courtesy of Perth & Kinross Libraries and W Davidson and Sons Ltd).

mainly by the staff and fieldworkers of Edinburgh University's School of Scottish Studies. Resulting from this, travellers nowadays are seen not so much as occupying the bottom rungs of society's ladder but as standing on a different ladder altogether. One of the energetic figures behind this re-evaluation was Blairgowrie-born poet and Marxist, Hamish Henderson, who, in spite of his public school and Cambridge background, thought nothing of pitching his tent with the travelling folk, gaining their acceptance and recording their songs, stories and traditions. He began his work in the 1950s and quickly realised that he was dealing not with mere fragments of a dying tradition but with a whole alternative culture shared by all travellers and which was invigorated annually at their coming together in his home town. Now, almost half a century later, the oral traditions of the Scottish travellers are regarded as virtually unequalled in Europe. Belle Stewart, who has since settled in Rattray, and her daughters, are leading figures in the world of Scottish folksong and several other members of this community have been encouraged to write and publish their stories. Duncan Williamson, Sandy Stewart and the late Betsy Whyte have produced remarkable insights into a way of life that has all but disappeared from the quiet corners and byways of Scotland. Hamish Henderson himself is now one of the most highly regarded authorities on this facet of Scottish life and a poet of considerable stature.

Another aspect of Scottish culture, also on the wane but fighting a rearguard action on the edge of the Highland line, was celebrated in great style in Blairgowrie in October 1996. Gaeldom's premier festival of song, verse and drama, the Royal National Mod, was described as the biggest single event ever to come to the town. In the run up, crash courses in Gaelic were held locally and even the late district council, normally prudent, was induced to part with £6000 to erect Gaelic street signs on the town's main thoroughfares. On the other hand, in terms of revenue from visitors to the Mod this figure was repaid a hundredfold and more although some traders would dispute this. But of course it is wrong to regard the event as a purely money-making exercise. Gaelic culture was the norm in north Perthshire until last century and there was a sense, if only for a week, that it had come home. Certainly it was good to hear the simple ethereal beauty of unaccompanied Gaelic song so close to Perth again.

Rattray, in some ways the poor relation, can boast at least one famous son. Donald Cargill was born in the town in around 1620 and spent much of his life as the influential minister of the Barony Church in Glasgow. The seventeenth century, however, was a time of upheaval in the Scottish church and when in 1661 Charles II re-established bishops in the hierarchy many staunch Presbyterians, including Cargill, spoke out loudly against them. He was duly removed from his charge and banished to the area north of the Tay, at a safe distance from both the capital and his parishioners in Glasgow. Thereafter he became an itinerant preacher and, having perhaps unwisely excommunicated the king, one with a price on his head. Tradition records his many narrow escapes from capture, the best known being when he jumped the foaming Ericht to escape the troops of Bonnie Dundee. He seems to have maintained a sense of humour in this dangerous period as, on being quizzed about his massive leap, he replied, 'Aye, but I had a long run to it. I ran all the way from Perth.' Cargill's Leap can be seen close to Keathbank Mill although, as a discouragement to others who might wish to emulate the feat, the span has since been widened. Cargill was eventually captured in 1680 and, having been found guilty of high treason, suffered a cruel death in Edinburgh the following year.

From Rattray the A93 heads north for Glenshee and Deeside, following in its early stages the writhing Ericht through a steep-sided gorge which in places reaches a height of around 300 feet. On one side, sheer above the river and visible through the bare trees of winter, is the mansion of Craighall, home to the Rattray family who have been resident in the neighbourhood since the twelfth century. Opposite, and higher up on the other side of the river, lie the lands of Mause which feature in a famous ghost story. It concerned a local man, William Soutar, who on several occasions between the years 1728 and 1730 met a strange black dog and always at the same place. Eventually the dog spoke and announced that he was the ghost of Soutar's uncle, that 35 years previously he had committed a murder and that he now wanted Soutar to bury the bones of his victim. At first Soutar was unable to find the location but after the dog had provided a better description, dogs being pretty good at locating bones, Soutar sure enough found the grisly remains which were then interred in Blairgowrie churchyard. The story, supposedly well documented, is not however the only one in Perthshire to feature a loquacious hound or a murderous ghost with unburied bones on his conscience. Leaving the 'ghaist o Mause' behind the road shadows the Ericht for a few more miles through a pleasantly green and soft landscape until it divides at Bridge of Cally, the A924 heading off towards Kirkmichael and Pitlochry, following the River Ardle for some of the way, and the A93 continuing towards Braemar, following upstream the Black Water initially and then the Shee Water. This area is described in more detail in the chapter on Highland Perthshire.

Coupar Angus, once known as the Queen of Strathmore, is today a rather dowdy lady. When even the editor of the local newsletter says in print that the interior of the town 'is sadly lacking in colour' it would seem wise not to expect too much from a visit. It has endured a lot in the last twenty years, not least of the indignities being the loss of the town council in 1975 and a growing sense of being trampled underfoot by armies of juggernauts and general heavy traffic thundering through the centre on the way to Dundee or Aberdeen. Few towns and villages can avoid the suffocating blanket of greyness which descends with such an excess of traffic. Since early 1997, however, its public face has been much improved and a measure of peace restored by the new relief road which now syphons traffic away from the town centre. Setting aside the inevitable chorus of complaints caused by the sudden diminution in passing trade this could be a turning point for Coupar Angus, for the town has much to offer. It has a history to be proud of, buildings to admire and a potentially attractive centre at the Cross. Away from the main roads the mediaeval pattern of the little streets, lanes and closes, which are such a pleasure to explore, has been described as one of the best preserved in Scotland. Hanging baskets, tubs of flowers in the streets, and some freshened paintwork would be a good start. The other drawback to the relief road, apart from the initial loss of trade, is that it should have been planned to scythe through the eastern portion of the town rather than bypass it altogether. This has left the tolbooth steeple, built in 1762 and one of the finest buildings in Coupar Angus, looking somewhat isolated from the centre.

The town was long considered to be a Roman foundation but the earthworks which gave rise to this belief are now thought, on balance, to have functioned as a boundary marker for the precincts of the famous Coupar Angus abbey. The Cistercian foundation dates from 1164 and in spite of having a complement of only nineteen monks became one of the richest and most influential organisations in western Strathmore. Just before the Reformation it had an annual income similar to that of Holyrood Abbey in Edinburgh and in excess of its well known mother abbey at Melrose. The *Rental Book* which the Grampian Club published in 1879–80 shows the full extent of its financial empire which stretched throughout Perthshire and Angus and even had interests as far afield as Banffshire. The Cistercians owned large estates in these counties and their reputation for improving land is borne out clearly by the *Rental Book*: for example, tenants of marshy land were required to drain it, peat had to be cut in a prescribed manner and crops had to be sown in rotation. The monks were also granted a number of important privileges including that of buying and selling unhindered throughout the kingdom, and of freedom from customs dues and ferry tolls. The mediaeval population must have regarded the abbey in much the same way as we do a multi-national business corporation today.

All that remains of Coupar Angus abbey, one of the great institutions of mediaeval Scotland. Where once the abbey would have stood within grounds extending to around 50 acres this surviving stone gateway is confined to a meagre enclosure measuring 10 yards square.

Eventually the crash came. As with so many Perthshire religious establishments the Reformation sounded the death knell for the abbey although, unlike most, the end was prolonged until the seventeenth century. But in accordance with good Christian doctrine the resurrection came when the townspeople used the redundant stone in the construction of new buildings and thus spread the deep pink of the old abbey walls throughout the town. All that remains now is a part of a wall and an arch which is in the ownership of the Earl of Moray. Perth and Kinross Heritage Trust have recently contributed to the cost of removing its blanket of ivy and of other urgently needed repairs.

Beside the ruins is the Abbey Church which dates from 1859 and is the second parish church on the site. It contains a number of interesting relics from the days of the town's greatness, including the tomb of Sir Gilbert Hay, 5th Lord Erroll and Lord High Constable of Scotland. The Hays, normally considered a Carse of Gowrie family, gave much land to the monks. The small oblong watch tower in the middle of the churchyard was built in 1822 at the height of the Resurrectionist scare when grave robbers, body snatchers and the infamous duo of Burke and Hare held the country in thrall.

The Perthshire-Angus county boundary cuts right through the middle of Strathmore, dividing what is essentially a single territorial unit into two distinct parts. Not only is each governed by a different local authority but the western part enjoys the added advantage of coming under the wing of the dynamic Perthshire Tourist Board. To mitigate the effects of split personality the Strathmore Association was founded in 1983 with the specific aim of looking at the problems and advantages of the area as a whole. Furthermore, because of the noticeable drop in the numbers of travellers passing through, following the opening of Perth's Friarton Bridge and the de-trunking of the A94 in favour of the A90, it has also worked hard to give the area a higher profile nationally. The organisation still exists today but, having apparently given up the unequal struggle, rather more as a social club than a pressure group.

The fact that the boundary line changes position every so often must place a strain on the loyalties of towns and villages which after centuries suddenly find themselves in an alien county. Coupar Angus had long been part of Angus (hence the name) before being swallowed up by Perthshire in 1891. Instead of lying at the fringe of a county which bordered the North Sea and extended to the Aberdeen hinterland the town woke up one morning at the edge of another county whose western extremities were within spitting distance of the Atlantic Ocean and the metropolis of Glasgow. The former Angus village of Kettins, just a mile south-east of Coupar Angus, went through the same experience in 1975 when it became part of Perth and Kinross District. A pleasant enough place, with a burn flowing through the middle, its most curious feature is the sixteenth century bell housed in an odd-looking structure in the churchyard. The bell, named Maria Troon according to the inscription, was cast in Belgium in 1519 and is one of several early Flemish bells to be found in Perthshire.

Midway between Coupar Angus and Meigle, and right on the county boundary, is the tiny village of Ardler, its nondescript appearance belying the high-minded principles which lay behind its foundation in 1835. George Kinloch, a radical thinker and champion of the ordinary man against the powers of the day, was the prime mover behind the project, although he never lived to see it completed. He intended Ardler to be a collecting centre for the produce of Strathmore and to this end sited the village on either side of the railway line which linked Coupar Angus with Dundee. He further intended that the village should commemorate the names of his political and philosophical heroes, with streets bearing the names of Jeremy Bentham, John Hampden, Benjamin Franklin and William Wallace. The village itself was called Washington, named after the American president who had led his country to freedom from British rule. The streets to the north of the railway were laid out according to plan but were never extended to the south. Washington in time gradually lost its name which, because of the close proximity of Ardler Station, became known simply as Ardler. Kinloch himself, on account of his beliefs, was actually declared an outlaw in 1819 and had to flee the country. He eventually returned, forgiven, and entered Parliament as the Member for Dundee in 1832, only to die a few months later.

Kinrossie, though small, is another of Strathmore's more noteworthy villages, consisting of two rows of cottages on either side of the village green which itself is bisected by a quiet country road. If this were not enough it still has its ancient market cross, old village pump and even a thatched cottage, all the ingredients necessary for a colour photograph to grace any Scottish shortbread tin. Twee, though, it is not, for Strathmore is a working community and has little time for unnecessary frivolities. It lies at the south-western end of the strath from where the fortifications on the top of Dunsinane can be clearly seen.

The southern boundary of Strathmore is marked by the gentle rising of the Sidlaws while the steep escarpment on the other side defines the northern limit of the Carse of Gowrie flatlands. This lava ridge stretches 12 miles eastwards from Perth to the county boundary and then for a similar distance into Angus. The unevenness of the ridge creates several distinct summits, including the more familiar ones of Dunsinane and Kinnoull, and where the average height of the Perthshire Sidlaws is around 900 feet, a few are well over the 1000 feet mark. King's Seat, above Collace, is the highest at 1236 feet. The hills, if not darkened by plantations of conifers, are bare apart from a covering of pale green grass. This is the best the poor soil can manage and makes the hills look cold and windswept even in summer. Several farmers scrape a living from this upland area but, unlike those enjoying conditions in the fertile Lowlands on either side, they cannot have an easy existence. Even so, some people love the Sidlaws and perhaps none more so than Dundee artist James McIntosh Patrick. No-one has a finer sense of the beauty of the hills, of their colours throughout the seasons, of the tree-lined winding roads, and of the fields and farms. His paintings bring out their special atmosphere and, with justification, fetch high prices.

Quarrying is the only commercial-industrial activity in the Sidlaws, a popular used car business in Abernyte having recently gone into liquidation. Collace Quarry was run by Tayside Regional Council and in 1991 suddenly found itself at the centre of a national controversy involving the arts world. What caused the rumpus was a planning application to extend quarrying activities to within 300 yards of Macbeth's castle on the summit of Dunsinane Hill. Local resident Professor Donald McIntyre, angered by this insensitive assault on one of the hallowed places of English literature, led a high-powered opposition which included vocal support from the likes of Dames Judi Dench and Iris Murdoch, Sir Peter Hall and Nigel Tranter. The following year, after the issue was given major coverage in the *Sunday Times*, the district council refused planning permission.

The Braes of the Carse, the southern limit of the Sidlaws, fall steeply away to the south, sheltering the rich Carse of Gowrie farmland from the severity of northern weather. The land here is fairly flat and low-lying, rarely exceeding a height of 50 feet above sea level. As such, it was under water during the post-glacial period and remained a waterlogged area until the eighteenth century when it was extensively drained. Clues to its aqueous past abound in local placenames with 'carse' itself believed to derive from a word signifying a marsh and several others beginning with 'inch', which comes from the Gaelic for 'island'.

The level countryside and the fast road and rail links between Perth and Dundee make it hard to appreciate just how difficult land-based transport used to be. The Tay, in fact, was the main means of communication between the two, and riverside villages such as Port Allen and the lovely Inchyra were much busier then than they are today. All this changed with the construction, firstly, of the turnpike road and the railway in the first half of the nineteenth century and secondly the new dual carriageway, completed in 1976, which has recently been renumbered the A90 after many years as the A85. Good roads also have disadvantages, the most obvious being the bypassing of the many communities between the two cities. Few tourists or motorists, sure in the knowledge that they can reach Dundee within twenty minutes of leaving Perth, or vice versa, are going to bother to turn off the dual carriageway to idle in Errol or stop for a coffee in Kinfauns. Fast roads and Intercity trains have done great things for the through traveller but little, if anything at all, for the villages and their inhabitants in-between.

Speeding along the A90, the motorist might form an impression of a gentle landscape dotted with peaceful communities, all dwelling amidst rich farmland bordered by the banks of the Tay. If so he would probably be surprised to learn that, with the possible exception of the area around Blairgowrie, the Carse of Gowrie has the greatest concentration of castles in the whole county. At the western end stands Kinfauns Castle, an impressive red stone edifice which was designed by Sir Robert Smirke in around 1822 for Lord Gray. In recent years it has provided hostel accommodation for an outdoors holiday company and in 1997 reopened as an hotel. At the other end is Castle Huntly, built by another of the Grays in 1452, which now functions as an adult open prison. Strung out between the two, some built in more elevated positions at the edge of the Sidlaws, lie Balthayock Castle of the notorious Blairs, the ruins of Evelick Castle, once a stronghold of the Lindsays, Fingask Castle, the former home of the staunchly Jacobite Threipland family, Fowlis Castle, yet another held by the Grays, Kinnaird Castle, Moncur Castle and finally Megginch Castle, long a possession of a branch of the Hays.

The Blairs, the Grays and the Hays have held sway in this area for many centuries and although most of the major Scottish families would prefer to forget certain periods in their histories the Blairs and Grays had more to hide than most. Nigel Tranter does not mince his words when he states that the Blair family 'was one of the most turbulent and lawless in the land' and, referring to the Grays, says that under their roofs 'some of the worst treacheries and Machiavellian misdeeds to stain even Scotland's history were concocted'. Why this pleasant, pastoral landscape should have witnessed such a long catalogue of violence, murder and treachery is indeed a mystery.

The Hays are one of Scotland's oldest families and as such could not escape the traditional musings upon the origin of their name. The story goes that the Scottish victory over the Danes at the possibly fictitious Battle of Luncarty in around 973 owed much to the leadership of a man with the anachronistically Norman-sounding name of De Luce. So exhausted was he after the battle that when found beside his plough by the king he could only say, like some tenth century hippy, 'oh hey'. The king, his country having just been saved by this hero, responded by saying, 'Henceforth Hay shall be your name'. (This story is only marginally less ludicrous than the one behind the name of Cumming, the progenitor of which family apparently had the unusual habit of responding to knocks on the door with the words 'Come in'!) Presumably at this point the king was made to realise that perhaps the new Mr Hay deserved a slightly more tangible reward and offered to endow him with lands that stretched from Scone to as far as a greyhound could run or a hawk fly. Hay staked his future on the hawk which, having set off eastwards, eventually alighted on what is still called the Hawk's Stane in the village of St Madoes.

Legend apart, the Earls of Erroll and Kinnoull both trace their origins back to the twelfth century William de la Haye who appears to have descended from the Norman family of that name. Sir Gilbert Hay (he who lies buried at Coupar Angus), 5th Lord Erroll and ancestor of the later earls, was created Lord High Constable of Scotland by Robert the Bruce and this office has been passed from father to son (and sometimes daughter) ever since, giving the possessor the status, according to *Burke's Peerage*, of 'the first subject by birth in Scotland after the Blood Royal'. Neither has this family been a stranger to violent death. The above-mentioned volume records that Josslyn, the 22nd Earl, was killed near Nairobi in 1941. Such a bland statement reveals nothing of the sex scandal which led to the probable murder of the earl by a jealous husband. The story, somewhat embellished, was played out in front of a much wider audience in the 1980s film *White Mischief*, starring Charles Dance and Greta Scacchi. The earl's grandson, now the 24th Earl, the 28th Lord High Constable of Scotland and the 33rd Chief of the Hays, as well as the Senior

Great Officer of the Royal Household in Scotland, is, perhaps disappointingly, a computer consultant living in Bedfordshire.

One of the most impressive of all buildings in the Carse, neither castle nor religious house, was Rossie Priory, the home of the Kinnaird family. It was designed in the Gothic style by William Atkinson, who had earlier drawn up the plans for Scone Palace. Unfortunately a substantial part of it was demolished in around 1949, although it still functions as a private house and is perhaps more noted nowadays for its fine gardens. Priory and palace, as well as sharing similar architectural styles, also boasted superb art collections which came from different parts of 18th century France. As far as the Priory is concerned, even 'superb' is perhaps too mild a term; with works by Michaelangelo, Leonardo, Raphael, Titian, Giorgione, Rembrandt, Veronese, Durer, Van Dyck and a host of others, this must have been in its time one of the finest private art collections in the country. The Kinnairds were a highly cultured family. Not only had they a good eye for a painting but the Hon. Douglas Kinnaird, a younger brother of the 8th Lord, became a close friend of Lord Byron, acting as both his banker and literary agent. A pleasant contrast from the other feuding families in the neighbourhood.

The village of Errol is the second-largest settlement in the Carse after Invergowrie and is situated on a slight elevation 11 miles from both Perth and Dundee. Its tall, square-towered church, known sometimes as the Cathedral of the Carse, confirms its primacy amid the surrounding villages. Here much of the non-agricultural industry of the area went on. At Inchcoonans, to the north-west of Errol, can be found the Errol Brick Company, a business which dates from 1855 and is the last surviving nineteenth century brickworks in Scotland. The estuarine clays deposited here during the post-ice-age period provided the raw material for the company which, together with a slightly older brickworks at Pitfour, supplied the red brick found in a large number of buildings throughout the Carse. The Pitfour business, in fact, was successful in winning the contracts to supply the builders of both Tay Bridges, the original order requesting a total of 10,000,000 bricks.

To the north-east is a former wartime airfield which was opened in 1942 and was used to train Russian aircrews. It was mothballed in 1945 and might well have been reopened in the late 1960s had plans to turn it into the main airport for Dundee

An early print of Errol parish church, the Cathedral of the Carse, which was completed in 1833. While the heritors felt able to pay the local constables for keeping the peace during the opening ceremony (a rowdy lot, the people of Errol) they were unwilling to reimburse the contractor who had lost a considerable sum of money on the work. The parish register dates back to 1553 and is the oldest in Scotland (Courtesy of Perth & Kinross Libraries).

not been vetoed by local residents. It is a curious coincidence that in the 1900s, long before an airfield was even considered, the site was used for the first trials of powered aircraft in Scotland.

The redundant airfield has now been transformed into a small industrial estate from which the Tayreed Company operates, supplying large quantities of thatch for use on the roofs of southern English cottages. The reed beds, which form part of a much larger Site of Special Scientific Interest along the nearby banks of the Tay, were originally planted in the 1780s by an enlightened landowner in an attempt to prevent further erosion of the river bank. The commercial harvesting of the reed beds has had a chequered history but at the moment, with southern home-owners turning in ever increasing numbers to the insulating qualities and attractiveness of thatch, the future seems reasonably secure. Of the 2000 acres of reeds by the Tay between 500 and 700 acres are harvested each year, usually between December and April. They grow quickly, in ideal conditions up to three inches a day, and generally reach a height of 6 feet 6 inches. Harvesting is now mechanised; whereas in Norfolk, the centre of this traditional rural industry, the reeds are generally still cut by hand, here in Perthshire it is done by huge machines which actually float on the surface of the river mud and apply less downward pressure, it is said, than a walking dog.

There are two museums in the neighbourhood worthy of a visit. One occupies a former bee-hive kiln at the brickworks at Inchcoonans and is devoted to the somewhat specialised interest of bricks and brick-making and the other can be found to the north of Errol at Errol Station. The railway between Perth and Dundee had its origins in the 1830s and owed much to the vision of Lord Kinnaird of Rossie Priory. The station at Errol was opened in 1842 and, having served the area well for 143 years, received its last regular passenger train in 1985. It was bought by the Errol Station Trust three years later and reopened in 1990 as a heritage centre, whereupon it almost immediately won British Rail's Premier Award for its preservation work. The interior of the station buildings, laid out with a fascinating collection of old tickets, railway posters and other ephemera, is marvellously evocative of a bygone era when the tendrils of a proper public transport system reached even the smallest of rural communities.

At the far end of the Carse is the village of Invergowrie, once famed for its quarries, which was welcomed back to the Perthshire fold in 1996, having been unwillingly transferred to the City of Dundee District in 1975. While most of the residents, it seems, are glad to have returned to their historic home county, some are not at all happy at being deprived of access to the local authority services provided by Dundee. The village has long fought against being regarded as a Dundee suburb, which in many ways it is, and the boundary change will doubtless help to deepen the desired division.

The attractions of the east Perthshire Lowlands are not as immediately obvious as those in other parts of the county. The absence of mountains and lochs and the paucity of particularly attractive towns and villages has effectively sidelined the area, with the notable exception of Blairgowrie, from the main tourist routes. The Sidlaws are so often ignored and the Carse of Gowrie is seen as little more than a fast corridor between Perth and Dundee.

Strathmore, without the mountain barrier that defines much of the county, merges almost imperceptibly with neighbouring Angus. But Perthshire is fundamentally an agricultural community and this part in particular has contributed much to the local economy. The mile after mile of rich productive farmland has a beauty of its own and like any landscape deserves to be looked at and read properly. There is much to be discovered here, from the Picts, King Arthur and Macbeth at one end to the heritage of Scotland's travellers at the other, from the mills of Blairgowrie to the castles of the Carse, and from the several powerful families which had influence over the area to an individual resident of Kettins, Dr James Tweedie, whose computing skills have had consequences for much of Europe. Why? It was his software invention which ensured that those tunnelling under the Channel from both ends actually met in the middle!

CHAPTER 8
STRATHEARN

S trathearn, to quote from Francis Groome's *Ordnance Gazetteer of Scotland*, a publication still unsurpassed in more than a century, 'forms, as a whole, one of the most exquisite tracts of country in Scotland, replete with every element of beauty, and exhibiting almost perfect specimens of very various styles of scenery'. Although the optimism of Victorian topographical writing generally tends to dazzle rather than illuminate, this description is as true today as it was then. The valley stretches in an east-west direction between the village of Lochearnhead, in the new Stirling Council area, and the confluence of the rivers Earn and Tay near Abernethy, close to the Fife border. In this favoured hollow of south Perthshire you will find one of Scotland's most beautiful lochs, river scenery of high quality, and mountains, hills and fertile fields transected by busy roads and almost forgotten byways.

The Earn is indeed a lovely river and, judging by the languid meanderings of its final stages, an old one too. It lies at a low level for much of its length of 61 miles and being without significant waterfalls or rapids is generally slow-moving. It is the antithesis of the Tay which is more Highland in character, sociable in the way it flows beside or through a number of towns and villages, and by its sheer size and volume dominant in the landscape. Not so the Earn which develops early its Lowland characteristics, shuns the main areas of human habitation, and whose hesitant course suggests a willing obedience to the dictates of the topography. If the Tay demands respect, the Earn appeals to the affections.

Even so, for a mild-mannered river, the Earn can be frustratingly obstructive. In the 1790s, when the nation's transport infrastructure was struggling to keep abreast of the demands made by the Agricultural and Industrial revolutions, the river was found to be far too shallow for cargo boats. Instead the planners and engineers of the time dreamt up the Perthshire Canal, which was intended to run east from Loch Earn via Crieff, Methven and Perth to the Tay, and south from the loch, through Glendevon, to the Forth.

Even more modern in concept was the intention to link the canal with turnpike roads to Stirling and Loch Tay, thus opening up a large part of north-central Scotland. Sadly for Perthshire it never saw the light of day, though it was sufficiently far advanced to appear on maps of the time as the 'proposed canal'. One person who did rise to the river's challenge was a Mr Clark, a forerunner of Jerome K. Jerome, who set off in a single-seater canoe amid the cheers and jeers of the locals to travel the length of the river — and more — between Lochearnhead and Dundee. His amusing, very readable and undeservedly little-known account, *Rocks and rapids*, was published in 1883, a full six years before *Three men in a boat*.

The loch itself, on a summer's day, appears as an oasis of shimmering beauty amid the fastness of the landscape of central Scotland. This is the place to rest the eyes after the close concentration demanded by the busy A85, perhaps on the views of Lochearnhead or St Fillans at either end, or on the wooded hills which slope attractively down to the water's edge. Or perhaps on the activity on the loch itself where the flash of a faraway sail indicates a yachtsman on a tack and where anglers sit gnome-like in rowing boats, their peacefulness occasionally disturbed by the drone of jet skis bobbing over the surface like angry mosquitoes or by the wash from waterskiers and their tow boats. This last-mentioned activity has been associated with the loch since the mid-1950s and many national events and championships have been held here. Environmentally incorrect though the sport may now be, it has been a part of the loch for so long that we must forgive its intrusion upon our reflective enjoyment of such a lovely stretch of water.

The simplest way to view the loch from all angles is to drive round it. The south road is very pretty but winding, undulating and wooded and the driver can easily imagine that he has stepped back half a century to the earlier days of Scottish motoring. The north road is much faster and busier. Perhaps incongruously, because it follows the water's edge rather more closely, it also offers better views.

At the east end, just offshore from St Fillans, is the tiny, tree-covered Neish Island, a former crannog which was the setting for one of the more barbarous episodes of seventeenth century clan warfare. The story, which may well have been based on fact, concerns a long-simmering feud between the Clan Neish, who lived on the island, and their archenemies, the Clan Macnab, who dwelt over the hills on the southern shores of Loch Tay. Things came to a head in 1612, literally as it turned out, when the Macnabs decided to take revenge on the Neishes for ambushing their Christmas supplies. 'The night is the night if the lads are the lads' said the chief, whereupon his twelve sons set off on the long trek over the hills, carrying the boat which was to ferry them out to the island stronghold. The Neishes were taken completely by surprise and all but a child were massacred before the Macnabs set off homeward, still heaving their boat with them. But the burden was to prove too heavy and they abandoned the craft whose remains, like many other legendary mementoes of clannish gory deeds, were supposedly 'still visible until recently'. The trophy from the night's raid was not the recovered Christmas turkey and crackers but the severed head of the Neish chief who to this day adorns the crest of The Macnab (the head, surely to the annoyance of all Neishes, is described heraldically as that of a savage). The surviving child was supposedly the progenitor of all who now bear the Neish name. Memories live long in the Highlands and some Neishes would doubtless have observed with satisfaction the decline and fall of the chiefly line of the Macnabs. Archibald, the 13th chief, was a failed banker whose debts obliged him to flee to Canada in 1821 along with a number of his clansmen. When he tried to raise a regiment in 1838 many of his followers, having tasted the freedom of the New World, turned against him, thereby illustrating the fact that at least some emigrant Scots were not at all sorry to turn their backs on the old country and its outdated feudal customs. Archibald eventually returned to Europe and died a pathetic figure in Brittany in 1860.

St Fillans is an attractive village stretching out at the eastern end of the loch and consisting of a mixture of hotels, bed and breakfasts and old cottages. In the early 1960s, just as they were becoming famous, the Beatles stayed briefly in a chalet attached to the Four Seasons Hotel, a visit which is still remembered with quiet pride. It is not too hard to imagine the Fab Four, far away from industrialised Liverpool, admiring the sunset over the loch and the peace of the unspoilt countryside and all the while remaining blissfully unaware, as are most visitors, of the underground hydro-electric power station virtually beneath their feet.

The small hill of Dundurn, only 200 feet above river level, may well have marked the western limits of Pictish influence. It seems likely that the ancient fort on the top would have retained its strategic significance until the ninth or tenth centuries whereupon, following the union of the Picts and the Scots, it was probably abandoned.

Following the truncation of Perthshire in 1975 St Fillans became one of the frontier villages of Perth and Kinross, and now looks wistfully westwards to what was once the sister village of Lochearnhead and the Braes of Balquhidder beyond. History has repeated itself as over a thousand years ago the same area was once the political, cultural and linguistic frontier between the Picts of eastern Scotland and the Scots of the west. The limits of Pictish influence were probably represented by the fort on the now grass-topped, craggy hill of Dundurn (or St Fillans Hill) which rises sharply, but to no great height, from the Earn at its foot. Most travellers are doubtless oblivious to the significance of the hill which can be seen a mile east of St Fillans on the south side of the road. Opposite is the locally famous 'crocodile', a brightly painted rock with ferocious teeth which has been a feature of this road for many years.

Leaving the loch behind, the peat-coloured waters of the youthful river flow gently between narrow tree-lined banks and can be glimpsed in places from the main road. But the river quickly reveals its shyness and within four miles loops south to

The graceful lines of the Bridge of Ross have spanned the Earn for 200 years, allowing access to the old weaving hamlet known as The Ross. The peace of ages was rudely broken in 1914 when a group of suffragettes set fire to three nearby mansion houses, including the House of Ross.

Comrie in the company of a little side road which plunges the traveller almost instantly into the depths of Perthshire *profonde*. The whitewashed Dalchonzie House is passed on the left and a little further, just visible behind the hedges on the right, is Aberuchill Castle, at the time of writing still under repair after the disastrous fire of 1994. Curiously enough, 80 years earlier and almost to the day, the more militant suffragettes of Perthshire nearly succeeded in reducing it to a pile of ashes along with two other Strathearn mansions. The most popular attraction on this little road, however, is the Drummond Fish Farm and Trout Fishery which provides a welcome relief from the outbreak of 'No Fishing' signs littering the roadside vegetation. Situated on a beautiful tree-shaded bend in the Earn, the farm draws water from the river to supply its several nursery tanks, rearing ponds and larger pools for learner anglers.

Continuing on, the road arrives at The Ross where the graceful arch of the old eighteenth century bridge, looking as if it would barely support the weight of a pedestrian let alone a car, leads into the old part of Comrie. In such an unusually rectilinear village this is just about the only curve to be seen. The main street, lined regimentally with two-storey village houses, runs almost unerringly straight through, and when at the west end the river forces a northwards deflection this is achieved geometrically by means of a couple of right-angle bends. Even the streets of Dalginross, linked to Comrie by the bridge over the Earn, are seemingly laid out on a grid pattern. This bridge, once admired for its advanced design, was built by Sir William Arrol's construction company in around 1905 and as a warning to heavy vehicles is now prominently labelled as weak. This deficiency only begins to cause concern when one realises that Sir William was also responsible some years previously for the construction of the present rail bridges over the Forth and Tay. The pleasant view from the centre of the bridge comprises the whitewashed old parish church (now a community centre but still known as the White Church) and further upstream the point where the Earn on the right meets with the Water of Ruchill, flowing out of Glenartney, on the left. At the east end of the village the Lednock also joins the Earn, a great meeting of the waters which is exactly what Comrie in its original Gaelic form means.

South of Dalginross and close to the site of a Roman fort is the Cultybraggan army training camp, notorious during the last war as a POW camp for some of the most fanatical of Nazi captives. In December 1944, with less than five months of the European war still to run, two of their number were accused of being informers and were beaten and hanged by their compatriots. After a trial in the summer of 1945 five of the murderers were themselves hanged at Pentonville Prison. The documents relating to the incident are scheduled to remain secret until 2045 which suggests that there might have been more to these events than presently meets the eye.

The popular Glen Lednock circular walk leads north from the west end of the village and includes in the itinerary the impressive waterfall known as the Deil's Cauldron where the Lednock thunders through a narrow wooded gorge. High above, on the summit of Dunmore, is the monument to Henry Dundas, 1st Viscount Melville, which towers over Comrie in much the same way that Dundas in life did over Parliament. Perhaps he towered too high. In 1805, believing him to have misused public money, Parliament voted in that year to initiate impeachment proceedings against him. His trial in the House of Lords — described as one of the trials of the century — took place in 1806 and, with the blame for various irregular financial transactions having being laid reasonably firmly at the door of a subordinate, Dundas was acquitted on all charges. Whether free of all guilt or not the charge illustrates a certain over-confidence on the part of Dundas which, together with his reputation for having a finger in every pie, earned him the nickname King Harry the Ninth. This was presumably a non-Jacobite designation as the titular Henry IX, Prince Charles Edward Stuart's younger brother, was alive, well and a cardinal in Rome until his death in 1807. Dundas's purchase in 1784 of the Dunira estate, just to the west of the village, explains the presence of a monument to a great politician in a spot somewhat remote from the centre of British politics.

Comrie's main claim to fame, apart from the earthquakes which are described in the first chapter, is the ancient Flambeaux procession. As each new year is chimed in the flambeaux, torches of rags held aloft by long and heavy poles, are lit and paraded through the village in an attempt to drive away evil spirits. The high spirits of Hogmanay remain, however, and after much merry-making in the streets the flambeaux are extinguished by being flung into the Earn from the bridge.

The main road to Crieff is unremarkable apart from the two mansion houses of Lawers and Ochtertyre on the left. Lawers, previously known as Fordie, derives its name from the village on the north side of Loch Tay. The Campbell lairds of this village, having been driven south by debt and the destruction of their property, took the name with them when they moved south to Strathearn. Designed in 1738 by William Adam, the father of the famous brothers, it is architecturally an impressive building and in its time has functioned as both a private home and an agricultural college. Ochtertyre dates from the later eighteenth century and, where for many years it was the seat of a branch of the Murrays, is now owned by a local businessman. During the last war it provided a safe location for the Seymour Lodge School which was evacuated from Dundee, and indeed several other independent schools, some from as far away as Cambridge, ended up in the stately homes of Perthshire during this same period. Ochtertyre may lack the classical proportions of Lawers but nevertheless enjoys a lovely situation amid woodland above Loch Monzievaird.

Between the two houses, on the right of the road, is a monument to General Sir David Baird, one of the heroes of the eighteenth century British struggle in India. As a young officer he spent four years in captivity in Seringapatam including a long period chained to a fellow prisoner. On hearing this dreadful news about the maltreatment of her son Baird's mother is believed to have exclaimed 'Lord help the poor chiel that's chained to oor Davy!' This is perhaps indicative of the strength of character which led to Baird's successful storming of Seringapatam in 1799, during the course of which was killed Tippoo Sultan, the son of his captor. In 1810 Baird married the Crieff heiress Miss Ann Campbell Preston and settled in the mansion of Ferntower, the site of which is now occupied by the greens and bunkers of the local golf course. In his later years, as president of the Strathearn Coursing Club, he participated in the then gentrified sport of dog racing and we can imagine with little difficulty the venerable general cheering on his dog, Harry, and willing him to beat one rival in particular; this was Tippoo, a dog which belonged to a neighbour with whom we can guess that relations were perhaps a little strained.

A more pleasant alternative to the A85 between Comrie and Crieff is a small road which runs parallel to it on the south side of the Earn. Here, in the early summer, the splashes of brilliant colour from yellow broom and purple rhododendrons are set against the white and lacy froth of may (or hawthorn) in bloom. It is indeed a pretty road whose finale is the best view possible of Crieff, tiered on its hillside and basking in the sun like a Mediterranean village. Having joined the A822 at the southern edge of Crieff, near to the Crieff Visitor Centre, there begins the long uphill climb over the Earn and up into the centre of the town. For no-one can be mistaken that Crieff is perched, almost precariously, on the side of The Knock, a hill of over 900 feet which can be blamed for the steady incline of the main street and the steep climb and sudden falling away of the roads on either side. The Knock, however, when seen as the object of a healthy walk rather than an obstacle to the daily shopping trip, can be easily conquered and the wide views from the top over much of Strathearn compensate for the contour problems of lower down.

Anyone first arriving in Crieff might be forgiven for assuming it was originally a Victorian holiday resort. The big villas, nursing homes and bed and breakfasts on the eastern and western approaches all seem to date from this period while the shops of the older, more central part jostle together to crowd out the few

James Square, open and south-facing, lies at the heart of the holiday town of Crieff.

remaining clues to its true antiquity. Its history, in fact, goes back at least to mediaeval times from which only the burgh cross, the Drummond cross and the town stocks have survived. At the time of writing there are plans afoot to move the crosses to the basement of the Tourist Information Centre, both for their protection and as the basis of a proposed Crieff museum, but as always in the late 1990s there is a large question mark over funding. From the days of Roman invasions up until 1746 the whole area of Strathearn, being a wide corridor into the heartland of Scotland, has seen the ebb and flow of numerous armies, and it was one of these, the retreating Jacobite army of 1716, which destroyed much of ancient Crieff. James, 3rd Duke of Perth and the Murray family of Ochtertyre played a significant role in its reconstruction and both are remembered in the town centre, James in the recently upgraded James Square and the Murrays in the fountain, at the heart of the square, which bears their name. Some places deserve to be enjoyed simply on account of their coffee shops, pleasant streets, parks and not too energetic walks, and Crieff, having made the best of a lack of visible history, is certainly one of them.

It is therefore fitting that the chief employer should be the Crieff Hydro, a sumptuous Victorian hotel which sits high above the eastern end of the town. Hydro is a shortened form of 'hydropathic' and is a clue to its original function as a sort of nineteenth century health farm where baths were a form of therapy and where the first guests were known as patients. The people of Crieff were in fact so health conscious at this time that they rejected early proposals to establish a hospital in the town, feeling that Perth — even in the days of horse-drawn transport — was quite close enough for an institution devoted to the sick. The Hydro is still regarded as a top-class hotel and, although perhaps unfortunate to be living in the shadow of the famous Gleneagles across the strath, can still boast an extremely high occupancy rate achieved with neither significant advertising nor, until recently, the attractions of a bar.

Leaving Crieff and the last vestiges of the Highlands behind, the wide expanse of Lower Strathearn suddenly unfolds itself to the east. Two miles beyond the town is the little village of Gilmerton from where the A85 proceeds rapidly towards Perth and the A822 heads north to the Sma Glen and Aberfeldy. The latter is a steady climb and offers fine views over the mountains to the west before levelling out at the head of Logiealmond. An attractive little detour branches left off this road just outside Gilmerton and leads past the gatehouse to Monzie Castle, lying beneath Kate McNieven's Crag. The unfortunate Kate was a local woman who suffered the usual penalty for witchcraft. The road continues through the pretty hamlet of Monzie and finally past the Glenturret Distillery before joining the A85 at the western edge of Crieff.

Three miles beyond Gilmerton is the historic village of Fowlis Wester, one of the tiny, hidden jewels of Strathearn. Formerly well-sited on the main road between Perth and Crieff this was a place of some importance until it was sidelined by the construction of the late eighteenth century turnpike road to which the present A85 has fallen heir. Today it enjoys the rare privilege for such a small community of having its own church and post office, its own historic monument and an unspoiled loveliness and air of centuries-old peace. Come here on a summer Sunday morning, listen to the hymn singing perfuming the village and enjoy that unique sense of God being in His Heaven and all being right with the world.

The replica of a Pictish cross stands behind its protective railings in the centre of the village and because of the natural light is easier to study than the original in the church. On the one side is a group of six standing figures which appears to have been executed from the top down, the tell-tale signs of a sculptor having forgotten to leave sufficient room for twelve feet being all too obvious. Behind the cross is the quaint post office with its shabby old sign, far more suitable than any freshly painted one could ever be, and next to this the churchyard with the graves of some of the local gentry, the Maxtone Grahames of Cultoquhey (one member of which family, under the pseudonym Jan Struther, wrote the wartime best seller *Mrs Miniver*). The church itself has been restored in recent years and with its combination of wood, stone and light must be regarded as one of the most attractive in the county. It is dedicated to St Bean which is why the Apollo 12 astronaut Alan Bean, when visiting the village in search of his ancestors, presented the church with a small piece of cloth, woven in the Bean tartan, which he had taken with him to the moon in 1969. It can be found framed on the vestry wall along with several photographs showing the donor himself, surely one of Perthshire's most travelled grandsons, on the moon. A narrow road continues north from the village, climbing steeply over the moor towards Buchanty and the panorama from here is superb. An equally narrow road with a similar fine view branches off to the east in the direction of Keillour Castle.

The A85 pushes on to Methven where the limits of Strathearn gradually evolve into the hinterland of Perth. Methven Castle, on the eastern flank of the village, is a magnificent building made all the better by the saltire flying proudly at the top. High above the road and standing four-square with a turret at each corner it is the archetypal Scottish mediaeval castle. Until recently, however, it looked decidedly emasculated, its ancient proportions and 'wha daur meddle wi me' stance having been ruined by the eighteenth and nineteenth century extensions at the sides. It took the expert eye of local architect Ken Murdoch to see its potential and several years of hard physical work to restore it to its original glory. The Murdochs now live in a flat within the castle, their son runs his architectural practice from the ground floor, and other parts are used for charity events.

At this point it might occur to the traveller through Strathearn to wonder what has happened to the river. In fact it now lies several miles to the south having been deflected from its course by the mass of the Gask ridge. The only significant flow of water in the immediate area is the Pow Burn which is actually two separate streams, the main one, the Pow of Inchaffray, flowing south-west towards the Earn and a smaller one, the East Pow, going in the opposite direction to link up with the Almond. The former can be viewed near the ruins of Inchaffray Abbey where it trickles through a deep cut, created by an Act of Parliament of 1696 to improve the drainage of waterlogged land. (A pow is a Scots word referring to a slow-moving ditch-like stream which generally drains marshy land. Thus there are several Pow Burns across Scotland.) The Augustinian abbey at Inchaffray was founded by the earls of Strathearn in the twelfth century, receiving its charter in 1200, and was known as the 'Insula Missarum' or the Island of Masses, an allusion to the wet surroundings as indeed is the 'inch' of the abbey name. Though it was never included in the top rank of Scottish mediaeval abbeys one of its abbots had the honour of blessing the Scots army at Bannockburn. Today only a high gable end survives, covered in ivy and standing close to an attractive modern house.

Nearby, but higher up on the Gask ridge, are the villages of Madderty and St Davids, the latter founded in 1832 by the widow of Sir David Baird from whom it takes its name. This old warhorse, hero of the above-mentioned victory at Seringapatam, may also have been responsible for giving a local crossroads the appropriate name of Quatre Bras (four arms) which is the name of a neighbouring village to Waterloo and which saw some of the fighting of 1815. (That great battle is itself commemorated in the name of a hamlet near Bankfoot).

Crossing the ridge and descending again to the Earn a narrow road leads down to the chapel and library of Innerpeffray, welcome touches of civilisation in an area which suffered more than most from the troubles of the Jacobite period. The red stone chapel was built by a Sir John Drummond in 1508 and served as a Drummond family burial place until the early years of last century. It still houses a rare pre-Reformation stone altar and on the walls and ceiling can be seen the remaining fragments of some fine mediaeval wall paintings, including one of a smiling sun. Standing only inches from the chapel are the white walls of Innerpeffray Library, the oldest public library (though not in the sense of a modern public lending library) in Scotland. The collection was founded in 1691 by David Drummond, 3rd Lord Madderty and the building erected in the eighteenth century by Robert Hay

Drummond who, at the time of inheriting the Innerpeffray estates, was the incumbent of the archiepiscopal see of York. As they might have said in the local hostelry, 'We don't get many archbishops around here'. The library and chapel are both open to the public at certain times and well worth a visit.

By following the Earn eastwards we pass the old Kinkell Bridge, erected in 1793 and two centuries on still one of the few crossing points of the river. It is a four-arched structure, attractive in spite of its almost clumsy bulkiness, and with its recently renovated piers looking as uncomfortable as anyone in brand new shoes. Kinkell was formerly a separate parish before being joined with that of Trinity Gask and had the possibly unique distinction of losing its minister to the hangman. In July 1681 the Reverend Richard Duncan became the focus of a church enquiry into rumours of scandal which, judging by his deposition the following April, were presumably found to be true. Shortly after he left the manse the body of a child was found beneath the hearth stone and the Reverend Richard suddenly found himself facing a rather more serious charge. In due course and just before his reprieve arrived he was turned off the gallows at either Crieff or Muthill, an event which gave rise to the following rhyme which is more frequently, though seemingly erroneously, attributed to the parish of Little Dunkeld.

> Oh whit a parish, whit a terrible parish
> Oh whit a parish is that o Kinkell!
> They hae hangit the minister, drooned the precentor,
> Dang doon the steeple and drucken the bell.

Legend has it that the precentor was drowned when trying to cross the Earn to get to the neighbouring church of Trinity Gask while the bell ended up in the church of Cockpen ('drucken' actually means 'drunk' which suggests that the good parishioners of Kinkell converted the bell into liquid cash and drank the whole lot). The fate of the steeple remains uncertain.

From the bridge the road steadily climbs the southern wall of the Gask ridge until, having negotiated two right-angled bends, it levels out along the spine and follows for several miles the straight course of an old Roman road. Beside the road at regular intervals of about one mile the Romans built a string of watch towers which were designed, or so it is assumed, to keep an eye on the native population and to provide a means of communication along the empire's frontier. With enough patience and a detailed map it is possible to find the sites of at least some of the towers although from personal experience it can be a tricky search.

To the south of the road is the estate of Gask, one end of the Jacobite axis which stretched along Strathearn from Drummond Castle at the other. But while the Duke of Perth, occupant of the castle, is primarily remembered for his military contribution, the most famous occupant of Gask probably achieved more by retrospectively romanticising the cause through her much loved poetry and songs. Carolina Oliphant, the daughter of Laurence Oliphant of Gask and granddaughter through her mother of Robertson of Struan, was born at Gask in 1766 and given a name which made no secret of the Jacobite loyalties of her parents. She first began writing in the 1790s but it was only after her marriage and subsequent move to Edinburgh that the poetry started to flow. Although she is best known for her Jacobite verse, such as *Will ye no come back again* and *Charlie is my darling*, she also penned *Land o the leal*, guaranteed to bring a lump to any throat, and the foot-tapping *Caller herrin* which was set to music by Nathaniel Gow. In 1824 the Nairne family was restored to its original rank in the peerage whereupon Carolina became Lady Nairne. Having long hidden behind the suitably gentrified pseudonym, Mrs Bogan of Bogan, her true identity was revealed to the world at large only after her death, at Gask, in 1845.

Another of her popular poems is *The auld hoose* in which she lovingly described the home of her childhood. Life in the house, however, was not the carefree idyll she depicted: it was demolished in around 1800, principally because it was so overrun with rats that not even the traditional remedy of requesting them by letter to leave would prove effective. The rather grander New House of Gask was built shortly after but it is the couthy Auld Hoose which has achieved immortality in a song so touchingly redolent of the happy, sun-filled days of youth. A century after the rats were evicted the Oliphants also succeeded in evicting themselves. The 11th and last laird, having had to contend with awkward and obstructive relations before he was eventually able to inherit the estates, took his ultimate revenge on the family by stating in his will that on his death (which occurred in 1902) Gask should be sold and that all the Jacobite heirlooms should be offered to the

The Auld Hoose of Gask, photographed in around 1935. This was the childhood home of Carolina Oliphant, Lady Nairne, who wrote a number of popular Jacobite verses and who immortalised these ruins in the poem of the same name (Courtesy of Perth & Kinross Libraries).

Society of Antiquaries in Edinburgh. This was duly done and the representer of the Gask branch of the Oliphant name is now Laurence Blair-Oliphant of Ardblair, near Blairgowrie, who is as well-known locally for his historical attachment to Jacobitism through the White Cockade Society as he is for his long grey beard, kilt and claymore. The Society of Antiquaries of Scotland did not in fact accept the Jacobite relics which are still in Oliphant hands.

Although Lady Nairne was quite capable of writing letters in the standard English of the period she clearly felt better able to express herself in verse in Scots, something which may come as a surprise to those who think of Scots as the language of the fields. And if she can be dismissed as merely a member of the rural gentry then the figure of the infamous Lord Braxfield, Scotland's hanging judge and eminent member of eighteenth century Edinburgh society, reminds us that Scots was formerly spoken by all classes and in all places. His way of sentencing one poor fellow to death — 'Ye're a verra clever chiel, man, but ye wad be nane the waur o a hangin' — still sends shivers up the spine. After two centuries of decline during which it was actively discouraged in schools, the twentieth century Scots literary renaissance, spearheaded by such luminaries as Hugh Macdiarmid and Willie Soutar, enabled the Scots language to take its rightful place as an accepted cultural medium, and one capable of the most sensitive and delicate expression. In the wake of this revival the recently founded Scots Language Resource Centre, based in Perth, is working hard to maintain the momentum of renewed interest in a language which was once spoken not only by the ploughboys and shipyard workers of Scotland but also by its bishops and kings.

The southern slope of the Gask ridge turns into the Cairnie Braes where the A9 slices through the peace of Strathearn and where business executives speed down its sweeping curve towards Stirling and slow lorries struggle uphill towards Perth. Nearby lies the old road to Stirling, now the B9112, which rises almost as steeply from river level up towards the hamlet of Aberdalgie from where some of the last memorable views over Strathearn can be enjoyed. On a summer evening the westering sun seems to flood the entire length of the strath with a warm mellow light, throwing the gentle contours of the hills into relief and causing the greenery below to shine with a vibrant intensity. Looking along to Abernethy and Newburgh, across the fields, trees and the twisting Earn this intimate rural idyll is Lowland Perthshire at its spellbinding best.

Moncreiffe Hill marks the end of our journey through that part of the strath lying north of the Earn. Getting there from Aberdalgie entails a pleasant three mile drive along the foot of Kirkton Hill to Craigend, then a brief encounter with dual carriageway before finally, with the whole of Perth laid out before you, turning right onto the peace of the Rhynd Road. The view from the top of Moncreiffe Hill was described by Pennant as 'the glory of Scotland' of which the sweeping panorama from this road, across the town to the Highlands and over the Tay to the woods and crags of Kinnoull, is but a foretaste. The road traverses the north side of the hill, passing through Rhynd and looking towards the confluence of the Tay and the Earn, before descending to river level and doubling back along the south side towards Bridge of Earn. Part of the hill was purchased by the Woodland Trust in 1988 and is now open to the public, access being gained from the south. The whole area is associated with the old Perthshire family of Moncreiffe whose most famous member in recent times was the late Sir Iain of that Ilk, a writer with a sharp, irrepressible wit and a surely unsurpassed knowledge of Scottish genealogy and heraldry. While his premature death may have denied him the top job of Lord Lyon, his statue adorns the entrance hall to the Lyon Court in Edinburgh.

By proceeding south from Crieff, instead of due east, we cross the river and join what was once an old military road leading towards Muthill. Midway between the two is Drummond Castle, now owned by a trust set up by Lady Willoughby de Eresby, daughter of the late 3rd Earl of Ancaster. The original castle, still standing high on a rocky outcrop, was built by the 1st Lord Drummond in the last years of the fifteenth century and was extended in the 1630s by his descendant, the 2nd Earl of Perth. Its most famous feature, however, is the formal Italian garden, embellished with statuary, which dates in the main from the early nineteenth century and which attracts not only a large number of visitors but regular visits from film crews too. The gardens lie far below the castle and are as impressive viewed from the terrace above as they are at ground level. At the centre of the garden is a remarkable obelisk sundial which was erected in 1630 and which can show the time in several capitals of the world.

Muthill suffered at the hands of the retreating Jacobites in 1716 in much the same way as Crieff, and with its row of two-storey eighteenth century cottages lining both sides of the main road is somewhat reminiscent of Comrie. A sense of architectural monotony, however, is dispelled in the summer by the hanging baskets and tubs of flowers which decorate the main thoroughfare. The real heart of the village lies away from the road around the ruined old parish church where a pleasant half-hour can be whiled away in admiring the architecture of the surviving arches and the distinctively tapering tower. Around the ruins are several well-preserved seventeenth century gravestones, some showing occupational symbols such as axes, T-squares, flails and hammers, and others the usual symbols of mortality, though judging by their depiction the carvers had clearly never seen a real human skull. Nearby is the new parish church, an ungainly spiky building in which taste has been sacrificed to size and which is out of keeping with the rest of the village. The small Episcopal church lies opposite, a reminder that Muthill has had a long history of Anglican worship

The ancient tower of Muthill old parish church, described as 'one of the best preserved...Norman towers in Scotland', has stood for close to a thousand years, surviving war, Reformation and rebellion. The church itself was a later addition and still in use as recently as 1818 when, following the construction of the new church, it was allowed to fall into disrepair.

and was once the focus for the many Episcopalians of Strathearn. It is sad that too often such churches are dismissed as 'the English church', a misnomer which fails to recognise that the Scottish Episcopal Church, while admittedly small and in a sisterly relationship with the Church of England, is no less ancient or Scottish than the Church of Scotland itself.

A grassy area known as Highlandman's Green can be found at the southern end of the village and takes its name from the drovers who used to rest their cattle here on their way to the tryst at Falkirk. Branching right at this spot the old military road climbs out of Muthill in the direction of Braco and in a mile or so crosses the Machany Water, on the one side of which lie the remains of the Mill of Steps and on the other the farm of Lurg. This is the setting for the well-known story of the country girl from Strathearn who ended up as Empress of Morocco. Helen Gloag was born in 1750, spent her youth at the mill and in her late teens struck up a relationship with the farmer across the burn. The story goes that she was so fed up with parental objections to this friendship that she decided to emigrate to America. Her ship, however, was captured by pirates and she was taken to Morocco. She was then bought as a slave and gifted to the Grand Vizier who eventually married her and who had two sons by her. Archie McKerracher, a local historian and writer, has done a great deal of research into the story and has uncovered enough evidence to suggest that there may be a lot of truth in it. That Perthshire may have supplied one Moroccan empress is just about believable; that the county has supplied two is stretching the bounds of credulity. Yet a remarkably similar, little known legend, comes out of the Glenshee area and concerns a local girl in the late seventeenth century who, having fallen in love with the wrong man, was tricked by her father into leaving the country. Sure enough, she too found herself in the slave markets of Morocco and eventually ended up as Empress, also bearing her husband two sons.

The unremarkable village of Braco is situated a further four miles down this road on the other side of the Tay-Forth watershed, a topographical division which is mirrored in the village's orientation towards Stirling. The shop windows carry posters advertising events in that town, the Stirling newspaper is on sale at the newsagents and the waters of the Knaik, flowing behind the houses on the main street, eventually merge with the Allan Water and end up in the Forth. The most remarkable feature within the bounds of the village is a freestanding clock tower, all that remains of the Free Church which was erected at the time of the Disruption in 1843 and which was demolished shortly after the congregation reunited with the Church of Scotland earlier in the present century. According to one local worthy it was only the presence of the clock which saved the tower from destruction and which is doubtless the reason why the clock is still working today! On the northern edge of Braco is the site of the great Roman fortress of Ardoch whose square formation and surrounding ditches have survived the centuries so well that this is one of the premier archaeological sites of Perthshire and a real treat for any fan of the Romans, child or adult. Braco is one of the most south-westerly villages of Perthshire, firmly anchored in Scotland's central belt, and as such is an appropriate place to remember that the wilds of distant Rannoch and Glenshee are also part of the same county.

Just to the north of the village a narrow road leads off towards Auchterarder and we begin here the long sweep through the towns and villages initially of Strathallan and then of southern Strathearn towards the mouth of the Earn and the border with Fife. Blackford nestles in the lee of the Ochils beside the Allan Water and like Braco divides its attention between both Stirling and Perth. The village was once on the main road between the two towns but has now been bypassed by the A9; thus the wide main street looks sadly abandoned while at the same time the air is filled with the constant sound of traffic noise, an ever present reminder to the local business community of lost trade. However, the gentle murmur of the Blackford Burn, which flows through the centre between the two parallel streets, and the distant views of Ben Vorlich and Stuc a' Chroin provide some relief from the worries and pervasive noise of the twentieth century. Blackford has successfully avoided becoming a ghost town since the opening of the bypass thanks to the three main drinks producers now based in the village. At the east end is the large Highland Spring works, at the west end the currently mothballed premises of the Tullibardine Distillery, owned by Whyte and Mackay, and in the middle the relative newcomer, Gleneagles Spring Waters, which started up in 1993 with a serious investment of £10 million and which is Highland Spring's main local rival.

The national press descended on Blackford in the spring of 1996 to cover the story of Ian Thomson and his protest against what has been described as the Blackford clearances. The Blackford Estate and the Highland Spring company are both in the hands of His Excellency Mahdi Mohammed Al Tajir and it was into an abandoned cottage on the estate that Thomson moved, in an attempt to draw attention to the apparent policy of allowing good properties to remain empty and fall into disrepair. The protest, in its several weeks' duration, received the tacit approval of a great many people, including several politicians who were probably unable to endorse openly an illegal occupation, while Thomson himself received, as he requested, a large number of potatoes through the post as symbols of support.

Aggrieved rumblings over land ownership have been a particular feature of Perthshire for well over a century. This may well have stemmed from the fact that a handful of individuals in the north of the county still own many thousands of acres, and that rural Perthshire, as can be seen from the Blackford case, is still fundamentally feudal in its socio-economic structure. The Duke of Atholl was challenged in a famous rights of way case in 1847 and today a few redoubtable campaigners continue to press for land reform. But the most famous of Scottish land reformers was John McEwen who was born in north-west Perthshire (and there witnessed as a child some of the more extreme inequalities of the landlord-tenant relationship) and who died in Blairgowrie in 1992 only two days short of his 105th birthday. He was a skilled and highly intelligent forester whose reputation for speaking his mind undoubtedly checked his career. Eventually, at the age of 83, he became a member of a team which produced the powerful pamphlet, *The acreocracy of Perthshire*, which was published by the Perth and Kinross Fabian Society in 1971. This was a hard-hitting investigative essay which attempted to expose the true extent of the ownership of the great estates of Perthshire and which at the same time took a Marxist tilt at the county's landed classes. The booklet ended with a tongue-in-cheek paragraph on the back cover: 'We would also be pleased to hear from any landowner with a *claim* [my italics] to 10,000 acres or over in the county whose name may have been inadvertently omitted from the list herein…'. This publication developed into McEwen's full length book *Who owns Scotland?* which first appeared in 1977 and which is regarded as a Bible for those now carrying his torch. The Duke of Atholl was shown to be by far the largest landowner in Perthshire with a total of around 130,000 acres, a revelation which, coupled with McEwen's figures showing that around 87% of the county was owned by around 0.2% of the population, may have prompted the 10th Duke, on his early death in 1996, to leave the bulk of his estates to a charitable trust.

The only practical route between Blackford and Auchterarder is the A9 which, crossing back into Strathearn proper, brings the motorist in past the Victorian villas and leafy gardens of the western approach to the Lang Toon. The nickname needs no explanation; the town's main street is over a mile in length, curving in places and sloping ever downwards past churches, shops, the Aytoun Hall and the Girnal House. It is a pleasant town and one of considerable antiquity, having been a favourite hunting seat of Malcolm Canmore, one of Scotland's royal burghs since the first half of the thirteenth century and briefly the seat of a sheriff, all of which explains why, in spite of the greater size and grander appearance of Crieff, it has a prior claim to be the chief town of Strathearn.

Tension has often existed between the rights of the common man and those of the landowner and Auchterarder has experienced its fair share. One such dispute in the 1830s earned the town an important place in the turbulent annals of Scottish church history. The cause of the trouble was the decision by the Earl of Kinnoull, the then patron of the town kirk, to present Robert Young as the new minister. The reverend gentleman, a good man in many ways, was regarded as a poor preacher and consequently rejected by most of his would-be parishioners. The case of the congregational veto ultimately went to the House of Lords and although the final judgment went in favour of Kinnoull and Young, this was followed almost immediately by the Disruption of 1843, a deep split in the church which saw a large minority of Church of Scotland ministers leaving to form the Free Church.

From the rigours of Presbyterian theology it is only a short distance to the other extreme, the comfort and splendour of one of the world's great hotels, Gleneagles. Although situated a mere two miles from the Auchterarder town centre the loveliness of the countryside surrounding the hotel and the range of facilities and luxuries within create an impression of being at the same time both miles from anywhere and at the centre of the universe. The origins of Gleneagles go back to 1910 when the general manager of the Caledonian Railway, Donald Matheson, spent a holiday in Strathearn and was so struck by its charm that he determined to build a hotel there for the travelling public. The architect James Miller (who was also responsible for the Peebles Hydro and the Turnberry Hotel) drew up plans and work began in 1913. After a long interruption caused by the war the hotel finally opened its doors in June 1924 and immediately ran into a storm of protest over the chosen name. The Haldane family, who owned the nearby Gleneagles estate, began a long and ultimately ineffectual campaign to persuade the management to refer to their establishment at all times as Gleneagles *Hotel*. As they said at the time, they had no wish to be confused with a modern railway hotel, a phrase which while terminologically correct was utterly damning of the new building.

The opening night, in which a concert from the ballroom, conducted by Henry Hall, was broadcast to the nation, set the tone for its modern, 'bright young things' image. The hotel was quickly adopted by society's elite who would think nothing of flying up from London for lunch and a round of golf before heading south again. It was pressed into service during the war, however, firstly as a military hospital and then as a convalescent home for injured miners, and in the years of post-war austerity never properly recovered its earlier carefree atmosphere. In 1977, following a meeting of Commonwealth leaders, it gave its name to the famous Gleneagles Agreement, by which all sporting links with the apartheid regime in South Africa were in theory severed. Four years later ownership of the hotel passed to a new company which immediately revamped the entire building and once again made Gleneagles synonymous with luxury living. The legendary Jack Nicklaus designed the Monarch's Course, the third of the great golfing Meccas in the hotel grounds, while Mark Phillips and Jackie Stewart have lent their names respectively to an equestrian centre and a shooting school. Even the great Jose Carreras was persuaded to give an open air concert in the grounds in 1995. The staff too have benefited from a £3 million accommodation and training centre.

Two of Perthshire's better known writers have links with the Auchterarder area. The prolific Naomi Mitchison came from the intellectually gifted Haldane family whose members included the Liberal statesman Viscount Haldane and several other eminent scientists, professors and philosophers. The other, James Kennaway, was the son of a local solicitor whose first novel, *Tunes of glory*, became a popular film which is still resurrected occasionally on television. Fate dealt an uneven hand: whereas Mitchison, at the time of writing, is in her 100th year Kennaway was killed in a motor accident in 1968 at the age of 40.

From the foot of Auchterarder the B8062 ducks under both the A9 and the main west coast railway line and continues towards Dunning, skirting the northern slopes of Craig Rossie. Beside the

Many mysteries surround this monument to Maggie Walls near Dunning. Who, for example, keeps the lettering freshly painted, why should a so-called witch have been commemorated so publicly, why by a Christian cross, and why is there no record of Maggie Walls in any official document?

road, a mile west of the village, stands a spine-chilling monument to the horrors of witchcraft. The crude white-painted lettering screams the message 'Maggie Wall burnt here 1657 as a witch'. The monument itself is tall and consists of a pyramid of rough stones surmounted by a stone cross, the overall shape being uncomfortably reminiscent of faggots around a stake and particularly so in the dusk of midsummer when a fiery red sky burns behind it. No-one knows who Maggie Walls was and why, in a period when so many poor innocent women were burnt, she alone should have been commemorated in this way. A well-built memorial with a neatly lettered inscription would have sanitised the evil work that was carried out here; instead, a tangible pent-up anger still simmers across the centuries, a raw wound which may have been sensed by the Moors Murderers, Brady and Hindley, who were apparently photographed (by whom, one wonders?) at this spot. The monument has a magnetic quality and there is a feeling of relief when one finally turns to move away.

The tower of St Serf's Church, very similar to the ruin at Muthill, signals Dunning's mediaeval origins, as indeed does the patron saint himself, one of a veritable army of missionaries which ventured across from Ireland and along through Strathearn in the earliest days of the Scottish church. The lowly-sounding Serf, whose existence is rather more probable than his legendary dragon-slaying antics, lived possibly as early as the 5th century and was clearly active in this part of the country as the church in Culross is also dedicated to him and an island in Loch Leven named after him (though the possibility arises that there may have been two St Serfs in the area at different times). The neighbouring village of Newton of Pitcairns, close to the residence of the mythical monster, was once known as the Dragon's Den and is still referred to locally as The Dragon. Dunning once enjoyed a prime location on the main Perth-Stirling road and as a major weaving town was one of the most populous centres of Strathearn in the eighteenth century. It has survived numerous threats to its existence — notably the Jacobite burning of 1716, the building of a new road away from its centre, and the decline of its staple industry — and has still managed to retain the air of a thriving village. Sufficient custom remains to justify the presence of shops and pubs and in the evening the youth of the village congregate on street corners while the more literary minded stroll along to the mobile library parked in the shadow of the church. Tucked behind the centre in Thorn Tree Square is the successor to the famous Dunning Thorn, originally planted to commemorate the events of 1716. With such a wealth of historical interest it is no surprise that the Dunning Parish Historical Society should be one of the most active of its kind in the county. Set up only in 1992 under the leadership of Lorne Wallace, a Canadian whose mother had been born in the village, the society publishes a regular

The village of Forteviot, with its attractive cottage architecture balanced by wide lawns, was rebuilt between 1925 and 1927, inspired by the ideals of an English garden city. The architect, James Miller, not only designed the magnificent Gleneagles Hotel but also the rather more mundane Perth Royal Infirmary.

newsletter, has produced a series of local history videos and in one of their recent field walks discovered a mesolithic flint scraper, one of the oldest artefacts ever found in Perthshire.

There is nothing at all in Forteviot, three miles north-east of Dunning, to suggest that this was once the seat of Kenneth MacAlpin and the capital of the embryo Scottish nation. Indeed, were it not for the presence of the church, the casual traveller would have every reason to believe it to be a comparatively modern settlement. The Forteviot of today owes everything to a king of commerce, the 1st Lord Forteviot, chairman of Dewar's and a son of the founder who, having acquired the Dupplin estate in 1910 from the impecunious Earl of Kinnoull, began to tackle the backlog of estate improvements, beginning with the village below his new Dupplin Castle home. He engaged an old Perth Academy friend, James Miller, to build a new village along the lines of the popular garden cities of England but, as with plans for Gleneagles (on which Miller had also been working), this had to be shelved with the advent of war. Between 1925 and 1927, however, a total of ten houses, a village hall, a carpenter's work-shop and a smithy were built and on completion the old village, which judging by photographs did not look particularly run down, was demolished. While the passing of the old cannot be whole-heartedly applauded, the attractions of the new are undeniable. The houses, characterised by large gables and dormer windows, are laid out round the carefully tended village green: on the other side of the tree-lined road are the non-domestic buildings, including the quaint little hall, opened by the great Sir Harry Lauder, and the estate workshops, one of which is now used by a local organ builder. The village is still owned by the Dupplin estate and the residents are only tenants of this pleasant union of landscape and architecture.

Just across the river is the famous Dupplin Cross, an eight-foot high example of fine Pictish craftsmanship which may possibly have been erected by Kenneth MacAlpin to mark the union of the Pictish and Scottish kingdoms. Standing quietly in a field to the east of Bankhead farmhouse its thousand-year repose was suddenly interrupted in 1993 by a controversial proposal that in order to protect it from further weather erosion it should be moved to Edinburgh where, rumour has it, the new Museum of Scotland (scheduled to open in 1998) was looking for that special some-thing to grace the entrance hall. There was strong opposition locally to such a move and at the ensuing public enquiry the Scottish Office reporter declined to come down in favour of either Edinburgh or of the two suggested alternatives, the churches of Forteviot or Dunning. While further developments are awaited with much interest, the cross stays where it is.

The B935 proceeds east from Forteviot through the village of Forgandenny and within the space of three miles passes the independent schools of Strathallan and Kilgraston. Between the schools to the south of the road can be found the Pitkeathly Wells, a group of springs which had long been famed for their healthy minerals. Even as early as 1711 the attractions of the springs were causing a major headache for the local kirk session whose deliberations, clearly forgetful of the story of Jesus healing on the Sabbath, are recorded in the New Statistical Account:

> Session met according to appointment and took into consideration
> the profanation of the Sabbath by people frequenting the
> medicine well of Pitkeathly, whereupon some of the elders

were desired to visit the well every Sabbath morning and dehort the people from coming to it on the Lord's day, and inquire what parishes they belong to, so that word may be sent to their respective ministers to discharge them; and John Vallance is forbidden to give them passage at Dunberny boat... and they are to be stopped by constables, by authority of the justices of the peace.

Such a heavy-handed reaction had little effect as the huge popularity of Pitkeathly in the early nineteenth century was a significant factor in the growth of the nearby village of Bridge of Earn. Schweppes took over the springs in 1910 but a fire in 1927 ended the bottling process there and in 1949 the wells ceased altogether to function as a spa, thus allowing the minister of 1711 to rest comfortably in his grave.

Bridge of Earn today suffers from being a dormitory village for Perth and even in the distant past, when it had more of an independent life of its own, the tolls from the original bridge went into the Fair City's coffers. But at least it is unlikely that the village will ever be swallowed up by Perth if only for the reason that the steep sides of Moncreiffe Hill, lying between the city and the village, would rule out any building development. The bridges have always been one of the main *raisons d'etre* for the village and this is reflected in the street pattern: the older houses in Back Street lead to where the Auld Brig once stood (the surviving arches, possibly mediaeval, were finally demolished in 1976) while the present main road takes traffic over the new bridge, built slightly further upstream in around 1822. The latest bridge carries the M90 which now takes almost all the through traffic away from the village, and while passing trade has dwindled the number of new houses in the present commuter age has soared.

In recent years, since the decline of the wells, the village has depended for local employment on Bridge of Earn Hospital. This collection of army huts was hastily thrown together in the years 1940–41 (appropriately enough on land belonging to the farm of Oudenarde, itself named after one of Marlborough's victories in 1708) to cope with an expected large influx of casualties of war. After D-Day in June 1944 it became particularly busy with the wounded beginning to arrive, some still in field dressings, only five days after the first landings — quite a feat of organisation within the chaos of the opening of the Second Front. In 1948 it

As can only happen in a small community the leading figures of Abernethy were divided in the early 1890s over the vexed question of whether the parish minister or the Town Council had the right to ring the bell in the Round Tower during the week, thus initiating a lengthy controversy about who actually owned the ancient tower.

was transferred to the National Health Service and notwithstanding its shanty town appearance developed into one of the main hospitals in the county until it was closed in 1993.

The two-mile Baiglie Straight, once part of the main Perth-Edinburgh road, leads south-east out of Bridge of Earn. Turning left at the Baiglie Inn the road then passes through the hamlet of Aberargie before arriving in Abernethy, an ancient and historic town which, while settled in a landscape that is North Fife in character, looks steadfastly across the Tay towards the heights of Moncreiffe Hill and Perth beyond. Immediately to the south-west of Abernethy is Castle Law, another notable hill which casts its shadow over the town for much of the day and which is known in the archaeological world for its ancient hill fort. The centre of the town lies hidden behind the dreary main road and is built around the famous Round Tower, an early mediaeval monument of mellow sandstone which over the years has been the focus of many questions and rather fewer answers. Who built it, when and for what purpose? Even today if you were to ask the name of the present owner the custodians, Historic Scotland, will decline to say, this silly state of affairs doubtless being a hangover from a well-publicised ownership dispute at the end of the nineteenth century. The 73-foot tower may possibly date from around the ninth century (although the Romanesque arches at the top suggest the eleventh) and may have been built as a refuge from Viking raiders who would have used the Tay as a channel of access into central Scotland. The tower would also have witnessed the visit of William the Conqueror in 1072 when he received the homage of Malcolm Canmore. The only other similar tower in Scotland is at Brechin although there are many more in Ireland. At the base of the tower is part of a seventh century Pictish stone, clearly bearing the familiar tuning fork symbol and below it part of a crescent and V-rod. Beside the stone and attached to the tower at head height are the mediaeval jougs. The nearby parish church is dedicated to St Bride and proudly proclaims an original though questionable foundation date of 457. Almost exactly a millennium later the town became a burgh of barony, hence the date 1458 at the top of the town cross. Abernethy is at its best in the late afternoon and evening when sunshine and birdsong again settle on the old houses and streets and when a real sense of antiquity, perhaps the most tangible in the whole of Strathearn, permeates the historic centre.

One of the enduring legends of east-central Scotland centres on Abernethy in the heyday of its Pictish power. It concerns the Nine Maidens, daughters of St Donevald, who in the eighth century were active in the Angus area, doing good works and living saintly lives, and who ended their days in Abernethy in a home provided by the Pictish king. They were buried beneath an oak tree which, even in the seventeenth century, was a popular pilgrim destination. The names of only two were known, one being St Fincana who is commemorated in the little hamlet of St

Fink in Strathmore. The group as a whole lingers in placenames such as Ninewells near Dundee.

For what is essentially a Lowlands range of hills the Ochils are a considerable barrier and indeed when covered in the mists and snows of winter look every bit as forbidding and dramatic as those much further north. In the summer, however, they provide fine walking with Craig Rossie, perhaps the best known of the Perthshire Ochils, being a popular local climb and offering excellent views over the patchwork fields of Strathearn and the Tay estuary towards the east. The Ochils form the southern boundary of Perthshire and are one of the least known parts of the county, perhaps because, as with most geographical barriers, they tend to be crossed as quickly as possible and not lingered over. But several roads climb and wind through them and one in particular, the low road through wooded Glenfarg, will be remembered in the annals of Scottish motoring in much the same way as the ferry over the Forth. It is hard to imagine that until 1980, when the last stretch of the M90 was opened, this pleasant little byway struggled to cope with almost all the through traffic between Edinburgh and Perth.

It is itself a comparatively recent road, dating from the early nineteenth century. Travellers before this time would have taken one of the higher routes across the Ochils, one in particular, the Wallace Road (deriving its name from the great Sir William who apparently led his army along it), being the proud possessor of one of the most beautiful views in the world. This extravagant boast comes from the pen of no less a figure than Sir Walter Scott and can be found in the introductory pages to *The fair maid of Perth*. Scott describes how at the age of 15 and on his first solo journey by pony he was mesmerised by the view from Dron Hill, a wonderful vista which apparently extends over lower Strathearn, through the narrow gap at Craigend between Kirkton and Moncreiffe hills and across to the Tay and the Inches of Perth. Scott actually gives the Wicks of Baiglie as the viewpoint but his memory seems to have been at fault here and few in Perthshire would presume to criticise a minor lapse when indirectly through his writings he contributed so much to the prosperity of the area.

Two of today's better known routes across the Ochils, apart from via Glenfarg, are the A823 from Crieff and Auchterarder and the B934 from Dunning, both of which meet at the village of Yetts o Muckhart in Clackmannanshire. The former cuts through the narrow Glen Eagles and then follows the River Devon on the first part of its contorted course towards the Forth while the latter takes a more direct route across ten miles of high ground, much of it wooded. The Ochils have long been a sparsely populated area and indeed the parish of Glendevon could only muster a population of 149 in 1801. Nowadays the most famous resident is probably Hercules the Bear who lives with his doting owners in the privacy and luxury which befits the star of many a television commercial.

CHAPTER 9
KINROSS-SHIRE

Kinross-shire and Perthshire make strange bedfellows. Leaving aside the unequal pairing of the Big County with the second smallest, Kinross-shire has for a greater part of its history enjoyed much closer links with Fife. Geographically, Perth and Kinross are divided by the substantial obstacle of the Ochils whereas between Fife and Kinross there are clear channels of communication which carry several major roads as well as the River Leven. The connection is perhaps most evident in the red pantiles of Fife which have strayed across the county boundary to adorn cottage roofs in the villages on the east side of Loch Leven.

The links are also there historically. In mediaeval times the Fife peninsula was divided roughly down the middle, the eastern half being known as Fife and the western half as Fothrif. This latter area included the present-day Kinross-shire, Clackmannanshire and part of south-east Perthshire. Until the mid-fifteenth century 'Fife and Fothrif' was a phrase commonly seen in old charters, since when Fife has gone on to greater things while Fothrif has evaporated from geographical consciousness. It is possible, however, that echoes of the name can still be detected in the name of the River Forth and perhaps also in Mills of Forth, the old name for Milnathort. As the shadowy concept of Fothrif gradually succumbed to the realities of mediaeval administration, so we begin to see the emergence of the county of Kinross. Its origins can be traced to the mid-thirteenth century when a sheriff was established in the town, his small domain extending to little more than the area around the Kinross and Milnathort of today. Most sources go on to state that the sheriffdom was formally embodied as the County of Kinross in 1426 although another, admittedly dating from last century but authoritative nonetheless, states that this is 'a pure historic fallacy'. Whatever the situation there seems to be little doubt that the county in its modern form was created in 1685 by the addition, to the original nucleus, of the former Fife parishes of Portmoak, Cleish and Tulliebole.

While Kinross-shire's main ties have historically been with Fife, other levels of local administration, such as the sheriffdom and parliamentary representation, have seen links with Clackmannanshire and even West Lothian. It was only in 1930 that Parliament, in trying to relieve the tiny county's heavy burden of local authority responsibility, sought to annex it permanently to Fife and was rebuffed by the councillors of Kinross-shire who made it clear that they, or at least a majority of them, preferred to throw in their lot with Perthshire. As the Provost of Kinross said, perhaps aware of the general feeling that a link with Fife would have resulted in higher rates, 'We will fare far better with Perthshire than we would have done with Fife'. Thus the Perth and Kinross Joint County Council was brought into being for the general administration of the two counties, while at the same time the continuing Kinross County and Town councils were allowed to perform a few remaining minor functions. In 1975 Kinross-shire was fully amalgamated with the greater proportion of Perthshire to form Perth and Kinross District. Even now, though, following the supposed rationalisation of local government in 1996, the county is still a bureaucrat's nightmare: it is governed from Perth, receives its water from the Glenrothes-based East of Scotland Water Board, police and fire services from headquarters in Dundee, shares its MP with Clackmannanshire, has a Kirkcaldy postcode and is included in both the Tayside and Fife telephone directories. And the electricity supply? I was informed by both Scottish Hydro-electric and Scottish Power, which between them serve the whole of Scotland, that it was the other which provided Kinross-shire with power. If ever a county needed an excuse for an identity crisis this is it!

In spite of being pulled in all directions Kinross-shire has nevertheless enjoyed a strong sense of community spirit, something which is perhaps easier for a small county than a larger one like Perthshire, and particularly so when its very existence has long been under threat. In 1970 the county suffered the first of two severe blows to its sense of identity when, after 123 years of reporting news to its 'ain folk', the *Kinross Advertiser* published its final edition and was taken over by the *Fife News* (now the *Fife Herald*). The second came five years later when Kinross-shire itself was effectively taken over by an alien authority. That any sense of community spirit should survive at all is due to the Kinross Community Council which has assumed the dual roles of county guardian and disseminator of local news. Formed in 1975 it is today one of the most active in Perth and Kinross, producing the

Kinross Community Council Newsletter which since its inception in 1977 has developed into the main forum for the discussion of local issues. It is published monthly and despite its title (it now covers the whole of the county) is essential reading for anyone with an interest in Kinross-shire.

In years gone by Kinross-shire was known as 'the sleepy hollow of Scotland', a designation which, while in some ways true, creates the false impression that the county is low-lying. Loch Leven, in fact, just about the lowest point of the county, is situated at an altitude of over 350 feet. Elevated though it may be, the hollow is formed by an even higher rim of hills which surrounds the county and which is visible from almost any vantage point. To the north lie the smooth-topped Ochils, stretching from east to south-west and gaining in height and hilly respectability as they recede into the distance. Opposite, defining the southern boundary, is the steeply rising Benarty Hill and further west the gentle slopes of the Cleish Hills where the Nivingston Crags bare their teeth and attempt to impress the passer by. The eastern boundary is formed by Bishop Hill whose long and level ridge mirrors that of Benarty. Within this basin lies the landscape of Kinross-shire which, in the space of a very few miles, displays a variety of characteristics. The most obvious is the expanse of Loch Leven which occupies about 6% of the county's acreage. Immediately to the west is the flat hinterland of Kinross which in turn gives way to the attractive wooded uplands around Cleish and Aldie. In the far west is a little boundary bulge containing some rather ordinary roadside villages as well as the magnificent Rumbling Bridge gorge.

It would be wrong to give the impression that Kinross-shire is in any way cut off from the rest of Scotland: there are gaps in the circle of hills which allow traffic to scurry through, heading for all parts of the country. The M90, for example, breaches the gap at the foot of Benarty Hill while in the south-west of the county there is a corridor between the Cleish Hills and the Ochils wide enough for both the A91 to Stirling and the A977 to Clackmannan. Indeed, it is hard to escape the conclusion, judging by the map, that most of the towns and villages in the county developed from their situation either on a major road or at a crossroads. Kinross and Milnathort, before being bypassed by the M90, straddled the Great North Road, the villages of Blairingone, Powmill and Crook of Devon line one of the main arterial roads between Kinross and central Scotland, and there would almost certainly have been a mediaeval road around the east side of Loch Leven to allow access to the healing waters of Scotlandwell. In contrast, the plain to the west of Kinross, almost at the centre of the county, is remarkably empty apart from a scattering of farms. The contrast between the traffic hurrying along these main routes and the peaceful lives of the inhabitants, coupled with the predominantly rural aspect of the county, may have given rise to the 'sleepy' tag. This centrality of Kinross-shire within the road network of east-central Scotland was put to good use in early 1997 when the Heart of Scotland tourist information centre was opened beside the M90 just outside Kinross. This state-of-the-art complex displays in photograph and video not only the attractions of Kinross-shire but also those of Clackmannanshire, Perthshire and Fife.

It could well be argued that the most recent assault on the Kinross-shire community has come from a rapidly increasing population. Statistics indicate that the town of Kinross currently stands at around 4500 and the county as a whole at around 9500, figures which by themselves make it the smallest county in terms of population in Scotland. But when comparisons are made with 20 or 30 years ago the situation is alarming. Kinross expanded by around 40% between 1971 and 1981 and by a further 28% in the following decade, while the overall population of the county increased by around 25% during the 1980s, compared with the Perthshire figure of 6%. This means in effect that a significant proportion of the residents have no historical attachment or particularly strong ties to the area. Council planners have also stated that while rural depopulation may no longer be a problem the 'rapid rate of expansion is perhaps of greater concern'. The same easy road links with Edinburgh, Dunfermline and Perth, which have turned Kinross-shire into a commuter suburb, also allow easy access to the bigger centres of shopping, leisure and entertainment, with the result that locally the range of shops and facilities is below what would normally be expected of the area. The danger of Kinross-shire turning into a dormitory county for the surrounding urban areas, with little to offer either resident or visitor, is very real. Indeed, in a period when Scotland is being extensively marketed as a tourist destination, the number of visitors to Kinross-shire has been falling in recent years. This worrying situation led Perth and Kinross District Council in 1995

*A view northwards along the pleasantly winding Kinross High Street with
the Steeple acting as a focus for the town. The fountain is on the right,
the Town Hall on the left, and just out of shot is the old tolbooth which
was restored by the architect, Robert Adam. One of the problems faced
by Kinross in the late 1990s, as perceived by the planners, is the dearth
of good shopping facilities — note the lunchtime rush in the county town!*

to draw up the *Kinross Strategy*, a detailed document which draws
attention to these problems and outlines possible solutions.

One of the potential problems highlighted in this report was
an over-dependence on the firm of Todd and Duncan, Kinross-
shire's biggest employer with a staff of around 350. Founded in
Alva in 1867 and based in Kinross since 1897, the company is the
world's largest dyer and spinner of cashmere and lambs' wool
yarns and supplies household names such as Pringle as well as
knitwear companies all over the world. The factory complex,
Lochleven Mills, and its popular factory shop can be found on

the southern outskirts of the town. Kinross-shire has had a history of dabbling in unusual industries. Apart from the processing of wool from Kashmir goats, Kinross was also known historically as a centre for the manufacture of cutlery, until the rise of the Sheffield industry put an end to it, and Kinnesswood for parchment, from where 'great quantities' were sent to Edinburgh and Glasgow. Mushrooms were also once grown commercially on a large scale in Kinross although the site now houses the popular Kinross Motor Auctions. The traditional mainstay of the county's economy, however, as with much of Lowland eastern Scotland, was linen weaving and agriculture, although by all accounts the county was unusually slow to embrace the agricultural reforms of the eighteenth century.

The county's main topographical feature is Loch Leven, the largest freshwater loch of Lowland Scotland in terms of surface area and the thirteenth largest in the country as a whole, although measured by volume the relative shallowness sends it a long way down the rankings. Most of the county drains into it, principally via the three main burns which flow from west to east, namely the North Queich and South Queich which both rise in the Ochils, and the Gairney Water which rises near Crook of Devon and flows along the foot of the Cleish Hills. The small size of the catchment area can be gauged by that slow-moving stream of no great width or depth, the River Leven, which flows out of the loch at the south-eastern corner of the county.

Two hundred years ago the loch was considerably bigger than it is today. Radical proposals to lower the water level were first suggested in the 1790s by Thomas Graham, laird of the Kinross Estate, who hit upon the idea of enlarging his territories by reclaiming land from the loch. By the time of his death in 1819 the scheme had hardly advanced beyond the surveying and discussion stage and it was left to his trustees, which included Sir James Montgomery, ancestor of the present owner, to push the proposals through to their conclusion. It was no easy matter. The boldness of Thomas Graham's vision was matched only by the scale of the difficulties faced by his trustees, not least of them the reluctance of the many mill owners on the river, downstream of the loch, to accept assurances that the reduction in water level would have no effect on the operation of their mills. Yet the scale of success in gaining their permission withers in contrast to the legal agreement made with the other landowners bordering the

The River Leven looking curiously lonely under a heavy sky. This view looks east towards Fife along the New Cut, a man-made channel over three miles in length, which resulted in 1832 in the level of Loch Leven being lowered by around four feet.

loch that all the land reclaimed would belong to the Kinross Estate; this in spite of the fact that they would be deprived of all access to the loch and their fishing and boating rights. Work eventually started on creating the three-mile-long New Cut in 1828 and ended in 1832 when the water level was lowered by four and a half feet. The completion of the scheme, described as one of the biggest water engineering undertakings in central Scotland in the earlier nineteenth century, resulted in the reduction of the loch's surface area by one quarter and the availability of new land on the eastern shore. Traces of the former water level still linger in the name of the farm of Lochend, now half a mile inland from the south-eastern

163

end, and in the tracks, still marked on Ordnance Survey maps, which lead towards the loch from the eastern side and which then seem to peter out in the middle of fields. Immediately to the south of Lochend the B920 crosses two bridges, the first one spanning the old river bed, now a narrow, meandering and overgrown trickle, and the second, known as the New Gullet Bridge, spanning the long straight of the New Cut whose stark linearity across the landscape is somewhat softened by the riverside vegetation.

The mills and factories bordering the loch and river made full use of the water both during their manufacturing processes and at their conclusion as a convenient drain for effluent. Little wonder, then, that there should have been a growing awareness of the modern environmental problem of water pollution, particularly regarding the river, as early as the middle of last century. By the 1930s it was considered one of the most polluted rivers in Scotland since when, perhaps spurred on by this ignominy, those responsible have successfully brought the quality of river water up to an acceptable standard. The pollution of the loch, on the other hand, being a less industrialised and much larger expanse of water, was less noticeable, although concern about the level of phosphates had been expressed way back in the early 1900s. The problem came to a head in the summer of 1992 when, in common with several other lochs and reservoirs, the surface was found to be covered in blue-green algae blooms. While this intensified the blue colouring of the water, to the pleasure of some observers, the algae were also releasing toxins and thus damaging the ecosystem of the loch. Ironically, on the very day that Scottish Natural Heritage, of all organisations, were to hold a festival at the lochside, the district council declared the water to be unfit for the planned water sports. The root cause of this sad state of affairs, perhaps the lowest point in the recorded history of the loch, was the high level of phosphates and nitrogen entering the water over a prolonged period, from local factories, sewage plants, farm fertiliser and ordinary clothes- and dish-washing powders. Steps are finally being taken to tackle this blight on one of Kinross-shire's loveliest natural features.

With such a long history of water pollution it is perhaps surprising that the quality of Loch Leven trout should be famed throughout the angling world. That doyen of anglers, Perth's P D Malloch, wrote in 1910 that the Loch Leven trout was reckoned to be the best in Britain, if not the world. So outstandingly good was it that many people regarded it as a distinct species in its own right though Malloch himself disagreed, taking the line that it was the richness of the food in the loch which accounted for both the superior taste and the unusual pink colouring of the flesh. Before pollution began to take its toll in the 1970s the annual catch would average around 40,000 trout, since when, in spite of attempts at restocking by Loch Leven Fisheries, the annual figures have dropped alarmingly to between 10,000 and 20,000. The nadir was reached in 1992 when the catch totalled 2,415, a paltry figure for a loch which used to host international angling competitions and which would annually attract around 50,000 anglers.

Pollution, according to Scottish Natural Heritage, seems to have had little effect on the bird population for which the loch is even more widely known. The shallow water and protective cover afforded by the reed beds and other vegetation have made the loch one of the most important sites in Britain for wildfowl. Migratory birds start to swell the population from June onwards until at the peak of the season there are as many as 25,000 geese, several thousand ducks and hundreds of swans all making a home by the loch. Indeed, the loch boasts the largest number of breeding ducks in the country and perhaps even in the whole of Europe. In 1967, for these various reasons, the Royal Society for the Protection of Birds purchased Vane Farm on the southern shores of the loch, nestling under the rocky crags of Benarty Hill, and turned it into a nature reserve which now extends to almost 600 acres. Here you will find bird-watching hides, a circular nature trail and for the keener ornithologist a number of organised dawn goose watches during which one can observe the unforgettable spectacle of thousands of geese taking to the air to feed in the surrounding countryside. Because of its fish and bird-life, and the presence close by of a number of rare plants and invertebrates, the whole of Loch Leven was declared a National Nature Reserve in 1964 under the watchful eye of Scottish Natural Heritage. Thus all sports except angling are outlawed on its waters.

Of the two main islands in the loch, St Serf's is the largest and takes its name from the saint, or one of the saints of this name, who was busy evangelising this part of Scotland in early mediaeval times. In around 950 a community of Celtic monks, or Culdees, who had already been living there for some time, made the island over to the Bishop of St Andrews in return for food and clothing, following which the community was developed along Roman, rather than Celtic, church lines and eventually made into a priory. The small ruin of the priory's chapel can still be seen and certainly predates the most famous prior, Andrew of Wyntoun, whose *Orygynale cronikyl of Scotland*, probably written in the priory in around 1400, makes him one of the earliest of Scottish historians. The historical writing, however, as is only to be expected of the time, was liberally laced with religion and legend and provided the source for Shakespeare's story of the three witches in *Macbeth*, although Wyntoun describes them as 'three weird sisters' rather than anything supernatural.

The smaller Castle Island has achieved lasting fame as the prison house of Mary, Queen of Scots although she was by no means the first person of noble birth to have been incarcerated there. Her turbulent reign effectively drew to a close in the months following her husband Darnley's murder in February 1567. The Earl of Bothwell was implicated in the crime and when Mary married him in May her enemies could stand no more and rose against her. She surrendered to rebels at Carberry Hill in June, and was immediately ferried out to the castle, from where in July she was forced to abdicate the crown in favour of her son, James VI. Her famous escape on 2 May 1568 was made possible by a young servant, Willie Douglas, who succeeded in stealing the castle keys by first covering them with a napkin while they lay unguarded on the custodian's dinner table. Willie unlocked the castle gate, led Mary to a boat and rowed her across the loch to her last, all too short, period of freedom. This gallant hero is remembered today in the name of a motor boat which acts as the island's ferry. Of all the many events associated with the history of Kinross-shire the romantic story of Mary's imprisonment and subsequent escape is the best known and it is doubtless for this reason that the castle 'represents' the county in the official Perth and Kinross Council crest. A boat trip to the island, leaving from the jetty at the far end of the Kirkgate Park, is a must for any visitor to Kinross, not just for its historic associations but for its green and leafy beauty and perhaps unexpected aura of peace.

Although Loch Leven is one of the main attractions of Kinross-shire, and has certainly been the focus for much of its history and wildlife, there is a lot more to the county than just this eastern corner. The following circular tour, which can easily be completed in a day trip, will give a flavour of the people, places and events associated with the area. Heading south from Perth, through Glenfarg, the old county boundary is crossed near the point where the B996 spans the M90, and as one descends into Kinross-shire the head and broad shoulders of West Lomond, standing sentinel on the Fife side of the border, are clearly visible to the east. Turn right onto the A91 then immediately left onto the B919 which is signposted to Scotlandwell. The first settlement on this road is Wester Balgedie which was promoted to the status of a conservation village in 1996; justifiably so, for its charmingly erratic arrangement of cottages appears to have been based on the configuration of a dice roll. It would be gratifying to think that Wester Balgedie sets the tone for the villages of Kinross-shire but unfortunately this is not the case as few attain the same level of attractiveness.

Nevertheless Kinnesswood, a mile along the road (now the A911), is not far behind. While the main street has little of note, the older part, running perpendicular to it, is worth exploring. The Cobbles is a pleasant mix of red pantiled cottages and newer housing which blend together remarkably well, in a haphazard sort of way, along the rising slopes of Bishop Hill. The road eventually dwindles into two footpaths, one heading up the hill and the other south to Scotlandwell. This side of the hill consists mainly of grass and tufts of gorse, overlaid with bird song and the sounds of rushing burns and always the splendid view over the loch and the 'sleepy hollow'. Occasionally the twentieth century will intervene in the form of the village school bell and within seconds the distant but timeless sounds of children at play. On the lower slopes of the hill and at the southern edge of Kinnesswood is the Bishopshire Golf Club whose name, as with Bishop Hill, reflects the ancient ties with the bishopric of St Andrews. The whole area to the east of Loch Leven was long known as the Bishopshire.

Kinnesswood was the birthplace of the poet Michael Bruce whose cottage, now a little museum, can be seen about half way up The Cobbles on the left-hand side. Born in 1746, the son of a humble weaver, he exemplified the great strength of the Scottish education system by proceeding direct from the village school to Edinburgh University. He left without graduating, as was apparently the custom of the time, and became a schoolmaster at Gairney Bridge where, curiously enough, the great Perthshire divine, John

The cottage on the left was the childhood home of Michael Bruce, the 'gentle poet of Loch Leven'. Behind looms Bishop Hill where he spent long summer months tending sheep and where he learned to love the local landscape which features so strongly in his verse.

Brown, of the *Self-interpreting Bible* fame, had occupied the same post some years earlier. Bruce did not last long here, resigning his post in order to pursue studies at the Secession Church theological 'college' at Kinross, after which he briefly took up another teaching post in Clackmannanshire. His tenure was tragically brief as in 1767, at the age of only 21, he fell ill with tuberculosis and returned to the home of his birth to die. By this time, however, he had already achieved a certain fame for his poetry, fame which was transformed by his premature death into local immortality. Some of his paraphrases are still sung in Scottish churches and an annual poetry competition keeps his name at the forefront of Kinross-shire's cultural history, even 230 years after his death.

Another native of the village was Alexander Buchan, born in 1829, who also began his career as a teacher but who was deflected by ill health into the less demanding job of secretary to the Scottish Meteorological Society. After many years of keeping weather statistics and using them to work out average temperatures he discovered that certain periods of the year, just a few days in length, had a tendency to be consistently either below or above the norm. These entered the British phraseology as Buchan cold or warm spells and are still occasionally mentioned by the likes of Ian McCaskill on the national weather forecast.

Less than a mile away is Portmoak Church, where Michael Bruce lies buried in the churchyard, and beyond it the village of Scotlandwell which in spite of its historic associations and ancient spring is an unprepossessing little place. Some writers, even in recent years, have claimed a Roman origin for Scotlandwell, citing as their reason the Latin name Fons Scotiae, the well of Scotland. But this is a fanciful piece of history as the Scots had nothing to do with Scotland until long after the Romans had left while Scotia itself was a name which referred originally to Ireland and only later, from the eleventh century, to Scotland. Nevertheless the village has had a long recorded history beginning with a community of Trinitarians, or Red Friars, which was founded here by a Bishop of St Andrews in around 1250. Many ancient wells across Scotland are associated with saints and it would seem reasonable to assume that this one, as a healing well (the story goes that Robert the Bruce later came here to be cured of his leprosy), should attract a new religious foundation. The well today is protected by a type of lychgate structure and at water level by a metal grille through which one can see the spring waters bubbling up through the silver-grey sand. But the bubbles seem so few and the surface water so still that it is a surprise to see how much water actually flows out of its nineteenth century stone cistern. Just to the west of the well is Portmoak Moss where the villagers used to graze their animals and cut peat. The area was bought by the Forestry Commission in 1947, laid out with trees and subsequently sold to the Woodland Trust in 1996.

The B920 leads south out of Scotlandwell, past Portmoak Airfield (the home of the Scottish Gliding Union), over the above-mentioned Old and New Gullet Bridges, and after a couple of right-hand turns leads onto the B9097 along the south side of Loch Leven. There is a large car park on the right from where the views across the loch are magnificent. Also visible from this spot is the sluice house on the shore line which was built at the head of the New Cut in around 1830 and which still regulates the outflow from the loch. A little further on the left is the entrance to the Vane Farm reserve and two miles beyond is the T-junction with the old Great North Road, now demoted to the B996.

By turning right here one sees almost immediately a tall obelisk at the side of the road. The inscription at the foot reads: 'To commemorate the formation of the first presbytery of the Secession Church at Gairney Bridge, 6 December 1733, for the maintenance of scripture truth and the rights of the Christian people'. The history of the church in Scotland is littered with divisions, breakaway sects, subdivisions of sects, partial reunions and stubbornly remaining rumps. This is well illustrated in the history of the Secession Church which, leaving aside the continuing Episcopal Church after the Presbyterian settlement of 1690, was the earliest to break away from the main stem of the Church of Scotland. This church later subdivided into Burgher and Antiburgher congregations and each of these later still into the curiously named Auld Lichts and New Lichts. The guiding light behind the events of 1733 was the Reverend Ebenezer Erskine who with three like-minded colleagues met at a house at Gairney Bridge, near where the monument now stands, to form the new church. The cause of the rift was a perennial problem for the democratically organised Presbyterian Church, namely who has the right to appoint a minister to a new charge.

A mile or so to the south of the monument lies the estate of Blairadam in whose name is commemorated one of the most eminent of British architectural families. Formerly known as Blaircrambeth, the estate was purchased by the architect William Adam in around 1733, at about the time his design for the Wade bridge at Aberfeldy had been completed, and was gradually transformed from an area of wilderness into a beautifully designed and tended garden. William himself enjoyed a high professional reputation but his sons, Robert and James in particular, were in their time even better known, particularly for their distinctively classical style of architecture and interior decoration. William's grandson, also William, was a distinguished politician and jurist, rising to become Lord Chief Commissioner of the Jury Court, a civil court whose jurisdiction was transferred to the Court of Session in 1830. He inherited the Blairadam estate and regularly entertained several leading figures of the Scottish establishment, including Sir Adam Fergusson, son of the Perthshire-born philosopher of the same name, and Sir Walter Scott. In 1817 the group, with a common antiquarian interest, decided to form the Blairadam Antiquarian Club with the intention of meeting annually to visit and discuss the historic sites of the area. The future literary giant was at this time plain Mr Scott although he was already well known as a collector of Scottish verse and as an eminent poet in his own right. It was his novels, however, which were to establish him as one of the greatest of Scottish writers although at the time, and for reasons known only to himself, he chose to publish them anonymously. William Adam, writing about the Blairadam Club in the 1830s, describes how ten years earlier he and his fellow members were among the first to suspect that their friend was none other than the author of the first few of the immensely popular Waverley novels. Not only had they recognised odd turns of phrase which had appeared both on his lips and in the novels, but they also realised that the author knew intimately the Blairadam estate. Upon being challenged by the group, in a very gentlemanly way, Sir Walter 'preserved profound silence, but there was a conscious looking down and a considerable elongation of his upper lip', by which I take it that Sir Walter was trying to stifle a wide grin. The ties of friendship allowed the secret, which had also been widely guessed by the literati of Scotland, to be kept for several years. Not until 1827 was Scott's authorship formally admitted, amid great excitement, at a public dinner.

From the old Great North Road we turn onto the B9097 and head for Cleish and one of the most attractive parts of Kinross-shire. Cleish is a little village of grey stone houses and mature trees, with a school on one side of the road and opposite it the parish church. When the playground is empty the sound of the wind rustling through the trees seems to fill the village. The churchyard has several mementoes of a bygone age, not least of them an eighteenth century sundial on the church wall, the remains of the 13th or 14th century village cross and several interesting gravestones. This wonderful sense of unspoiled rural peacefulness was compounded, on my last visit there, by finding the church unlocked, a rare treat in these security-conscious days. Should you have the same opportunity then do go inside, not for any particularly outstanding feature but for the simple pleasure of sensing the bonds which hold this little community of rural Kinross-shire together. Read the chronology on one of the walls, about the minister who was caught up in the ill-fated Darien Scheme and died at sea, or about Sir Walter Scott and his friends at Blairadam who used to worship in the previous church before its destruction by fire in 1832. Read also of the appointment of William Michie as schoolmaster in 1790, the same who was immortalised in a clever quatrain by Burns which, because of my own Michie ancestry, I feel duty-bound to quote:

> Here lie Willie Michie's banes:
> O Satan, when ye tak him
> Gie him the schulin o your weans
> For clever deils he' ll mak them.

Willie, whose name appears as Ebenezer in some editions, was apparently a friend of Burns who penned the lines, long before the subject of the epitaph had died, in friendly revenge for having fallen asleep at a party in the Bard's lodgings. This may possibly have been in Kinross's Red Lion, a popular roadside inn.

The road out of Cleish takes us westwards along the lower slopes of the Cleish Hills. The landscape here is not just hilly but beautifully contoured, with wide open views across long, gentle slopes to the higher Ochils behind, now much closer than before. The House of Aldie, the former home of a branch of the Mercers, appears on the right across the valley floor. Here, in the early years of the eighteenth century, the Scone-born 'silver-tongued Murray', the future Lord Chief Justice of England, spent his last night in Scotland when still no more than a boy. Just before turning right onto the A823 we cross into Fife and then, within a mile and a little short of Powmill, return to Kinross-shire. Powmill and its neighbour Blairingone, two miles south-west on the A977 trunk road, are the southernmost villages of Perth and Kinross. In a leafy lane near Blairingone in December 1865 a local vanman was murdered, shot by one Joseph Bell, a footloose native of Derbyshire, who was quickly apprehended and hanged. His execution in front of the Speygate prison in Perth in May 1866 was the last to be carried out publicly in Perthshire.

North of Powmill the A823 peels off to the left for Rumbling Bridge, once on the list of essential sights for any eighteenth century traveller doing the grand tour of Scotland. Nowadays, were it not for the signpost and the curious name, no-one travelling by car would have any inkling that 120 feet below the present rather nondescript bridge is one of the most impressive natural sites in the whole of Perth and Kinross. The car park is in the grounds of the adjacent nursing home, a little beyond the bridge, and is only

The unusual double structure at Rumbling Bridge in western Kinross-shire. At a height of 86 feet above a deep and narrow gorge and with no parapet, it would have taken a brave man or a drunken one to cross the original brig at night.

a short stroll from the viewing platforms and the woodland walks, all of which have been restored in recent years by the army. The bridge, however, is not the main object of the visit although the curious double structure, whereby the original Rumbling Brig of 1713 (built 86 feet above the water and without a parapet!) was surmounted by the present one of 1816, is certainly worth a look. What is truly memorable is the breathtaking power of the River Devon as it roars and thunders through the steep-sided, moss-covered walls of a deep and narrow gorge. So towering are the sides, so ancient the dripping moss and so tenacious the thin trees in their grasp of the vertical rock face, that the romance of the

173

scene could have been taken straight from Ossian. Even more memorable is the sheer volume of noise, hence the name, which is magnified many times by the rocky walls and which is akin to standing close to an aeroplane engine at full throttle. Another walkway spans the narrowest part of the gorge from where a huge jet of white water shoots out almost horizontally before crashing into the pools below. This is known as the Devil's Mill, so called because the power of the rushing water, seven days a week, was particularly reminiscent of a millrace. And as no God-fearing miller would think of working on the Sabbath then it must have been the devil at work, grinding his corn.

Some would say that the devil really was at work further upstream at Crook of Devon, a little roadside village which takes its name from the sharp bend, of almost 180 degrees, taken by the river at this spot. Away from the heavy traffic of the main road the village is pleasantly peaceful, yet between April and October 1662 it witnessed a sickening excess of judicial murder when a total of twelve women and one man were accused of witchcraft, tried locally, and all but one, it seems, strangled and burnt at the stake on a hillside outside the village. Records show, in fact, that in that same year another 15 residents of Crook of Devon were tried for the same crime although their fate is not known. Across the county, on the side of Bishop Hill, stands a tall rock pillar known as Carlin Maggie ('carlin' being the Scots word for a witch or an old woman), a surviving relic of Kinross-shire's macabre fascination with witchcraft.

From Crook of Devon the A977 leads north-west towards Kinross passing on the way the giant 'golf ball' at Balado. Originally a World War II airfield used for training pilots Balado is now owned by the Ministry of Defence and since 1985 has been functioning as a NATO ground satellite station with radio aerials apparently housed inside the spherical structure. Another part of the airfield successfully hosted in the summer of 1997 one of the great open-air Scottish pop festivals, T in the Park, a curiously old-fashioned contrast which brings to mind the 1960s clash between militarism and flower-power.

Hemmed in by the loch and built alongside the old Great North Road Kinross could have no shape other than that of a long thin town. The older part lies towards the southern end while the more modern housing, dating from Victorian times to the present day, stretches out to the north, built over what was once the Muirs of Kinross where sheep and cattle used to graze. With the recent construction of the leisure centre on the northern edge the town seems to be stretching out hungrily towards Milnathort now less than 400 yards away.

First impressions of Kinross are not inspiring. It looks like many a small Scottish town with little to distinguish it from the rest. The real Kinross has to be looked for and once found does not disappoint. The street names, for example, are full of character. Look for Parliament Square, just off the High Street, a little less grand than its namesakes in Edinburgh or London, but doubtless of greater relevance to the local inhabitants and so called from the town worthies who used to congregate here to discuss the issues of the day. Or Swansacre which was built on land belonging to a Mr Swan or Currat's Wynd, possibly named after an Episcopal priest in the town who in bygone days would have been known as the curate. Or Piper Row, well, who knows how that originated?

The centre of the town seems to huddle round the Steeple, a landmark whose prominence owes almost as much to its red stone as to its height of 80 feet. When a new parish church was built in the High Street in 1742 a committee was formed to oversee the erection of an accompanying steeple which was finally completed in 1751. The Steeple Committee, instead of disbanding when their work was done, continued until 1865 as a sort of unofficial Town Council. On one side of the Steeple is the fountain, which was inaugurated in 1886 amid much rejoicing and dancing in the streets, and on the other, where the above-mentioned new church once stood, the Town Hall which was built in 1841. A stone plaque on this building records that the Kinross Market Company, which was originally formed for the purpose of erecting a market hall on the site of the demolished church, presented the building to the town of Kinross in 1946 as a memorial to the dead of World War II. More or less opposite, on the other side of the road, stands the old County Building or tolbooth where the town's prisoners used to be held. This was restored in 1771 by the architect Robert Adam, then the Member of Parliament for Kinross-shire, and is notable for its narrow, classically designed, bowed extension. A plaque at the top commemorates his beneficence though whether the design is in keeping with most of the town's architecture is perhaps debatable.

The classical proportions of Kinross House are complemented by the formal gardens in front. The house looks over Loch Leven towards the castle where Mary, Queen of Scots endured eleven months of captivity. Kinross House, described as 'one of the most important houses in Scotland', is the home of Sir David Montgomery, the present Lord Lieutenant of Perth and Kinross.

Not far away, and certainly inspired by the same classical principles, is Kinross House. Far from being a typical stately home, hidden in the depths of the countryside, this one is easily visible from the town centre at the end of a long straight drive. Its oblique angle in relation to the High Street is due to the alignment of the house and formal garden with Loch Leven Castle. The house was designed by another of Kinross-shire's great architects, Sir William Bruce, and built between 1679 and 1693. With Bruce having already contributed to the building of Holyrood Palace, in his capacity as Royal Surveyor in Scotland, and later to Hopetoun House, the pedigree of the architecture is beyond dispute, particularly as he was building the house for his own use. It is a well-proportioned building of neat symmetry and yellow-grey stone (from the Cleish Hills), its ground-floor rustication and pilastered frontage labelling it unequivocally as of the classical style. In its 300 years of existence remarkably few alterations have been carried out, bolstering the house's reputation as one of the finest of 17th century Scottish stately homes. Earlier this century one of the Montgomery lairds laid out the grounds which are now open to the public, although the house itself remains private.

Situated within the walled garden of Kinross House and with fine views over Loch Leven is Rachel House, the first children's hospice in Scotland. After a massive fund-raising campaign which touched the hearts of many across Scotland, the building was opened by the Princess Royal in 1996 and won a top architectural award the following year. Just outside the main gates to Kinross House is the hospice's shop and information centre.

Nearby, branching off the High Street, is Burns Begg Street which commemorates one of the town's greatest figures of last century. Robert Burns Begg was a great-nephew of the Bard and a much loved lawyer, antiquarian and poet in his own right. The street named after him (he himself was the moving spirit behind its construction) leads into the Kirkgate which follows the lengthy boundary wall of the Kinross House grounds to the Kirkgate Park and the shores of the loch. Opposite the jetty and on a slight elevation is the town cemetery in the middle of which stands a small mortuary chapel. It bears the date 1675 and is the only surviving part of the original parish church of Kinross, the one which was finally declared redundant in 1742. Inside are the remains of Sir William Bruce, his wife and his son. Nearby is the Burns Begg memorial, complete with a carved likeness of the man himself, looking out over the cemetery wall and across the loch he loved so much. His gaze is focused on the site of an ancient crannog which he himself discovered in 1887. He died in 1900 and his funeral was described in the local paper as 'perhaps the largest ever seen in Kinross'.

Milnathort lies a little to the north of the county town and is centred on the crossroads formed by the old Great North Road and the road connecting north Fife with the Scottish heartlands. The presence of two tall steeples and the two-storeyed architecture of the place give the impression that Milnathort is rather more than the large village it really is. One of the steeples is actually named the Town Hall, though no Town Council ever sat within its walls. Even until recently, with the streets busy with traffic and brightened by a number of well-patronised shops, it could have passed with little difficulty for a small country town. But nowadays, with both main roads having been bypassed by a single motorway, the wide thoroughfares look forlornly empty and Milnathort's dreams of

Not, perhaps, the best known castle in Kinross-shire, but an impressive ruin nonetheless. Burleigh Castle lies a little to the east of Milnathort and was formerly the home of the infamous Master of Burleigh who appears to have got away with murder not once, but twice.

modest grandeur have awoken to the grim reality that the twentieth century passed through but did not stay.

Outside Milnathort there are several places of interest. To the north-west stands the huge Ochil Hills Hospital, a former TB sanatorium which like its alpine counterparts was built at a reasonably high altitude to take advantage of the purer air. At the time of writing there are plans to turn it into a nursing home. Not far away is the estate of Ledlanet, formerly the home of the Calder family who owned the Stronachie distillery higher in the Ochils. In the estate's shooting lodge, the publisher John Calder staged the popular Ledlanet Nights in which a series of concerts, ranging from folk-song to grand opera, was given by well known musical names. These were held between 1963 and 1971, when fire regulations effectively ended this ambitious cultural experiment in the heart of rural Kinross-shire.

Two ancient monuments stand to the east of Milnathort, both approached by the A911 to Wester Balgedie. The first of these is the ruined Burleigh Castle, its sixteenth century red stone ruins jutting so aggressively into the twentieth century that the road has to take an obvious loop around them. The castle is associated with the Balfour family whose most infamous member was Robert, son of the fourth baron. In 1707 this young man had fallen in love with a pretty girl who came from a rather lower station in life and in consequence had been sent abroad by his family so that his ardour might cool. Perhaps he went to France and learnt something of the *crime passionel* as on his return in 1709, and on discovering that she had married the Inverkeithing schoolmaster, he went straight to the schoolmaster's house and shot him. Robert was arrested, tried and sentenced to death but managed, or was perhaps even allowed, to escape. He is recorded as having sided with the Jacobites in 1715, whereupon the castle was forfeited to the Crown, but little is known of this romantic antihero after this. A mile or so beyond the castle, and just visible from the road on the left-hand side, are the standing stones of Orwell, two reminders of the county's prehistoric past.

From here it is less than a mile to Wester Balgedie and the completion of the circular tour through the so-called sleepy hollow. Reflecting on stories of passionate young noblemen, an imprisoned queen, great engineering works, witches, church divisions and murder, Kinross-shire is surely anything but sleepy.

CHAPTER 10

CENTRAL PERTHSHIRE:
THE ALMOND AND THE BRAAN

The following two chapters consist of a circular tour through the heartlands of Perthshire, starting and finishing in Perth. The first takes us through the relatively unknown areas of Glenalmond and Strathbraan to Birnam, and the next continues from Dunkeld, through the ancient lands of Stormont to Scone and Perth. In a world where the remote and the unknown go hand in hand it is odd that this part of Perthshire, much of which lies between the populous Lowlands and the popular Highlands, should be less familiar to many than the further reaches of the county. Whatever the reason, and it cannot be for want of attractive countryside or notable history, there is much to be discovered in this quiet and unspoiled part of the county.

The background for the first half of this chapter is provided by the Almond, a small river in terms of volume in spite of its length of over thirty miles. The source can be found high above the village of Ardeonaig, only three miles from the southern shores of Loch Tay, from where the young river begins its journey through the hilly moorland landscape of Glenalmond and the Sma Glen. Although nowadays the whole length of the river valley is frequently called Glenalmond, the name traditionally applies only to this its Highland section. Crossing the Highland Boundary Fault the middle stretches tumble along beside the foothills of the southern Highlands in an area properly known as Logiealmond. This area, overshadowed by the brooding presence of the hills, has a distinct atmosphere of frontier unease; indeed, a local historian, Dr David Forrester, described it rather more poetically as 'a Lowland spearhead thrust into the Highlands, but not of it'. Finally, in the vicinity of Harrietfield, the river turns its back on the hills and heads south-east, now through a Lowland landscape, to a final union with the Tay upstream of Perth.

From a point near Almondbank a channel of river water, known as the Town Lade, is led off from the main flow and for four miles heads in a more southerly direction to link the Almond with the

A less common view of Huntingtower Castle, taken from the rear. The central section with the clearly visible pitched roof was a later addition which linked the two earlier mediaeval tower houses. This was the gap, now known as the Maiden's Leap, which was jumped by a girl torn by the conflicting demands of love for a young man and duty to her parents.

very centre of Perth. This historic waterway, probably constructed in mediaeval times to power the city's corn mills, discharges into the Tay at a point just slightly downstream of Perth Bridge. Although for most of the way through central Perth it flows beneath street level, it can still be glimpsed in the open behind St Ninian's Cathedral, beneath the glass-panelled floor of the City Mills Hotel and at the recently improved Horse Cross.

An excursion by car from Perth into Logiealmond can be a delightful way of spending a sunny morning. Leaving the city by the A85 road to Crieff, one's attention is immediately caught by the high walls of Huntingtower Castle on the right. Formerly known as the House of Ruthven, this was the seat of one of the most powerful families of later mediaeval Scotland. It stands above the Almond at the top of a steep slope and consists of two originally separate tower houses linked by a much later central section. The story goes that before the towers were joined a young female member of the family, having ignored a parental ban on meeting an unsuitable suitor and on the point of being discovered, jumped the span of over nine feet in an attempt to get back to her bedroom before her disobedience could be proved. The place of this remarkable feat, 60 feet above the ground, is known as the Maiden's Leap. The castle is now in the care of Historic Scotland and can boast a fine pre-Reformation painted ceiling and some late fifteenth century wall paintings.

In 1487 the Ruthven family was raised to the peerage and in 1581 the 4th Lord Ruthven became the 1st Earl of Gowrie. The following year the ultimately ineffective Raid of Ruthven took place in which Gowrie and others held the young James VI in the castle for ten months in order to persuade him to abandon his support for a rival political faction. Hardly surprisingly James quickly changed his mind after his release, had Gowrie executed in 1584 and took his revenge in a big way in 1600 in the events of the Gowrie Conspiracy. Briefly, for several lengthy volumes have been written about the affair, James was advised by the Master of Ruthven, the younger brother of the third Earl of Gowrie, to hurry to Perth from his hunting base at Falkland to investigate the discovery of a large quantity of gold. This, he was told, was to be used to foment Catholic unrest. James made the journey to the Gowrie House in Perth where a supposed assassination attempt was made. Whether there really was an attempt on the king's life or whether it was a Machiavellian scheme to discredit a too powerful family may never be known but the consequences are beyond dispute: the third and last Earl of Gowrie (of the Ruthven creation) and his younger brother were both killed, their estates forfeited and the Ruthven name proscribed. The Murrays of Tullibardine were given the castle which, under the new name of Huntingtower, remained a part of the Atholl estates until 1805. In spite of John Buchan's connections with Perth (he was born at 20 York Place) his novel of this title has nothing to do with this part of Scotland.

A mile beyond Huntingtower take a right turn at the hamlet of Lochty and head for Almondbank where, at some considerable distance from the coast and from the nearest naval base, one may be surprised to find the Royal Naval Aircraft Workshops, a major employer in the area. This arm of the Ministry of Defence was established here during World War II when, following heavy bombardment in the south, the navy decided to look for safer places for its storage depots. Logistics dictated that one should be positioned north of the Forth and Almondbank, with its tree cover, was felt to be suitable. In the 1960s the workforce totalled about 1000 but defence cuts since then have whittled that figure down to less than half that number and on several occasions have even threatened its very survival. In 1992, however, when the Government finally recognised the workforce's pre-eminence throughout Europe in the field of repairing helicopter gearboxes and rotor-heads, the threat of closure was lifted and the foreseeable future now seems secure.

Beyond Almondbank the road descends into the pretty village of Pitcairngreen, at the heart of which lies a large grassy area bordered by several mature oaks. Some fine old houses and a number of modern ones surround the green, each enjoying a picture postcard prospect of old-world peace and contentment. The land on which Pitcairngreen stands formed part of the estate of Thomas Graham of Balgowan who in 1786 planned and initiated the development of this new settlement. His strict instructions about the size of the village green and the relationship to it of the surrounding houses, and indeed about the dimensions and construction of the houses themselves, may have resulted from his observations of some of the lovely old villages near Oxford, where he had been an undergraduate.

Born in 1748 Thomas Graham spent the first half of his long life as an enlightened landowner. Following the death of his father, and after a brief spell at Christchurch, the new young laird returned to Scotland to take over the family estates. In 1774 he married Mary, the second daughter of the ninth Lord Cathcart, whose eldest daughter, Jane, married the fourth Duke of Atholl at the same ceremony. Mary was regarded as one of the finest beauties of the age and is immortalised in the world-famous full-length portrait by Gainsborough, 'The Honourable Mrs Graham', which was completed in 1776 and now hangs in the National Gallery of Scotland. To refute the suggestion that anyone would have looked just as beautiful had they been wearing the same gown, Graham instructed Gainsborough to paint a second, little-known, portrait with his wife this time dressed as a housewife complete with broom in hand. The marriage was obviously one of intense happiness and had Mary not died prematurely in 1792 Graham would probably have lived out his days on his nearby estate of Lynedoch, playing cricket (he took part in the first properly recorded game in Scotland in 1785) and perhaps, in accordance with the spirit of the age, planning other villages like Pitcairngreen.

Instead, stricken by grief, Graham turned his attention to politics (he was the Whig M.P. for Perthshire for several years) and military affairs and surprised himself by showing a particular aptitude for the latter. He raised the Perthshire Volunteers in 1794 and thereafter played an increasingly prominent role in the war against France. In 1809 he was present in Corunna at the death and burial of Sir John Moore, whose aide-de-camp he had long been, and indeed it seems to have been one of the dying Moore's recommendations that led directly to Graham's long awaited promotion to general. Following his victory over the French at Barossa in 1811 the honours came swiftly: in 1812 he was knighted, a preferment superseded two years later by his elevation to the peerage as Baron Lynedoch of Balgowan. In 1821 he was promoted to the rank of full general. He eventually retired to his Perthshire estate, resumed his interest in farming and stockbreeding, and died there, much loved, in 1843 aged 95. Prior to his death he declined the honour of a Westminster Abbey burial, choosing instead to lie beside his beloved Mary in the churchyard at Methven.

Ten years later a monument to his memory was erected near Perth by the Murray of Murrayshall family, to whom the Grahams were closely related. A century and a half further on that addition of a needle-like sharpness to the top of the rounded Murrayshall Hill has proved ineffective in keeping the great man's memory alive: whereas the name of the Duke of Wellington is well enough known throughout the country, few even in his native Perthshire are familiar with the name of one of the Duke's most senior officers. The monument itself, at an elevation of around 900 feet, has been fully exposed to the damaging effects of wind, frost and rain for the past 150 years and has only recently undergone much needed repairs.

Turning left at Pitcairngreen the westward journey into Logiealmond begins. The road winds and rises through pleasantly leafy countryside with the occasional shimmering haze of springtime bluebells on the right, and on the left, from the bridge at Dalcrue (one of Graham's last projects on his estate), a fleeting

Thomas Graham of Balgowan, later Lord Lynedoch, was a man of huge ability and simple taste. This plain, unadorned monument, highly visible on top of Murrayshall Hill, is — perhaps unintentionally — a very appropriate memorial.

glimpse of the river far below. At this point the road is briefly deflected from the river only to resume the relationship a few miles further on beyond the farm of South Ardittie.

Proceeding further west, with the Highland ramparts on the right becoming increasingly obvious, the countryside very quickly assumes a more northerly air. There are fewer trees on the higher ground and the soil is less productive; the road is alive with pheasants and rabbits, and in the distance can be made out the entrance to the Sma Glen, with the appearance of a mountain having been cleft in two by the blow of a giant axe. The pinky-grey walls of the Glenalmond College quadrangles can be made out from a couple of miles away as can the later additions, including the newly constructed girls boarding house. West of the college the road begins a gentle descent to river level at Buchanty, passing on the way a noteworthy dwelling called Tulchan Garden Cottage. Whitewashed and with a weathervane atop its central tower this attractive little cottage presides like a mother hen over an equally pretty and productive garden. As far as can be ascertained it existed in the later eighteenth century as a tower, purpose unknown, before being turned firstly into a doocot and then, in around 1830, with the addition of the wings, into a cottage. It is now quite rightly a listed building.

Buchanty, where the road divides, is as well-known for its seventeenth century high-arched bridge as it is for the dangerous waters which it spans. Here the Almond moves turbulently through a succession of narrow gorges and deep pools creating a view from the bridge parapet which should not be missed. Slightly further upstream is the infamous Buchanty Spout, a beautiful place for a picnic or a walk but where the treacherous river current over many years has claimed a number of lives.

From Buchanty, having crossed the bridge, it is possible to return to Perth along the north bank of the river. Lined with oaks, the sun-dappled road winds peacefully through a scene of rural tranquillity enlivened only by the rich variety of bird life. On the right the Almond and some of its tributaries have forced deep channels through the fields. Curiosity is aroused by the names of the neighbouring farms of Williamston, Louisafield and Francesfield, all in close proximity to the little village of Harrietfield. Was this the work of a local landowner choosing to commemorate the names of his children in a novel way? Although the guide books will say that Harrietfield is a corruption of Heriotfield, it is hard to believe that personal names are not behind the others.

The old red telephone box, shaded by a variegated holly tree, says much about the character of sleepy Harrietfield. Indeed it would be easy just to note its charm and drive straight through, but to do so without a backward glance would be to miss out on an important piece of Scotland's literary heritage. In 1875 a Free Church minister, John Watson, was inducted to his new charge in the village and, in the two brief years he spent there, was unlikely to have made a lasting impression on the minds of his parishioners. In fact, rather the opposite was the case. Writing as Ian Maclaren,

Watson became a huge overnight success with his 1894 publication, *Beside the bonnie brier bush*, a collection of tales of rural life in which many of the people and places of Logiealmond, weakly disguised, were featured. Harrietfield itself appears as the village of Drumtochty, where many of the tales are set. The book opens with the following couplet:

There grows a bonnie brier bush in our kail-yard
And white are the blossoms on't in our kail-yard.

It is hard to conceive of a more inauspicious start to a book. Yet it was the word 'kailyard' which caught the critics' attention and which was later applied to a whole genre of Scottish writing, characterised by an idealised, almost sentimental, vision of rural village life. The Kailyard School originally consisted of Maclaren, J M Barrie and S R Crockett, three immensely popular writers whose work in this style, in spite of its success (or perhaps because of it), was never totally accepted by the literary establishment. The pejorative undertones of a word which means 'cabbage patch' are never far from the surface.

In an old brown envelope behind the bar of the Drumtochty Tavern in Harrietfield can be found the *Drumtochty Visitors Book*, a highly browsable testimony to the popularity of Watson's creation. Dating from June 1895, only months after his book first appeared in the shops, it contains the names, addresses and comments of many of his readers, including several from Liverpool, where he had ministered for the previous eighteen years, and a number from the States — 'pilgrims', as they described themselves. In stark contrast to this adulation the few remaining Watson memorabilia in the village, including letters, books and even the man's church robes, were found to be mouldering in a box in the recently closed (1995) church. At the time of writing, the plans to establish a Watson 'shrine' in the church at Methven seem to have come to naught.

Watson would probably have been surprised and perhaps even a little disappointed to find that today he is best remembered for his Perthshire stories. He was, after all, a native of Essex and spent most of his clerical life south of the border, particularly in Liverpool where he was one of the leading figures in the establishment of what later became Liverpool University. He played a similarly important role in the founding of Westminster College (a theological college in the Free Church tradition) in Cambridge and indeed his appointment as its first principal was to have been announced on the very day he died. Such is fate.

A mile east of Harrietfield the briefest of detours down a road to the right will lead to the splendid semi-circular Millhaugh Bridge. Built sometime after 1779 its remarkably steep gradient, about 1 in 10, used to cause travellers many problems, particularly when the ground was icy. About the turn of this century a more functional but far less graceful bridge was built beside the old one, its only redeeming feature being the fine view of the redundant structure, whose roadway is now thickly covered with grass.

Another mile further on, a small road leads off to the left, heading north up into Little Glenshee which, apart from the name, has no connection at all with the winter sports complex on the Perthshire-Aberdeenshire border. The contrast between the softness of the Lowland scenery of eastern Logiealmond and the sudden reappearance of a certain Highland harshness along this single track road is a sharp reminder of the closeness of the Highland Boundary Fault. Not for nothing was it called the old Highland Road. After three miles the road abandons its northwards thrust and veers off to the right in the direction of Tullybelton and Bankfoot, leaving a mere footpath to take the traveller over the hills and into Strathbraan.

A little further still, on the left bank of the Almond and unfortunately inaccessible to all but the most persistent, lie the earthly remains of Bessie Bell and Mary Gray — or so legend would have us believe. A popular ballad recounts the bare facts of how the two 'bonnie lasses' of the title lived together beside the Almond and how they died together following a visitation of the plague. Prevented from being buried beside their families in Methven churchyard they were instead interred near their lonely dwelling place. Other versions of the story tell of how the girls had sought to escape the plague by moving away from habitation but that the lover of one, on finding where his sweetheart was living, came to visit her. He presented her with a silk handkerchief which, unbeknown to him, had been contaminated with the fatal disease. How much truth lies in the story is uncertain. Plague did devastate Perth and its neighbourhood in the 1640s, which is when the events of the ballad are believed to have taken place, and a contemporary legal document confirms the existence of a Patrick Gray who held land in Methven parish at that time. The riverside grave itself is strong evidence that the events of the ballad may have some basis in fact. Over the years several landowners have kept a watchful eye on this melancholic spot, including Thomas Graham of Balgowan, whose home at Lynedoch was nearby. He placed railings around the grave and over it a stone, which is now apparently hidden beneath the surface. Today the Scone Estates own the burial spot and application should be made to them at Scone Palace by anyone wishing to visit it.

In 1993 a Glasgow-based film company, with financial backing from the local council, came close to making a feature film of the story. Having lined up, according to the press releases, a number of well-known names including Hannah Gordon, David McCallum and Tom Conti, the plans had to be shelved when a wet summer made filming impossible. Perhaps one day the story will hit the silver screen and, if so, the blurb writers may wish to borrow the Hollywood-esque epitaph which Thomas Graham had inscribed on their stone — 'They lived, they loved, they died.'

At this stage the short tour of Logiealmond can be brought to an end by returning to Perth either via Moneydie and Luncarty or via Pitcairngreen and Almondbank. The longer excursion continues westwards from Buchanty towards the site of the great Roman fort at Fendoch, strategically positioned at the head of the pass through the Sma Glen. Although hardly any surface traces of this fort survive, the low-lying grassy plateau where it once stood is visible to the south-east of the junction of the Logiealmond road and the A822. True aficionados of Roman remains will probably wish to take a five-minute stroll from this spot up to the site of a small watchtower, probably once the main look-out post for Fendoch, from where a much better view of both the fort's location and the pass can be had. On a winter's day, standing here in the heather with the circular ditch around the tower still quite obvious, it is easy to imagine the feelings of Roman soldiers at a posting such as this on the northern frontier of the empire. With the ever present threat from hostile Caledonians, not to mention the severity of the winter weather and the possibility of attack by wolves and bears, the average legionary must have asked himself many a time what he was doing there and what the point of the whole military campaign actually was.

A drive through the Sma Glen used to be a popular activity for Perthshire people, at least for those who had cars, in the days when driving was once enjoyable. Nowadays the road is much busier although the attraction of the scenery is as strong as ever. The steep-sided, scree-covered hills are not particularly high although the narrowness ('sma' means 'narrow' in Scots) of the glen probably creates the opposite impression. The relatively wide bottom through which the Almond flows, the classic U-shape, shows that it was once the path of a glacier.

Many places in Scotland claim a connection with Ossian and this part of Perthshire is no different. Ossian was a legendary third century warrior and poet, the son of Finn or Fingal, whose stories were deeply embedded in the Gaelic culture of western Scotland and Ireland. For want of a more appropriate label, the Ossianic legends could be regarded as a Celtic equivalent of the Arthurian cycle. Once again the ubiquitous Thomas Graham of Balgowan had a small part to play in the literary sensation centred on the poems of Ossian. At the end of the 1750s Graham's father, not wishing to send his son away to school, instead employed a tutor for him, one James Macpherson. This young man, having moved to an area steeped in Ossianic legend, then shook the literary establishment to its very foundations by claiming to have translated some of the bard's poetic works. It is more than likely that some of the inspiration for Macpherson's publications came from the many excursions he and his pupil would have made together into the country around Logiealmond and the Sma Glen where, it is reported, he took a particular interest in the local folklore. An area known as the Field of Fingal, for example, was somewhere in the vicinity of Buchanty, and the bones of the bard himself were long believed to be lying under a massive stone in the Sma Glen. An illustration of the depth and richness of Ossianic culture comes from the pen of David Stewart of Garth who, in one of the earlier accounts of Highland life, recounted the common custom in Highland villages of asking strangers if they could speak of the days if Fingal. If the answer was affirmative then the whole village would gather round and listen well into the night. There was clearly a huge reservoir of Ossianic oral tradition extant in the eighteenth century Highlands and it was into this that Macpherson tapped.

Although the mid-eighteenth century witnessed a growing interest in the old Gaelic tales of Scotland, Macpherson's desire to publish may have been stimulated by the work of a Dunkeld schoolmaster, Jerome Stone, who regularly throughout the 1750s (until his death in 1757) submitted translations of ancient Gaelic poetry to the *Scots Magazine*. Macpherson's first book, *Fragments of ancient poetry collected in the Highlands of Scotland*, appeared in 1760 and was followed in 1762 with *Fingal* and in 1763 with *Temora*, which claimed to be a translation of some of Ossian's work. These publications were to have a tremendous influence not only on the romantic movement in Europe, and in particular in Germany where literary giants such as Goethe and Schiller were great admirers, but also on the way in which Scotland was perceived by outsiders. The grossly romanticised view of Scottish history and culture, the blame for which is so often assigned to Sir Walter Scott and George IV, in fact owes much to Macpherson.

In Britain the main interest stimulated by the poems concerned not so much the intrinsic merit of the literature as its authenticity. The celebrated Dr Johnson, perhaps not the first to regard the translations as a hoax, was one of the most vociferous in his denunciation. Macpherson's cause was not helped by his inability to produce the manuscripts he claimed to have used, although several people provided written testimonies as to their existence. The controversy rumbled on for over forty years until the Highland Society of Scotland published its definitive opinion on the matter in 1805. The findings concluded that Macpherson had freely translated ancient Gaelic poetry to which he had added various passages of his own creation, and this is broadly the view today.

Ossian's stone, where Macpherson must have lingered and pondered in the years before he changed the literary landscape of Europe, can still be seen standing close to the A822. Eight feet high and cuboid in shape, it lies about two miles north of the T-junction with the Logiealmond road, and, although without any identifying signposts or plaques, is quite visible on the right (northbound). A later bard, William Wordsworth, who in 1803 was doing the almost obligatory 'grand tour' of Scotland (and incidentally whose nephew Charles Wordsworth became the first warden of nearby Glenalmond College) paused here and reflected on the contrast between the turbulent and romantic man of legend and the tranquil loneliness of his supposed resting place. This is the first stanza from *Glen Almain; or, the Narrow Glen*:

> In this still place, remote from men,
> Sleeps Ossian, in the Narrow Glen;

In this still place, where murmurs on
But one meek streamlet, only one;
He sang of battles, and the breath
Of stormy war, and violent death;
And should, methinks, when all was past
Have rightfully been laid at last
Where rocks were rudely heaped, and rent
As by a spirit turbulent;
Where sights were rough, and sounds were wild,
And everything unreconciled;
In some complaining, dim retreat,
For fear and melancholy meet;
But this is calm; there cannot be
A more entire tranquillity.

One would have thought that, shielded by the weight of such a huge rock, Ossian's tranquillity would have remained for ever undisturbed. Not so. Whoever had deposited the stone in that place could not have anticipated the determination of General George Wade, that genial road-building Irishman, to move it. For it seems clear from the physical evidence that Wade deliberately chose to desecrate the supposed tomb of a legendary Highland hero, either out of personal archaeological curiosity or from politically-motivated vandalism. A contemporary account by Edward Burt, one of Wade's engineers, states that the roads were planned to follow wherever possible the most direct route across country and that Ossian's stone, lying in the way, had to be moved. Nothing wrong with that, one would think, yet a glance at a detailed Ordnance Survey map shows that the most sensible route for this stretch of road would have followed the modern A822. Why did a skilled engineer like Wade plan a route which necessitated firstly the removal of an enormous rock and secondly, within yards of this rock, the formation of a sharp bend to the left to avoid the river? And if for some reason now unknown this genuinely was the most obvious route, why did Wade not bend the road to the left *before* he reached the stone? All in all the facts suggest that Wade, or whoever was responsible for this particular section, was well aware that this was no ordinary lump of rock. Credence to the theory is added by a third-hand account of these events, which is now held in the library of Glenalmond College, and which states that the motive for moving the stone was the

A wonderful example of indifference to history! Who, with any sense of awe, could daub Ossian's grave with a 'no dogs' sign? Doubtless Bran, Ossian's fabled hound, is turning in his own grave.

possibility of buried treasure beneath. But Wade was wrong and legend right, at least to some extent, as a number of bones were, in fact, discovered beneath the stone. To whom they belonged is a very different matter although at the time the inhabitants of the glen were in no doubt. They carefully removed the remains of Ossian from the hitherto hidden chamber and reburied them with much ceremony on the top of Dun Mor. This steep hill, forming the east side of the Sma Glen, has an ancient fort which had long been associated with Ossian's father, Fingal.

At Newton Bridge, less than a mile beyond *Clach Ossian*, the road parts company with Glenalmond and pushes north towards Amulree and Aberfeldy. The bridge itself, widened in around 1835, was originally another Wade construction, a simple, single span over quite a small river. There are picnic tables here between the road and the riverside, although for those wishing to eat in quieter

Not a mere farm track this, but the remains of one of the great civil engineering projects of eighteenth-century Scotland. This is a section of General Wade's road between Crieff and Dalnacardoch, built in 1730, where it joins with the A822 through the Sma Glen. The Young Pretender himself travelled this road in February 1746.

surroundings, the initial stage of the footpath leading west through the upper reaches of Glenalmond offers a good alternative. The path follows the Almond most of the way to its source and then heads off, through some wild countryside, towards Ardtalnaig on the southern shore of Loch Tay.

The high, bare and bleak landscape to the south of the path once hid the lair of the Thief of Glenalmond, marked on Ordnance Survey maps as the Thief's Cave. Being the subject of a ballad which, as usual, has several different versions, it is now almost impossible to be sure about who he was, what he did, and where he died. A distillation of traditions, however, indicates that his name was Alastair Bane and that he lost an ear either at the Battle of Sheriffmuir in 1715, or as a result of the primitive justice of those days. A stealer of cattle and sheep, who successfully evaded capture over a long period, most accounts agree that he was captured in his cave, quite literally *in flagrante delicto*, with a sheep roasting over an open fire, and was subsequently hanged at either Crieff or Perth. One cannot help thinking that, were it not for the need to protect livestock, a worse punishment for this folk hero would have been to let him live out his days in his cave, at an altitude of over 1500 feet and at the mercy of bitter Highland winters.

Beyond Newton Bridge the road climbs a little and, leaving the Sma Glen behind, travels the few miles northwards to Amulree through a broad, spacious and heathery landscape. The village consists of a cluster of houses, a shop, a church and a hotel and yet, judging by the number of picture postcards emanating from here in the early years of this century, was obviously a destination popular with tourists. It occupies a prime location at the point where the north-south Aberfeldy to Crieff road meets the west-east route of Glen Quaich and Strathbraan, and for this reason acted as one of the gathering places for the Jacobite clans in 1715. Shortly after this the builders of the military road pushing steadily towards the heart of the Highlands would have met the Highland drovers cajoling their seas of cattle in the opposite direction towards the great tryst at Crieff. Later still, in the early weeks of 1746, the bedraggled followers of the Young Pretender would have been observed trudging broken-spirited to their final rendezvous with history at Culloden. And here, almost a century later, the crofting families from Glen Quaich would have paused for a last look at their beloved glen before turning south for Glasgow and the ships to Canada. Amulree has witnessed some sadness indeed.

Although the Highland Clearances are more often associated with the north-west of Scotland than with Perthshire, the county did not remain completely untouched by this agricultural and social upheaval. Glen Quaich in particular suffered a classic textbook clearance when the 2nd Marquis of Breadalbane, on the advice of one of his estate managers, not only evicted a number of families from their crofts to make way for more sheep, but in true Sutherland fashion torched some of their homes to prevent their return. This led to a war of words conducted through the press and pamphlets of the period in which the marquis was obliged to defend himself against accusations of trying to exterminate the Scottish peasant. Other contributing factors, such as poor living conditions and general social unrest, combined with posters and advertisements extolling the tremendous opportunities available in Canada to 'labourers and those with small capital', resulted in a mass exodus from the glen. Between the census years of 1841 and 1851 the population of Dull parish (in which Glen Quaich is situated) fell by 17%, a sudden decline which must have caused chaos in the local economy. 300 people from the glen alone are believed to have emigrated at this time to what would have been initially an even tougher life in the developing south-eastern corner of Canada, near lakes Huron, Ontario and Erie. And as so often happened throughout the former British colonies these settlers quickly gave a tangible form to their emotional link with the old country by giving the familiar names of home to their new abodes, with the consequence that Amulree and Perth County have become well established on the map of Canada. There is a fascinating little exhibition in the porch of Amulree Church, much of it devoted to the Glen Quaich emigrants. The displays reveal the close bond between the present-day inhabitants of the glen and those of over a century ago. *Sheila*, a novel by the erstwhile popular writer Annie Swan, provides a vivid and dramatic account of the Glen Quaich clearances.

Even now Glen Quaich has an empty, almost haunted, feel to it. Derelict cottages can still be seen and contribute much to the underlying yet powerful sense of abandonment. Perhaps this is also due to the fact that some maps depict the glen, wrongly, as leading nowhere. For as well as being an old drove road it was once the main thoroughfare between Kenmore and Crieff, and indeed, if one is willing to open and shut the few farm gates which bar the way, it is still possible to drive right through the glen to Kenmore. Snow can also add to the difficulties and for this reason the road beyond the first gate (about half way through and just past the lovely old bridge over the River Quaich), which marks the start of the ascent to around 1750 feet, should only be attempted with caution between December and April. But in the summer it is a beautiful ribbon of a road, snaking its way over the roof of Perthshire, and offering the traveller near the crest a wonderful

Amulree Church has a spiritual simplicity quite in keeping with its lonely surroundings.

view straight down Glen Quaich and across Loch Freuchie. The river, from which the glen takes its name, flows into the loch, where those with an eye for archaeological detail will notice the probable crannog origins of the small tree-tufted island near the shore.

The white-painted Amulree Church, perched above the meandering Braan (which flows out of Loch Freuchie), has an almost alpine appearance from the outside. Its interior is equally attractive with light-coloured walls, a deep richness to the wood of the pews and a glorious stained glass window at the east end. The beginnings of the church go back to 1741 when the Society in Scotland for Propagating Christian Knowledge (an organisation better known for its funding of schools in the Highlands) advertised for an itinerant preacher to cover a huge area of central Perthshire, from Glenalmond up to the southern shores of Loch Tummel. Having had no interest from prospective applicants, the Society then added the area of Rannoch to the job specification, clarified the question of a manse for the successful candidate (there wasn't one), and waited expectantly for the arrival of a pile of applications. The upshot, of course, was a major rethink and the subsequent construction at Amulree of both the church, completed in 1752, and a manse.

The journey through Strathbraan commences two miles north of Amulree where the A822 bends sharply to the right and the A826 carries on towards Aberfeldy. The landscape at the western end of the strath is that of a gently sloping valley, bounded by the Logiealmond hills to the south and the woods and uplands of Craigvinean Forest to the north. The scenery is pleasant though not outstanding and only increases in interest beyond the little village of Trochry. On the east side of this village a narrow road to the left, part of an old military highway linking Amulree with Dunkeld, takes the braver motorist on a short detour high above the strath where the views are well worth the risk of meeting another car coming in the opposite direction. Winding through the farm steading of Lagganallachie and past the nearby ruined church and graveyard, the road descends again to recross the Braan at Rumbling Bridge. This was built in 1774 following a not over-generous grant of £10 from the Commissioners of Supply (a forerunner of the County Council) and should not be confused with the bridge of the same name in Kinross-shire. In terms of its setting, spanning a river which crashes through a deep and wooded gorge, and its remarkable height above the water, this is one of the most impressive bridges in the county and a memorable place to pause before rejoining the main road.

From this point it is a mere two miles to Birnam and the choice of several routes to explore. But before either joining or crossing the A9, take a little while to stroll around the village of Inver which lies peacefully sandwiched between the Braan and the Tay. In the days before railways and major trunk roads Inver was a significant point in the Scottish transport and communication network, and indeed the former coaching inn, built around three sides of a square, still dominates the centre of the village. It was also one of the three places from where a ferry could safely cross the Tay to provide access to Dunkeld, a city of political and ecclesiastical importance from the early days of Scotland's recorded history. The path to the right of the former inn leads uphill past the cottages of two of Inver's most famous inhabitants, Niel Gow and Charles Macintosh, both now commemorated by plaques on the appropriate walls.

Niel Gow was born near Inver in 1727 and, through the brilliance of his playing and with the encouragement and patronage of the Duke of Atholl, became the best known of all Scottish fiddlers. He was in constant demand to play at all types of occasions, from village dances to glittering balls, and yet, for someone who was used to rubbing shoulders with the aristocracy or receiving the acclamation of his peers, derived as much pleasure from sitting with his fiddle beneath a favourite oak tree near the Inver ferry. It was his mastery of bowing technique which singled him out from the crowd and which gave such life to his music that one contemporary was moved to state that even amongst a hundred fiddlers he would always recognise Niel's bow. The tradition and heritage of Scottish fiddle music, so memorably admired by the great Yehudi Menuhin himself, was transformed by Niel Gow and his second youngest son Nathaniel. Not only did Niel's method and style become established in time as the correct way to play but he and Nathaniel together published several volumes of collected fiddle music and composed many tunes of their own. *Niel Gow's lament for the death of his second wife* is truly a haunting melody. Niel died in 1807, his celebrity status having been confirmed by the four portraits of him by Raeburn. His gravestone was restored in 1950 and can now be seen in the Chapter House Museum at Dunkeld Cathedral. His fiddle is on display at Blair Castle, the home of his Atholl patrons, and is still occasionally played today. Those who have heard it have commented on the quality of its tone, in spite of the doubts about its authenticity.

For such a small village Inver produced a remarkably large number of fine musicians, of which the Gows were the best known. Another was the greatly loved Charles Macintosh, a giant of a man in not just the physical sense, who achieved eminence in a very different field. He was born in 1839, eight years after the death of Nathaniel Gow, and began his working life in a saw-mill at Inver. When an accident at work removed several of his fingers he rather wisely looked for alternative employment and ended up with a new job as the local postman. Traversing the countryside all around Dunkeld on foot, covering many miles every day, he found himself with the opportunity to indulge his passion for natural history. By his mid-thirties Charlie was acknowledged locally as an expert in ferns, mosses and fungi. It was also at around this time that he first made the acquaintance of the very young Beatrix Potter, who with her family was to spend many summer holidays in the neighbourhood. In her journals Beatrix wrote warmly of Charlie and was undoubtedly much in awe of his knowledge and skill as a naturalist. A charming correspondence developed between the two, during the course of which she would send him specimens of fungi which she had gathered, the latest books on their mutual interest, and a number of her own exquisite paintings. He would reciprocate by sending similar parcels south and commenting on her investigations. Beatrix in time became an expert on fungi and was saddened that as an amateur she never won the professional recognition she sought and which she certainly deserved. Charlie, all through their long correspondence and brief meetings, was probably her main support and mentor in her scientific endeavours, and, although they eventually lost touch, she acknowledged her debt to him in a simple tribute after his death in 1922.

Charlie was also a gifted composer and musician, being equally at home on the fiddle and cello and in leading the congregational singing in church. He had a particular interest in Scottish fiddle music, something he shared with Lady Dorothea Ruggles-Brise, the eldest daughter of the 7th Duke of Atholl. Henry Coates, Charlie's biographer, recounts the following story, given to him by Lady Dorothea, in which Charlie had offered to give her an old manuscript book of jigs, dated 1733, which was of no further interest to him. Lady Dorothea, in reply, suggested she pay for it, an offer kindly meant but one by which Charlie felt so insulted that he flung the volume on the fire. It was rescued only just in time and now forms part of the valuable Atholl Collection of Scottish music which was left by Lady Dorothea to the Sandeman Library in Perth. The collection is regularly consulted by musicologists from all over the world, one of whom, on receiving a copy of this nearly incinerated volume (*William Dixon's Tune Book*) pronounced it to be the earliest surviving manuscript of bagpipe music in the United Kingdom and duly published it in 1995 with the perhaps over-optimistic title, *The master piper: nine notes that shook the world*. It is a merry collection of rollicking pipe tunes, rather than mournful pibrochs, and indeed some of the tune titles would make a grown man blush, never mind a maiden. The only indication of the manuscript's provenance is a brief note in Lady Dorothea's handwriting inside the front cover — 'Given me by Charles Macintosh, Inver. October 1909'. The only indication of its near brush with the ash pan is the faint whiff of wood smoke when shutting the volume.

Immediately to the west of Inver is a beautiful woodland walk leading alongside the Braan to a folly known as the Hermitage.

The Hermitage or Ossian's Hall as seen from the banks of the River Braan near Dunkeld. The tiny building dates from 1758 and originally had three windows where the open viewing platform now is.

Usually approached from the A9, this popular attraction was gifted to the National Trust for Scotland in 1943 by Katharine, Duchess of Atholl, in memory of her late husband, the 8th Duke. The Hermitage, also known as Ossian's Hall, was built in 1758 by the future 3rd Duke and has little if anything to do with the legendary bard. Perched on a rocky outcrop high above the thundering waterfalls of the Braan, it was designed to function not merely as a country retreat but also as an amplifier, unnecessary though it may seem, for the natural sights and sounds of this breathtaking spot. The echoing acoustics of the gently domed ceiling can still be appreciated, particularly when stepping into the second room, but the mirror-clad walls, which were positioned so as to magnify the spectacle of falling water, have long since disappeared. (Professor William Hooker, the man behind the botanical expeditions of David Douglas, memorably described the illusion as 'a trickery and buffoonery of art insufferably out of keeping with the majesty of such scenery'.) Further on and of a similar age is Ossian's Cave, a pseudo hermit's cell created in the main from naturally lying rocks. In the earlier nineteenth century the Hermitage walks developed into a popular visitor attraction, but the fact that they remained open seven days a week stirred the stricter Sabbatarians of the locality into action. The 'proper authorities', having listened to the grievances, agreed to shut the walks 'during divine service' only, a remarkably modern response of capitalism paying lip service to Christianity.

The last stop on this tour of west-central Perthshire is at Birnam, an essentially mid-Victorian village, in spite of the ancient link with Shakespeare's *Macbeth*. Its making was the arrival of the steam locomotive and the fact that the northern terminus of the Highland Railway was situated here for a full seven years before it was advanced to Pitlochry. The result was a huge influx of visitors stepping off the train, all keen to follow in the footsteps of Queen Victoria and experience something of the Scottish Highlands. Accommodation for those passing through was speedily erected, impressive turreted stone mansions, to be used as boarding houses, appeared on the main street and the imposing Birnam Hotel took its place at the centre of the village. The grey-beige stone buildings have mellowed over the course of a century and today the village nestles comfortably between the heights of the pine-clad Birnam and Newtyle hills, the Gateway to the Highlands, offering a warm welcome to those travelling north on the A9.

Mr and Mrs Rupert Potter of South Kensington, with their children Bertram and Beatrix, were early visitors to the area, returning year after year though not always to the same accommodation. Rupert must have been a man of some wealth and social standing as he regularly rented large properties for the summer months and entertained some of the better known figures of late nineteenth century society. One such person was the artist Sir John Everett Millais who apparently spent some time encouraging the young Beatrix in her painting. And anyone who has seen her water-colours of fungi will appreciate that she was indeed highly gifted.

Beatrix had a pet rabbit, Benjamin Bouncer, who, on his demise, was replaced by one Peter Piper. In 1893, while spending the summer at Eastwood, a country house on the left bank of the Tay opposite Birnam, Beatrix wrote and illustrated a short story based on her new rabbit which she herself eventually published in 1901. The following year it was taken on by the publishers Frederick Warne, since when *The tale of Peter Rabbit* has been a worldwide children's favourite. A few years ago I was privileged to be shown a number of Potter family photographs, now in private hands, amongst which was one of a rabbit. I would like to believe that this was Peter himself, as it may well have been, but sadly there was no inscription on the back.

Other characters in her books appear to have been modelled on real people. Mrs Tiggywinkle, the be-aproned hedgehog, was almost certainly based on a Dalguise washerwoman, Kitty MacDonald, while Jeremy Fisher and his boat probably have their origins in family fishing trips on the Tay. It has even been suggested, and backed up with photographic evidence, that Mr MacGregor was none other than Charlie Macintosh. Some of these characters in statue form can be seen opposite the Birnam Hotel in the recently and most attractively laid out Beatrix Potter Garden. It is gratifying to see that Perthshire has finally laid claim to a fair share of the Potter heritage which for so long had been almost monopolised by the English Lake District.

Behind the hotel and accessible via the aptly named Oak Road is a riverside walk leading past the famous Birnam Oak. Tradition has it that this is the only surviving tree from Birnam Wood which, according to writers earlier than Shakespeare, provided the leafy camouflage for the army of Malcolm Canmore, so essential for the final but almost certainly fictitious victory over Macbeth at Dunsinane. If the story had been true then the tree should be at least 900 years old. The plaque in front, however, sensibly only commits itself to stating that it has an age of several centuries. For all its supposed antiquity it is not a tree of particularly great height, although its branches extend a long way and many are now supported by posts. Through its leaves can be seen the silent-flowing Tay which divides the new village of Birnam from the ancient city of Dunkeld, and which brings this tour of west-central Perthshire to an end.

CHAPTER 11

CENTRAL PERTHSHIRE: DUNKELD TO SCONE

Most visitors to Dunkeld arrive via the A9 and peel off this caravan-clogged road to cross the Tay by way of the Dunkeld Bridge. A more pleasant approach, however, is via the A984 from Caputh, a quiet tree-lined road which borders the Tay and gives the new arrival a fine view of this lovely bridge. It is ironic that such a graceful structure, funded mainly by the Duke of Atholl as much for the benefit of the local community as the travelling public, should have been the cause of so much bitterness and strife. It was built to a design by Telford and opened in 1809, complete with a tollgate, the root cause of the trouble, at the south end. The duke had been authorised by Parliament to recoup his outlay by levying a toll on all foot passengers and this was paid, not without murmurings of discontent, for nearly half a century until eventually a louder voice of protest was raised by Alexander Robertson. Better known simply as Dundonnachie, the name of his house near the Hermitage, this writer, businessman and would-be philosopher argued that the duke, having received in tolls far more than his original expenditure, had no further right to pontage. The war of words eventually escalated into physical violence when a crowd late one night tore the tollgate from its post and flung it into the Tay, from where it was fished out a few days later near Perth and replaced. Such action was repeated on several occasions and in 1868 even led to a detachment of the Royal Highlanders being called in to keep the peace. Dundonnachie finally won a moral victory in the Court of Session, which decreed that the debt claimed by the duke should be reduced by a massive £60,000. The tolls were abolished in 1879 but not before they had levied their own sad toll on Dundonnachie himself. The courts found that he too had strayed onto the wrong side of the law and sentenced him to a period of imprisonment, an experience from which he mentally never recovered. He died in 1893, his last journey being to cross the bridge, free of charge, on his way to burial in the nave of the cathedral.

The long ecclesiastical history of Dunkeld may have begun as early as the sixth century with the founding of a Columban monastery, the 'keld' of the placename being taken by some as signifying the presence of the Celtic monks later known as Culdees. There is stronger evidence to show that in around 820 the Pictish king, Constantine I, founded a church here, and that thirty years later Kenneth MacAlpin, the first king of the united Picts and Scots, moved some of the bones of St Columba (others went to Ireland) from Iona to this same spot. This ensured a steady stream of pilgrims converging on the town which thus became for two centuries the ecclesiastical capital of the Scottish nation. Its leading position is illustrated by the fact that Crinan, lay abbot of Dunkeld, a powerful political figure in spite of his lowly-sounding position, married the daughter of Malcolm II and was the father of the ill-fated Duncan I. Even now the Episcopal and Roman Catholic churches in Scotland each have a bishop of Dunkeld (the church having been elevated to the status of cathedral by David I in 1127), while the Church of Scotland and the Free Church have presbyteries centred on the town.

The construction of the present building began in the mid-twelfth century with the choir at the east end. The nave, used primarily by the laity, came next, followed by the south porch, the chapter house and finally, in 1501, the 96-foot clocktower. After a quarter of a millennium spent in building, the cathedral survived intact for less than six decades. In 1560, during the upheaval of the Reformation, the Privy Council ordered the removal from the cathedral, and the burning, of all altars and idolatrous images with the proviso that there should be no unnecessary damage to doors, windows, furniture, glass and metalwork. This meant nothing to a mob fired by religious bigotry who proceeded with terrifying ferocity to tear the cathedral apart, an act of iconoclasm from which it has never fully recovered. In 1600 the choir was reroofed, the first of several repairs, following which it effectively became the local parish church. The rest of the building, apart from the clocktower, remains a roofless shell and serves as a stark reminder of a troubled past which the idyllic setting, surrounded by trees and lawns sloping down to the banks of the Tay, may soften but cannot hide.

The guiding principle behind the last major refurbishment of the interior was the restoration of the choir to something like its original form. This work was funded in 1908 by the shipping magnate Sir Donald Currie as a thank-you to the parish minister's daughter who had tended him through a serious illness. A number of military flags and plaques now decorate the walls, including one in memory of a former parish minister who drowned in the wreck of the *Forfarshire* in 1838, in spite of the heroic efforts of Grace Darling. Behind the impressive oak screen, designed by Sir Robert Lorimer and situated at the east end, is the tomb of the notorious Alexander Stewart, the fourth son of Robert II and better known as the Wolf of Badenoch. For someone who took his revenge on two northern bishops by burning the towns of Forres and Elgin in 1390, he did remarkably well in finding a final resting place in one of the country's foremost cathedrals. Even by the standards of the time he was a voracious womaniser, to the extent, it has been asserted, that almost all the Stewart families in north Perthshire descend from this one man.

One other grave of particular interest, to be found in the ruined section of the cathedral, holds the remains of General Charles Edward Stewart, Count Rochenstart, who claimed to be a grandson of Bonnie Prince Charlie. This unfortunate fellow, the self-styled Last of the Stewarts, died in the town in 1854 following an accident to the carriage in which he had been travelling. Apart from the fact that the Wolf, his supposed ancestral uncle, is also buried here he had no other known connection with the town.

The Chapter House Museum, in a room off the main body of the kirk, has been recently restored by the Friends of Dunkeld Cathedral and now houses an excellent display recounting the history of both the cathedral and the town. A massive wall memorial to John, Marquis of Atholl (who died in 1703), the father of the first duke, occupies a large part of one wall and is surrounded with family coats of arms, each freshly painted in brilliant colour.

Cathedral Street lies on the other side of the splendidly ornate wrought iron gates which, until 1832, used to guard the entrance to the grounds of Dunkeld House, a former home of the Dukes of Atholl. Most of this street consists of the award-winning, white painted 'little houses' which, having been threatened with demolition, were so effectively restored between 1954 and 1965 by the National Trust for Scotland in partnership with Perthshire County Council. In one of these houses, number 9, a nineteenth century premier of Canada, Alexander Mackenzie, spent his early childhood.

A view of Cathedral Street in Dunkeld as seen from the cathedral gates. Their original function as gates to Dunkeld House, a former home of the Dukes of Atholl, is indicated by the ornate letter A at the top.

Perhaps better known nowadays, even in Canada, is the man behind Dunkeld Records, a small shop on the other side of the street. Dougie MacLean in recent years has carved out a reputation as one of Scotland's most popular singer-songwriters, regularly filling concert halls on both sides of the Atlantic. *Caledonia* was a tremendous hit, partly on account of it being the accompaniment to a popular television beer commercial. His wife Jenny provides the artwork for his album covers and her paintings frequently grace the shop window.

The other end of Cathedral Street opens out onto the bell-shaped High Street with The Cross, dedicated to the memory of the 6th Duke, occupying a prominent position at the wider end.

There are several buildings of note here, including the Ell Shop (deriving its name from the measuring gauge dated 1706 attached to the outside wall), the Duchess Anne (a former girls school erected by the wife of the 6th Duke in 1851), and the Museum of the Scottish Horse Regiment. The 8th Duke was behind the raising of this regiment which originally recruited amongst Scotsmen living in South Africa at the time of the Boer War. Having fought in that and in the two world wars the regiment was amalgamated with the Fife and Forfar Yeomanry in 1956.

Virtually nothing of the old town, apart from the cathedral, survived the horrendous events of the Battle of Dunkeld in 1689. This took place a month after Bonnie Dundee's victory at Killiecrankie when a Jacobite army of 5000, pushing south towards the open Lowlands of Scotland, came face to face with a 1200-strong contingent of Cameronians, garrisoned at Dunkeld. Heavily out-numbered, the Cameronians only won the day after locking the Highlanders into the houses they had occupied and setting fire to them, thus visiting a dreadful death on the enemy and almost total destruction on the town. Phoenix-like, Dunkeld began to rise from the ashes with the building of the quaint 'little houses' which date from shortly after this time. Dunkeld today is one of the most historic and attractive towns in Perthshire, owing much to its beautiful riverside location and former close associations with the ducal house of Atholl.

The area to the east of Dunkeld, with its concentration of woods and lochs, wildlife and history, is a little-known corner of Perthshire begging to be discovered. There are two reasons for its anonymity. Firstly, it lies almost forgotten between two heavily-used trunk roads, the A9 for Inverness and the north and the A93 for Aberdeen and the north-east; secondly it is effectively cut off from the Perth hinterland by the path of the Tay which, instead of continuing in a generally southerly direction from Dunkeld, suddenly sweeps eastwards towards Meikleour before turning south-west again for Perth. Stormont was the ancient name for this compact corner of the county, and one which still lingers locally in street and pub names as well as in the family of the Earl of Mansfield whose eldest son bears the Viscount Stormont title.

Stormont is traversed latitudinally by two main roads, the A984 which shadows the Tay between Dunkeld and Meikleour, and the more northerly A923 which follows the Highland foothills between

Dunkeld and Blairgowrie. Between them lies one of the loveliest attractions of Stormont, a whole necklace of little lochs threaded by the Lunan Burn which itself flows into the Isla. Here also are a number of small unclassified roads which provide the most enjoyable means of exploring this hidden part of Perthshire.

To continue the tour which began in the preceding chapter, take the A923 out of Dunkeld and then branch off to the right after a mile to skirt the southern side of the Loch of the Lowes. This is the biggest of the Stormont lochs and is best known as one of the few Scottish breeding grounds of the osprey. Reasonably common up until the earlier nineteenth century, the combined effects of egg collecting and recreational shooting eventually took their toll and by the early 1900s these magnificent birds had ceased altogether to breed in this country. It was only in the late 1950s that ospreys again attempted to breed in Scotland, at Boat of Garten in Inverness-shire. And perhaps as a result of some avian sense of safe haven they chose in 1969 to settle at the Loch of the Lowes, only weeks after the nature reserve had been established. Here, beside a shallow loch with a plentiful supply of fish and with surrounding tall trees ideal for nesting, they found a comfortable home.

The Scottish Wildlife Trust owns and runs the nature reserve and provides excellent facilities for viewing the nesting birds. Right on the shore of the loch and partially hidden by tree foliage they have constructed a simple two-storey hide well equipped with binoculars and benches where, if it is not too busy, the keen ornithologist can watch to his heart's content. Further back from the water's edge an exhibition centre presents a series of informative displays. The other main activity of the staff and their team of volunteers is to provide a round the clock nest watch to prevent the eggs from being stolen. Although such raids are infrequent the thieves have been known to plan their work with some care. Genuine bird watchers should also plan their visit with care as the ospreys are rarely in residence much before the end of March or after the middle of September.

The only access to the loch, apart from via the visitor centre, is along its southern side, where cars can be tucked into any of the small lay-bys which are only yards from the water's edge. Continuing along this road towards Clunie, it is worth making a short detour north to the A923 from where a steep and narrow road leads up the lower slopes of the Forneth Braes to the farm of Over Forneth.

From this quiet spot you can drink in one of the most outstanding views of central Perthshire. Fields of golden summer corn slope away to reveal below the deep green of the woods, the brilliant blue of the lochs, and a dusty yellow patchwork of fields. The distant horizon is formed in the east by the uneven profile of the Sidlaws and, swinging round to the west, by the level ridge of the Ochils and the more rugged southern Highlands. The near perfection of the scene makes it easier to ignore the line of electricity pylons crossing the foreground!

The hamlet of Clunie lies at the heart of Stormont, its small size and apparent absence of any ancient building belying its historical significance. Yet the clues are there. The mausoleum-type structure in the churchyard incorporates a Romanesque doorway which dates from the late twelfth or early thirteenth century and would presumably have belonged to one of the earlier churches on this site. The present church building, with its elaborately decorated finials, dates from the nineteenth century and has recently been threatened with closure. The churchyard itself contains a number of fine memorials including several tablestone graves and some interesting carvings. Leaving the church and heading towards the loch, a second glance at the hill immediately to the right will reveal the site of a royal castle, one of the earliest to be constructed of stone in this part of Perthshire. It was built in around 1141, possibly as a base for hunting in the nearby royal forest of Clunie, and although it has long since been demolished the level top and terracing around it can still be seen. Beyond the castle, in the middle of the loch, lies a small island on which, surrounded by trees, are the ruins of the sixteenth century tower house of the bishops of Dunkeld. The last pre-Reformation bishop, Robert Crichton, rightly fearing the imminent confiscation of his Clunie lands, had them conveyed as a long-term loan to his relation, Robert Crichton of Eliock. Thus it was that the latter Robert's son, James, better known as the Admirable Crichton, spent his early childhood on the island. With its crannog origins the island has had a long history of human habitation and, as an early historical source suggests, may perhaps have been an important political or ecclesiastical centre in the Dark Ages.

The tranquillity of the loch owes much to its position away from the road and the lack of obvious access to it. Whereas on a hot Saturday afternoon in high summer the 'quiet' side of Loch

Earn will be crawling with traffic searching, usually without success, for a peaceful picnic spot, the empty grassy banks of Clunie Loch, overlooking waters lazily dotted with water lilies and swans, provide a haven of peace.

From Clunie the itinerary turns south-west towards the great Roman legionary fortress of Inchtuthil on the north bank of the Tay. Aerial photos reveal with some clarity the layout of the external fortifications and even some of the internal buildings, but unfortunately little can be seen nowadays at ground level. In spite of the thorough post-war excavation and all the subsequent reports and learned articles the single find which caught the attention of the public was the hoard of almost 900,000 iron nails, which had been buried during the evacuation of the camp probably to prevent them from falling into the hands of the native tribes. These nails still turn up occasionally at local auctions.

Two miles to the north-east of Inchtuthil can be found the Cleaven Dyke, a remarkable earthwork once thought to have been built as a line of demarcation between Roman and native authority. While radiocarbon dating has finally assigned it to a period no later than 3600 BC, firmly in Neolithic times, its purpose remains even more of an enigma. Consisting of a low earth wall, almost a mile in length, running between two shallow ditches about 50 yards apart, its very size and antiquity make it an archaeological site worth visiting. It is best approached by the pathway leading from Carsie Road in the village of Meikleour, along which a ten minute walk through the woods will lead you to the Dyke, visible in a large clearing on the left.

Meikleour itself was described in a publication of 1883 as one of the most beautiful villages of Perthshire and, while this may be regarded as a slight exaggeration today, it is still an attractive settlement. It was once a local centre of some importance, boasting three cattle fairs a year, a tron for the weighing of wool and, as visible reminders of the need for fair trading, a whipping post and jougs (iron collars attached to a stone pillar). The only surviving clue to its historic past, still *in situ*, is the weathered late seventeenth century village cross outside the post office.

Today Meikleour is best known for its beech hedge which runs for 600 yards alongside the A93 and which, according to the *Guinness Book of Records*, is the tallest hedge in the world, rising to a height of between 80 and 120 feet. The precise height, of course, depends on the date of the last trim, an operation which, if complicated nowadays, was decidedly hazardous a century ago. The process required foresters in those days to strap themselves to near the top of the hedge and then flail around with a billhook in the direction of the highest branches; by contrast, the 1988 trim engaged the skills of five men and required an aerial platform with a reach of 150 feet and a budget of around £16,000. According to tradition the building of the wall in front of the hedge was interrupted by the uprising of 1745 when a number of workmen rallied to the Jacobite cause. The hedge, it is believed, was planted the following year and was well-tended for the first 40 or 50 years of its life. Thereafter it was allowed to grow wild until its increasing obstruction of the main road necessitated some remedial action by the estate foresters. It is quite possible that at this time the height of the hedge was already becoming a tourist attraction.

Hidden on the other side and beautifully situated by the banks of the Tay is Meikleour House, home of the Marquis of Lansdowne. Architecturally, the house is a mixture of styles, the original Georgian mansion having been extended and given a continental air by the addition of roofs which would have been more appropriate on a Loire chateau. Since 1362 the lands of Meikleour have belonged to the Mercers, one of the oldest of Perthshire families. They entered recorded history in the later thirteenth century at a time when they were already influential burgesses of Perth, the antiquity of the family being hinted at in the saying that 'the Mercers aye are aulder than auld Perth'. Long distinguished in a variety of fields, from civic and national government to diplomatic and military service, it is a little surprising that the family only allied itself to the ranks of the aristocracy in the second half of the eighteenth century when the daughter of Colonel William Mercer married Viscount Keith.

At the southern-most point of the beech hedge a small road bears off west, crossing the Tay, and entering a part of Perthshire once known as West Stormont. Having the shape of an inverted triangle, its bounds are roughly defined by the Tay along the top and right-hand sides, by the A9 along the left, and by the mouth of the Almond at the bottom. It is an area characterised by quiet roads, peaceful farmland and woods, generally low-lying but with an area of higher ground, the Muir of Thorn, in the north-western corner. The villages of Luncarty, Stanley, Bankfoot and Murthly are arranged around the perimeter.

Bankfoot, so named from its position at the foot of this rising ground, is clearly visible from the new A9 where traffic on this long incline can suddenly slow to a crawl. To the south-west of the village is the estate of Tullybelton, birthplace of Robert Nicoll, a lad of great but unfulfilled poetic talent whose early death places him on a par with Kinross-shire's Michael Bruce and England's Thomas Chatterton. He was born in 1814 and by the age of 13 was the *Perthshire Advertiser's* chief correspondent in Bankfoot. As he grew into adulthood he developed an interest in politics and at the age of 22, a year before he died, was appointed one of the first editors of the popular radical newspaper, the *Leeds Times*. His poetry gained a wide readership after his death and only then was a monument erected to his memory near the place of his birth.

Stanley, situated on a stretch of the Tay where the river doglegs between high wooded banks, is one of Perthshire's planned villages, dating in conception from the early 1780s. Its English name derives from the Stanley family, Earls of Derby, who were related through marriage to the Dukes of Atholl, the owners of the land on which the village was built. The village in fact was a secondary consideration, the main project being the new cotton mill which was set up by the 4th Duke in consortium with Richard Arkwright (a pioneer of mechanised spinning) and a few local businessmen. As the cotton industry at this time was booming in the west and spreading ever nearer to the linen stronghold of the east, the construction of such a large mill must have been regarded as a reasonably safe entrepreneurial gamble. Although Arkwright quickly bowed out it was a generally successful venture which became the main employer in the area for over 200 years. In 1989 the machinery stopped for the last time and the whole complex turned overnight from a mill into a metaphoric millstone. The company briefly investigated the possibility of converting the huge six-storey building into flats and when this fell through a public enquiry was held to discuss its future. Following a major fire in the summer of 1995 Historic Scotland stepped in and, with National Lottery funding being made available, plans are now being drawn up to preserve this important piece of Scotland's industrial heritage.

The village of Murthly lies along the top edge of the afore-mentioned triangle, on the south bank of the Tay. It deserves a

The Stanley Mill complex, viewed from the opposite bank of the Tay, is currently being renovated by Historic Scotland with the help of National Lottery funding. One of the early discoveries, which caused much excitement amongst industrial archaeologists, was a pit about 36 feet deep which housed one of the original water wheels.

particular mention, if not for having the former county mental hospital nearby, then at least for being the seat of one of the most colourful of nineteenth century landowners. The Murthly estates in 1615 came into the possession of the Stewarts of Grandtully, a family distinguished in the nineteenth century by acts of recklessness, bravery and Bohemian romanticism. In 1826 the grounds around Murthly Castle witnessed new building work which, according to family legend, sprang from a wager between Sir John Stewart, the 6th Baronet, and the Marquis of Breadalbane as to who could build the better castle. If better was to be equated with bigger then the marquis, still building the new Taymouth Castle, was on a fairly safe bet. Perhaps Sir John realised this and lost heart for his New Castle was never completed. The unfinished shell was eventually demolished in 1949, leaving the old castle, part of which dates from the fourteenth century or even earlier, to enjoy its return to the splendid isolation of former times.

Sir John's younger brother, William Drummond Stewart, having been denied financial help from the family, consequently went out to North America in 1832 to make his fortune. He became a skilled hunter and survived several years in the Wild West, returning in 1839, following the death of his brother, to claim his estate and concomitant wealth. There arrived with him in Murthly two North American Indians, eight buffalo and one grizzly bear, which, at a time when Indians were regarded by European civilisation as little more than savages, must have caused something of a stir locally. Stewart's carefully cultivated image of a wild Scottish cowboy, with overtones of gunslinging and shoot-outs at the Och-Aye Corral, is at odds with the devout Catholicism of the inner man. Whilst in America he fell seriously ill and was nursed back to health by Jesuits. As a result of this he was baptised into the Roman Catholic faith in 1837 and in 1846, having returned to Murthly, built the Chapel of St Anthony the Eremite. Tragically, one of the first services held in this richly decorated building was the funeral of William's younger brother, Thomas, who had become a Benedictine monk and who had been murdered overseas just prior to the chapel's opening. William himself died in 1871 and was also buried in the chapel. His son, George, was a survivor of the famous Thin Red Line at the Battle of Balaclava in 1854, and three years later, having participated in the Relief of Lucknow in India, was one of the earliest recipients of the Victoria Cross. George died in mysterious circumstances before his father, possibly as a result of a sword-swallowing experiment which had gone drastically wrong or as a result of a duel. No-one seems to know.

Recrossing the Tay and four miles south of Meikleour, sandwiched between the river and the A93, lies Stobhall, the ancestral home of the Drummonds. As the true origins of this great Perthshire family will probably never be uncovered, the romantic story of legend will have to suffice. Margaret, the bride-to-be of Malcolm Canmore, arrived in Scotland in 1068 in the company of a group of Hungarian noblemen (Margaret's mother was Agatha of Hungary and Margaret herself had been brought up at the Hungarian court), one of whom, Maurice, possibly a grandson of King Andrew of Hungary, was granted the lands of Drymen in Stirlingshire. Authorities on Scottish surnames tend to agree that the name Drummond derives from this placename. By 1384, however, the Drummonds had moved north-east to Perthshire and were in possession of the estates of Cargill and Stobhall. A century later, in 1487, Sir John Drummond was elevated to the peerage as the first Lord Drummond and immediately began work on the construction of Drummond Castle, a more prestigious seat which is situated near Muthill to the south of Crieff. Following the completion of the castle in the 1490s Stobhall became a satellite of the Drummond estates, acting for some time as a dower house for the widows of deceased lords and later as a home for the estate factor. Jacobite revolution and female succession then conspired to place both Drummond Castle and Stobhall in the hands of the Earls of Ancaster. In 1954 the 3rd Earl sold Stobhall to the present head of the Drummond family, the Earl of Perth, who has since carried out the restoration of the buildings.

The strategic setting of Stobhall, on a high ridge overlooking the Tay, would admirably lend itself to that of a Scottish baronial castle. In contrast, the open plan arrangement of four separate buildings around a courtyard, one of which is a chapel, gives Stobhall an unmistakably monastic air. The chapel is probably the oldest surviving building, dating from the fourteenth or fifteenth centuries, and is the proud possessor of a splendidly painted ceiling which, although heavily repainted in 1858, is believed to have been originally completed in 1642. The dower house provided the main living accommodation, while the other buildings were used for a variety of domestic purposes ranging from a brew-house and bakery to a kitchen and laundry.

A mile beyond Stobhall a road to the right, signposted to Stormontfield, provides a pleasant and quiet alternative to the traffic of the A93. Those with an interest in ecclesiastical history should pause at the farm of Cambusmichael where a track leads through the steading to the now ruined church of the same name. Perched high above the Tay, it began life in the twelfth century as a chapel attached to Scone Abbey, achieving the status of a parish church in the fifteenth. Despite being a ruin for around 300 years, many of the original features can still be seen, including the small round-arched doorway and the lower sections of several of the windows. The ivy-smothered gable ends, the sounds of the river beyond the trees and the occasional visit by deer create an impression of a holy spot now completely forgotten by man. On the way back to the farm a steep path on the left leads down to the riverside and the best possible view of the huge Stanley Mill complex on the opposite bank.

South of Cambusmichael the road, originally Roman, follows a reasonably straight course towards the villages of Stormontfield

The ruined mediaeval church of Cambusmichael stands above the Tay opposite Stanley Mill, seemingly losing its battle against the encroaching vegetation. Like many other churches dedicated to St Michael it enjoys an elevated situation.

and Colenhaugh. The latter is a new settlement which revives the old pre-nineteenth century name for Stormontfield, and is an excellent example of how well-planned modern housing can result in a particularly attractive hamlet. Near here, in 1853 and lasting over several years, a major experiment in salmon farming began which caught the attention of piscatologists throughout Europe. Such an enterprise is quite taken for granted nowadays so it is with some surprise that one reads in contemporary accounts of the genuine amazement that living creatures could be sown and harvested in much the same way as a field of corn. Similar investigations on a lesser scale had taken place in France a few years earlier, but it was only as a result of the Stormontfield experiments that proof finally emerged to show that parr (young salmon which have not yet ventured out into the open sea) and full-grown salmon (which have returned from the sea to their original spawning grounds) were indeed the same fish. Only a few years previously such a suggestion had been thought ridiculous. While the specially constructed fish tanks are still marked on

The Waulkmill ferry, three miles upstream from Perth, viewed from the west bank of the Tay. The ferry operated until 1964 although, with passengers becoming increasingly scare, the County Council latterly had to pay the ferryman's weekly wage (© Dr W H Findlay).

current Ordnance Survey maps (although by all accounts they are sadly overgrown) the barrier across the access road suggests that visitors, other than those on foot, may not be entirely welcome.

Past Stormontfield the road edges again towards the river. The old ferryman's cottage still stands at Waulkmill, just off this road, complete with a table of charges dated 1920 occupying a large part of one wall. For much of the seventeenth and eighteenth centuries Perth itself had been served by two ferries, one at the east end of the High Street and the other, the Kincarrathie ferry, at the north end of the North Inch. The opening of the Perth Bridge in 1771 made these both redundant, leaving the Waulkmill ferry as the only means of crossing the river between Perth and Stanley. Remarkably, it continued in operation until 1964. There is an attractive walk from Waulkmill, following the river south to the Scone Palace race course and skirting on the left the site of the Roman marching camp at Grassy Walls.

River frontages and stately homes go well together and while Scone Palace may sit slightly back from the Tay the grounds extend as far as the river. The ancient abbey of Scone originally occupied the site and it was very near to the abbey ruins, destroyed in 1559, that the first Scone Palace was built. The second and present building was constructed in the early years of last century to a design by William Atkinson, he who later planned part of Taymouth Castle near Kenmore. The palace is unquestionably a large dwelling yet architecturally it sits lightly amid its acres of parkland and even with the crenellations has a warm and open countenance, quite unlike the almost aggressive bulk of Taymouth. Outwardly Gothic in detail, with pointed arches over windows and doors and splendid vaulting supporting some of the interior ceilings, the spirit of the building has not strayed far from the classical ideals of balance and proportion. The palace is open to the public between the spring and autumn of each year and should be on the list of essential sights of any visitor to, or indeed resident of, Perthshire. Particularly rich in its holdings of ivories, porcelain, and French furniture, it also had until recently a magnificent collection of Vernis-Martin ware which was considered to be virtually unsurpassed in this country, if not in the world. It had been acquired in the mid-eighteenth century during the 2nd Earl's appointment as British ambassador to France (much of eighteenth century British diplomacy was in fact handled by Scots), at a time when the lacquer work of the Martin brothers was at the height of its popularity. Unfortunately a large proportion of the collection was stolen in a well-planned burglary in 1994 and although the thieves were caught shortly afterwards the pieces themselves have never been recovered.

The rise of the Mansfields dates back to 1600 when Sir David Murray, who shared common ancestry with the Murray Dukes of Atholl, helped to protect James VI during the events of the Gowrie Conspiracy. The official (or royal) version would have us believe that Murray first calmed an angry Perth crowd, baying for blood following the death of their popular provost, the Earl of Gowrie, and then spirited the king out of the town and safely back to Falkland. His loyalty was formally recognised in 1605 when he was granted the title of Lord Scone and invested with large estates, some of which had previously belonged to the Earl of Gowrie. As these included sizeable parts of Stormont, Murray took that name when he was created a viscount in 1621.

Scone Palace, viewed here from the south, has been home to the Murray family, Earls of Mansfield, for almost 400 years. The building dates in its present form from early last century and with its rich decoration and furnishing is one of the finest stately homes in Perth and Kinross.

In the palace in 1705, exactly a century after that first elevation to the peerage, the wife of the 5th Viscount gave birth to a son, William, who was destined to become one of the towering figures of the eighteenth century English legal establishment. He began his studies at the Grammar School in Perth where his early promise prompted his father to send him to London to further his education at Westminster School. Never again did he set foot in Scotland. An eloquent speaker, the 'silver-tongued Murray' was called to the bar at the age of 25 and quickly rose through the ranks of his profession to become Solicitor-General in 1742, Attorney-General two years later and in 1756 Lord Chief Justice of England. This last-mentioned appointment was accompanied on the same day by his ennoblement as Baron Mansfield in the county of Nottingham, a title formerly held by his friend and political ally, the Duke of Newcastle, who may have suggested he adopt it. In 1776 he was advanced another two steps up the aristocratic ladder by his grant of the earldom of the same name. In the last months of his life, however, a misinterpretation of the law of succession resulted in him being recreated the Earl of Mansfield in the county of Middlesex, and to this day the present holder is referred to in *Burke's Peerage* as the Earl of Mansfield and Mansfield.

The 1st Earl died in 1793 and, at his own request, was buried in Westminster Abbey. He had given judgment in a number of well-known cases, perhaps the most contentious centring on the negro slave, James Sommersett. This poor fellow had been bought in Virginia, subsequently sent to England and had then made a bid for freedom by running away. On his recapture, and on the point of being shipped out to Jamaica in chains, his case — and with it the whole question of whether slaves could lawfully be kept in England — came before Lord Mansfield. His judgment, in 1772, that the very idea of slavery was so repugnant that it could only be legal if a law existed to say so (and no such law existed), resulted in the liberation of around 15,000 negroes, including Sommersett, and was a major step towards the eventual abolition of that inhuman practice.

Almost nothing can now be seen of the Royal City of Scone, which a thousand years ago was one of the most important settlements in the country. It had already been an important town to the Picts, prior to their subsumption by the Scots of Dalriada, and in the ninth century, with the Stone of Destiny at its heart, became the chief town in the newly enlarged kingdom. With the founding by Alexander I of an Augustinian monastery in the early twelfth century Scone, in terms of status, must have enjoyed an aura of virtual impregnability. But it was not destined to last. The first indication of waning influence came in around 1125 when nearby Perth was granted the rights and privileges of a royal burgh. This was doubtless because the Tay was (and is) navigable as far as Perth and water in those days provided the quickest and most effective means of transport and communication. Certainly by 1209, the date of the earliest surviving charter, Perth had become a thriving commercial town.

If Scone was thus becoming marginalised in a kingdom where trade was assuming an ever greater importance, it suffered a second assault on its esteem in 1296 when Edward I of England removed the famous stone to Westminster Abbey. With it, in the minds of the Scots, went the very symbol of the nation's sovereignty as well as the confidence and stability of the Scottish monarchy itself. Kings continued successively to be inaugurated here up until

1424 (James I), the setting of the ancient ceremony having to suffice in the absence of the historic stone. The coronation of the exiled Charles II in 1651, while Cromwell ruled supreme in England, was the last to take place at Scone.

The third and final blow to Scone was the destruction of the abbey in 1559 by a mob of religious reformers, incited, it is said, by a colourful metaphor attributed to John Knox that 'the best way to keep the rooks from returning was to pull down their nests'. For the next two and a half centuries Scone withdrew into itself, overshadowed by a town which in turn was being overtaken in size and prestige by Edinburgh. The final indignity, following the construction of the new Scone Palace, was the removal of the village to its present site, a mile or so to the east, to allow the proper landscaping of the palace grounds. The old stone gateway and the village cross were left in position, where they can still be seen, prompting the remark that while it was not uncommon for a village to lose its cross, it was somewhat unusual for a cross to lose its village.

In under two centuries New Scone, with a population in 1991 of just over 4500, has blossomed into the fourth largest settlement in Perth and Kinross, behind only Perth, Blairgowrie and Crieff. Indeed, because it has never had a town council (although it has all the facilities of a prosperous small town), it has been called the largest village in Scotland. Apart from the hazards of the busy A94 and the absence of an historic centre, it is a pleasant place to live, as many of the working population of Perth will testify.

The high profile which Perthshire has enjoyed within the history of the nation owes much to the priceless relics which Kenneth MacAlpin brought over from the west. Neither Columba's bones nor the Stone of Destiny remained here for long, yet without them Dunkeld and Scone could not have become the main centres, albeit briefly, of ecclesiastical and political power within the kingdom. Columba was undoubtedly a remarkable man — a man of royal blood, of courage, vision and holiness, whose biography by Adamnan turned him into arguably the greatest figure in the history of the Scottish church. Without the miracle stories few indeed would have made the pilgrimage to Dunkeld.

In a similar way, the immense pulling power of the stone, even today, stems not just from its use in the inauguration ceremonies of Scottish kings but from the legends which link it, through thousands of years and over thousands of miles, with the stone which the Biblical Jacob used as a pillow. Considering the significance of this precious relic, it is difficult to play down the frequently made point that the stone recently returned to Scotland from Westminster Abbey may not be the real one. Is there any reason to suppose that thirteenth century Scots, when faced with imminent invasion, would not send national treasures away from the capital to places of comparative safety, as indeed their twentieth century counterparts did during World War II? The simple fact that the stone which now lies in state in Edinburgh Castle consists of old red sandstone, the rock-type predominantly found in Lowland Perthshire, suggests strongly that it is indeed a thirteenth century copy. Or perhaps even a twentieth century copy. Over Christmas 1950 the stone was repossessed (I refrain from using the word 'stolen' as the police, rather wisely in view of the events of 1296, never pressed charges of theft) in an audacious raid by four Glasgow University students. A stone which satisfied the Abbey authorities was recovered shortly after, but rumours abounded that once again this was only a copy which was allowed to be found. Meanwhile, what may have been the real stone was apparently found in an underground vault on Dunsinane Hill in 1818 and sent to London for analysis. Judging by reports of its discovery it bears comparison with descriptions of the mediaeval stone; unfortunately it disappeared somewhere on its way to the capital and no-one will admit openly to having seen it since. All things considered, Edward I has a lot to answer for. The pedigree of the stone which was used in the coronation of the present queen in 1953 can only go back with reasonable certainty to 1951. And the real stone? No-one knows, but perhaps after seven hundred years it is still waiting to be rediscovered beneath the sweeping lawns of Scone Palace.

CHAPTER 12

HIGHLAND PERTHSHIRE

An attempt at defining the boundaries of the three historic divisions of Highland Perthshire, namely Atholl, Breadalbane and Rannoch, is the equivalent of not only sticking one's head in the lion's mouth but sending him an invitation to dinner as well. The problem is well illustrated by the fact that Aberfeldy, known as the capital of Breadalbane, is, according to an authoritative source, quite definitely not in Breadalbane. It has also led one recent writer to suggest that Pitlochry marks Atholl's southern boundary, by which definition the historic centre of administration (at Logierait) was several miles outside. And no-one seems to be sure about the status of Rannoch, whether it is still properly a part of Atholl, as it once was, or if it has evolved into an 'independent' region in its own right. These uncertainties are further compounded by the flexibility of the Atholl and Breadalbane estate boundaries which conformed only loosely to those of the ancient regions. Confused? Most people are. Suffice it to say that Atholl occupies the north and east of Highland Perthshire, Breadalbane the south and west, and Rannoch the far north-west. In broad terms Schiehallion conveniently acts as a cornerstone for all three.

The distance between the eastern and western boundaries of Highland Perthshire is in the region of 50 miles and the scenery in this swathe of upland becomes richer and more conventionally Highland the further west one travels. Atholl is characterised by smoother-topped mountains set amid wide heathery moorland while Breadalbane possesses the slightly higher, more rugged peaks and the largest Perthshire loch. Rannoch is a huge basin formed by the mountains of Breadalbane, Badenoch and Glencoe and which has two contrasting types of landscape centred around the loch and the moor.

The quickest way to get from Perth to the north of the county is to travel up the A9, a generally fast combination of single and dual carriageway which can nevertheless be reduced to a virtual crawl by summer caravans, autumn tractors and winter snow, particularly on the approach to Drumochter. The Scottish Office, after several years of pressure from local authorities, still declines to upgrade it to full dual carriageway status. Even so, for a modern road, it passes through some splendid countryside with the afforested hills around Dunkeld providing a theatrical curtain behind which lies the dramatic spectacle of the Perthshire Highlands.

North of Dunkeld, just after the exit for the Hermitage, the B898 turns off the A9 and heads at a more leisurely pace towards Aberfeldy. This pretty and quiet road has Craigvinean Forest on the left and good open views of the Tay valley on the right. Two miles beyond Kinnaird a road to the right leads into the village of Logierait which, along with the seemingly equally insignificant villages of Dull, Weem and Moulin, has little to indicate its former importance. It is a curious fact that today the main towns of Highland Perthshire, Aberfeldy and Pitlochry, are of comparatively recent development while the former centres of authority are now almost forgotten, surviving only as small villages and in parish names.

Logierait and not Blair Atholl was for many years the seat of justice in the regality of Atholl, the village being situated at the confluence of the Tay and the Tummel and reasonably central to the whole of the Atholl domain. The courthouse no longer survives but was reckoned to be over 70 feet in length and in its time one of the finest buildings in the county. The regality prison stood close to the village inn and many an unfortunate Highland thief would have breathed his last on the nearby gallows tree. The churchyard, lying between the large cream-coloured church of 1805 on one side and the quiet waters of the Tay on the other, has a number of interesting old gravestones and in a little stone enclosure three iron mort-safes. These metal cages, presumably covering the graves of a young child and its parents, were intended to prevent the theft of the bodies by resurrectionists in the early nineteenth century. At the west end of the village is the former Atholl, Weem and Breadalbane Poorhouse, a supposedly haunted and still forbidding building in spite of its mellow stone walls but which has now been turned into a much happier Childhood Heritage Centre. It is well stocked with toys and memorabilia of former times and being a little off the beaten track needs public support.

Following the Tay upstream the A827 proceeds west from Logierait and, passing several small sporting estates, arrives at Grandtully, an historic village known for its nearby pre-Reformation church and castle. The latter was a former stronghold of the

Stewarts of Grandtully, a family now represented by the Steuart-Fothringhams of Murthly Castle. By crossing the Tay at Grandtully and looking down at the foaming rapids and the markers suspended above, one can see why the village has been described as the finest centre for natural slalom and white water canoeing in the United Kingdom.

The bridge leads uphill to Strathtay, a lovely little village which has appropriated to itself the name of a wider area stretching along the north bank of the Tay between Aberfeldy and Logierait. The lands of Strathtay are as attractive as the village, and the undulating road, which is much prettier than the main approach to Aberfeldy, looks down on a cool, dark Tay, bordered by dense woodland. The Himalayan gardens of Cluny House are situated high above (600 feet above sea level to be precise) and are worth a little detour, particularly in early summer when the garden is at its best. Here you will find Tibetan cherry trees, a fine collection of Asiatic primulas, an extensive woodland walk and a bog garden, all of which have been created over the past fifty years out of a virtually empty field.

A little further on and the appearance on the left of a golf course and an intriguingly modern footbridge, apparently the first bridge in the world to be made of fibreglass, indicates the proximity of Aberfeldy. By turning sharp left at the junction with the B846 and then proceeding along an avenue once lined with tall poplars, planted in 1897 to mark Queen Victoria's diamond jubilee, one can cross the Wade Bridge and make an almost triumphal entry into the town. The bridge was designed by the architect William Adam and completed in 1733. Despite Adam's reputation as one of the greatest Scottish architects of his time the design of the bridge, with the two rather odd and certainly superfluous pillars at each end, was not universally admired. This apart, it was for many years the only bridge over the Tay and was thus as important to Wade's network of military roads as it was to the travelling public of north-central Scotland.

The pleasant grassy area on the Aberfeldy side of the bridge is dominated by the huge Black Watch Memorial which commemorates the first mustering of the regiment in 1740 but not the actual spot; as the staff of Castle Menzies will gently point out, this took place on Menzies land on the opposite bank. The Black Watch, perhaps surprisingly in view of its outwardly Highland character, developed from a number of independent companies charged with keeping

The kilted figure of Farquhar Shaw stands resolutely against the Aberfeldy sky. The Black Watch Memorial, one of the most impressive of Perthshire monuments, was erected in 1887 at a cost of around £500, a huge sum for the time. Special trains brought people in for the opening ceremony from as far away as Edinburgh and Glasgow.

an eye on potentially troublesome Jacobite clans and was therefore initially a tool of the London government. Loyalties were quickly changed, however, when in 1743 the regiment was lured south of the border and almost sent overseas. Having been promised on enlistment (or so they genuinely believed) that they would never be required to serve outside Scotland over 100 of the men abandoned their officers and headed north again, only to be rounded up and court-marshalled. Three of their number were eventually executed on Tower Hill and the rest sent abroad, a shameful episode which two years later did little to endear the Highland Perthshire population to the Hanoverian cause. The figure of the great kilted Highlander on top of the memorial is believed to represent Farquhar Shaw, one of those shot.

In common with other Scottish regiments the Black Watch was at the forefront of British colonialism in the later eighteenth and early nineteenth centuries, fighting with honour in America, India, Africa and Europe, and thus contributing in no small measure (from a Hanoverian viewpoint) to the reappraisal of the Highlander as hero rather than rebel. Of the many battle honours inscribed on the Aberfeldy monument the name of Ticonderoga is associated with the following ghost story which features with minor variations in several regimental histories. Whilst out walking on Ben Cruachan in Argyll in the summer of 1755, Major Duncan Campbell of Inverawe chanced upon a fugitive who begged to be sheltered from his pursuers. Campbell agreed to protect the man and promised not to reveal his whereabouts. Learning shortly afterwards that the man had just killed his (Campbell's) foster-brother, Campbell was trapped by his honour into saying nothing. His silence understandably incurred the wrath of the murdered man's ghost who in vain tried to persuade him to divulge his secret. In the end, the murderer having slipped away, the ghost too departed with the prophetic words, 'Farewell, Inverawe, till we meet at Ticonderoga', a name which at the time meant nothing to Campbell. Three years later, and by this time serving in America, Campbell was again visited by the ghost who revealed that the place where he was presently stationed, Fort Carillon, was known to the native population as Ticonderoga. With horror Campbell suddenly foresaw his fate and announced to his colleagues that he was certain to die that day in battle which is exactly what happened. An earlier version of the story, however, mentioned almost in passing by David Stewart of Garth, has an unnamed colleague of Campbell as the subject of the story and gives the names of the officers to whom he recounted his premonition. Unlike many ghost stories there appears to be an element of truth in it.

Whatever shades may haunt the monument by night the town of Aberfeldy by day is as lively and bustling as any popular holiday centre should be. The sights of Aberfeldy are well distributed through the town, with the bridge and monument at the north end, a distillery at the east end and the famous Birks o Aberfeldy at the south. At the heart of the town is The Square where a number of roads meet and where most of the shops are to be found. Leading off The Square is the entrance to the Birks, a beautiful woodland walk which appears to end rather abruptly but which, after a short interlude along a metalled road, is continued in the 'Big Birks'. There is a large car park here, several picnic tables and at the far end the Falls of Moness which were somewhat pedantically, if not lazily, described by Pennant as 'an epitome of every thing that can be admired in…waterfalls'. Burns a few years later did a better job in his eponymous poem though this appears to have been adapted in part from the earlier song, the Birks o Abergeldie (in Aberdeenshire), to which tune the Bard's words more or less fit.

The town, without denigrating Blairgowrie's role as host to the Royal National Mod in 1996, is one of the last enduring outposts of Gaelic culture in Perthshire. At least one native speaker of the much maligned Perthshire Gaelic still survives (in spite of press reports a few years ago to the contrary) and more will doubtless remember common phrases learnt at a grandmother's knee. Standard Gaelic, in its supposedly purer form of the West Highlands, is taught at Breadalbane Academy and a peripatetic teacher travels round the feeder primary schools to prepare those who wish to pursue it. In the early summer of each year the Perthshire and Angus Provincial Mod is held in the town and gives the residents of north Perthshire, and further afield, young and old, a chance to polish their Gaelic or to perform on the fiddle, accordion and pipes.

The Tourist Information Centre is situated in The Square and shares a building with Locus Breadalbane Ltd, a community company which has its roots in the 1970s and which even today seems ahead of its time. As one of the founders told me, it aims to look at Highland Perthshire in a holistic way through encouraging business and tourism while at the same time fostering the environment and the culture of the area. Tourists were not seen as walking purses to be dipped into as they passed through, an attitude which was felt to demean and abuse both sides of the economic equation, but rather as visitors who would be encouraged to return as friends. This alternative approach to managing a local economy may sound idealised and unworkable, but the fact that it has been mirrored in other ventures and featured in prestigious economic journals is testimony to its success.

Locus, in fact, is just one of several Highland Perthshire organisations which have sprung up in recent years. If the existence of pressure groups can be taken as a sign of something under threat then the proliferation of other bodies such as the Highland Perthshire Communities Partnership, the Highland Perthshire Training Company, The Cairngorm Partnership, and many smaller ones, not to mention the new landscape protection designations such as the Loch Rannoch and Glen Lyon National Scenic Area and the Breadalbane Environmentally Sensitive Area, suggests that Highland Perthshire may be living on an economic and environmental knife edge. It is certainly true to say that, while the casual visitor may form the impression that the area is pleasantly well off in a stable, timeless sort of way, the reality of life in Highland Perthshire is the struggle to find decent employment, to stimulate the local economy away from a dependence on tourism, to support and sustain existing businesses and to keep an overall healthy balance of diversity in employment and age groups. When in early 1997 Esso was granted planning permission (after a public enquiry) for a roadside services complex at Broxden near Perth, the outcry from Highland Perthshire, and particularly from businesses close to the A9, was huge, vividly illustrating how a whole community can feel threatened by a single business operation many miles down the road.

The local community magazine, *Atholl and Breadalbane Community Comment,* which in the past has had a loose connection with Locus, provides both detailed coverage of the main issues facing Highland Perthshire and perceptive insights into the local way of life. It is one of the quickest and best ways of finding out what makes Highland Perthshire tick. The contents have ranged from detailed articles on the pros and cons of a proposed barytes mine to an amusing series which poked gentle fun at the 'white settlers' in the area. Buy it if you can. Playing a similar role in the fostering of community spirit is the Pitlochry-based Heartland Radio which itself was pioneered by *ABC Comment*. It has been operating from a corner of the curling rink in Pitlochry since 1992 and claims to be Britain's smallest independent local radio station. The staff are almost entirely volunteers and manage to broadcast for three hours each weekday evening and all day at weekends. Some of its output has been so popular that tapes of programmes have been sent to radio stations as far afield as America and

Australia for broadcasting to the ex-pat community. The continued success of both the magazine and the radio station demonstrates that Highland Perthshire, in spite of the inevitable difficulties which arise from its situation on the margin of the central belt, still has a vibrant life of its own and a strong community spirit, and in no way should be regarded as a moribund backwater of the county.

From Aberfeldy the suggested route recrosses the Wade bridge and returns to Weem, a village which at first sight would appear to have been built around its large hotel. Historic though it may be (part of the building dates from 1527 and another part may have acted as General Wade's headquarters in 1733), the oldest surviving building is actually the Old Kirk which, although rebuilt in around 1500, was traditionally founded by St Cuthbert in the mid-seventh century. In 1836 it ceased to be the parish church and began a new life as the Menzies family mausoleum, which role, being generally bare, gloomy, cold and damp, it performs very well.

The chiefs of Clan Menzies (pronounced 'Mingis' — as with most Scottish names the 'z' is silent, but don't take this too far when trying to find Edinburgh Zoo) have possessed lands in this area from the thirteenth century and chose in 1488, having been burned out of their former stronghold some miles away, to build a new castle on the western side of Weem. It too suffered a similar fate in 1502 (a proficiency at arson obviously being one of the social graces of the time), and the replacement, re-erected some years later, now forms the nucleus of the present structure. Castle Menzies, judging by the thickness of the ground floor walls, was designed to last and has certainly outlived the chiefly family which built it. On the death in 1918 of the last Menzies of the direct line, the clan found itself leaderless and the castle was sold. In 1957, however, the Lord Lyon approved the claim of a distant relation to the chiefship and in that same year the Clan Menzies Society purchased the castle and began the long and expensive process of restoration. Apart from pictures on the walls, a few furnishings and some interesting display material the interior is bare, allowing the visitor to appreciate the true nature of a fortified house beneath the usual patina of domestic furnishings acquired over the centuries. This is a Scottish castle *par excellence* and not a stately home!

Castle Menzies is a difficult act to follow and it is therefore doubly unfortunate that the second village along the road, after Camserney, is signposted Dull. The inhabitants have doubtless endured a lot of leg-pulling but in a sense they have the last laugh as the village enjoys a lovely outlook over the Tay valley and the rich flatlands of Appin of Dull. Appin means 'abbey land' and is just about the only surviving reference, albeit well-disguised, to the great abbey which flourished here in the Middle Ages. Tradition has it that the founder was St Adamnan, who is said to be buried in Dull and who is best known as the hagiographer of St Columba; this may be true as he was active in the area and is remembered in other placenames such as Milton Eonan (Eonan equates with Adamnan) in the heart of Glen Lyon, Ardeonaig on the shores of Loch Tay and Kilmaveonaig near Blair Atholl. Legend tells of how over the centuries the abbey became one of the most important centres of learning in mediaeval Scotland and that it ultimately came under the wing of St Andrews University. There is a belief that until recently a stipend was paid to the incumbent of Dull by St Andrews but neither the archivists nor the financial officers of the university have been able to confirm any such link.

West of Dull the tree-clad Drummond Hill, better known as the lovely wooded backdrop to the village of Kenmore, deflects the road towards the north and a parting of the ways at Coshieville. The main B846, to which we shall return later, climbs northwards in the direction of Tummel Bridge while the left fork leads into Glen Lyon, one of the most beautiful glens in Scotland but tainted by two of the more infamous names in Scottish history, the Wolf of Badenoch and Robert Campbell of Glenlyon. The first of these is Alexander Stewart, better known as the Wolf of Badenoch, whose wicked deeds have been mentioned elsewhere and whose almost impregnable stronghold of Garth Castle, now a private home, lies a mile away from the road high above the Keltneyburn. Beside the bridge, near where the burn joins the Lyon, stands a memorial to the above-mentioned General David Stewart of Garth who, as a descendant of the Wolf and the last Stewart of this particular line, did much to redeem the name. A brilliant and brave officer of the Black Watch he is remembered today for his much sought-after book, *Sketches of the character, manners and present state of the Highlanders of Scotland*, which was first published in 1822 and which gave one of the earliest accounts of Highland life from the perspective of a Highlander.

Fortingall is the next village along the road and the historic centre of one of Scotland's largest civil parishes. Covering an area

These cottages, which one might with good reason have expected to find in the depths of rural England, in fact nestle amid Highland hills in the village of Fortingall. It is testimony to the skill of James MacLaren that his architecture, if unusual, is not out of place.

of over 300 square miles it is bigger than nine of the old Scottish counties and larger than Kinross-shire and Clackmannanshire combined. Many archaeological remains have been discovered in the vicinity of the village, testifying to its antiquity, and yet the overriding impression is one of early twentieth century home counties rather than ancient Highland. The reason for this anomaly lies with the wealthy shipping magnate, Sir Donald Currie, who bought three estates in the neighbourhood of the village in 1885 and immediately set about the business of improvement. He employed the architect James MacLaren who, combining elements from sources as diverse as traditional Scottish architecture and the thatched cottages of Devon, produced a very successful series of buildings in the village. But MacLaren died young and it took almost 80 years for architectural historians to appreciate quite how influential he had been on the early development of Charles Rennie Mackintosh. The curious English-style, rose-bedecked thatched cottages which are such a hallmark of the village are therefore of considerable significance in the annals of Scottish domestic architecture. The cream-coloured hotel and church also date from around this time, the latter containing a seventh-century Celtic hand bell. Currie, a self-made Irishman, MP, friend of Gladstone and public benefactor, died in 1909 and is buried in a family enclosure beside the church.

Fortingall is famous on two further counts, the first one chronologically being the tired old yew which grows behind its protective railings next to the church and which rests its weary limbs on stone walls. Having an estimated age of 3000 years and believed to be one of the oldest living organisms in Europe it first took root at around the time when David was King of Israel and would already have been a mature tree at the time of the traditional founding of Rome. Pennant recorded its girth in 1769 as being an astonishing 56 feet which in a straight line is close to the length of a cricket pitch. Coming forward in time to the start of the Christian era Fortingall is also associated in legend with the birthplace of Pontius Pilate, his father supposedly having been stationed at the nearby Roman camp. Common sense tells us that this is nonsense and the facts back this up; the Romans did not establish a presence north of the Tay until around AD 80 and the earthworks which for centuries were assumed to be Roman are now reckoned to be mediaeval. But the legend itself is remarkable, however little truth may be in it. Who first linked Pilate and Fortingall in one sentence and with enough conviction to make it stick? Was it simply an insult dreamed up by a neighbouring settlement and passed down the generations to show what a wicked place Fortingall was? A little postscript to the story apparently occurred in around 1902 when the church was in the process of restoration; workmen digging in the churchyard found a stone slab several feet down with the initials P.P. inscribed thereon, and this was taken as proof that Pilate had not only been born in the village but had returned there to die.

Immediately to the west of Fortingall the wooded hills on either side of the Lyon rise sharply up to enfold the traveller in the full glory of the glen. It is a breathtakingly beautiful combination of rugged Highland grandeur softened, at least at the eastern end, by old woods and rushing water. Even so, for those with a knowledge of Scottish history there is a stain on the character of the glen which the scenery cannot altogether hide. For Chesthill, three miles west of Fortingall, was home in centuries past to that branch of the Campbell family which took part in the infamous massacre of Glencoe. While contemporary records disprove the legend that the massacre was actually planned here there can be no glossing over the fact that the person charged with carrying out the deed was Captain Robert Campbell of Glenlyon. The letter addressed to him on 12 February 1692 began: 'You are hereby ordered to fall upon the Rebells, the McDonalds of Glenco, and putt all to the sword under seventy. You are to have speciall care that the old Fox and his sones doe upon no account escape your hands. You are to secure all the avenues that no man escape'. The order was executed in barbaric fashion early the following morning and even by seventeenth-century Highland standards was quite indefensible, particularly in view of the hospitality received from the Macdonalds immediately before. In mitigation, however, there had been a history of ill-feeling between the two parties and this may have been the reason why Robert Campbell was selected for the task.

Further into the glen the trees are left behind and the steepness and height of the hills become more evident. South of the river are the lands of Roro, formerly one of the main stamping grounds of the Macgregors whose ghostly presence is also indicated by the well known Macgregor's Leap near Fortingall. The parish church for Glen Lyon is situated at Innerwick and although an ancient foundation the present building only dates from 1828. Inside can be found the 1200 year-old bell of St Adamnan and from the churchyard outside the views along the glen are superb. Finally, at Bridge of Balgie, one begins to appreciate exactly what is involved in exploring Scotland's longest cul-de-sac glen for the end of the road at Loch Lyon is still a further 11 miles distant. Only the most determined of travellers continue towards the bitter end, perhaps on a business excursion to the hydro-electric power stations, perhaps to do a bit of trout fishing on the loch or perhaps to look at the remains of a string of castles built, according to legend, by Fingalian warlords of many centuries ago. If so, they are in for a disappointment as archaeologists have recently shown that the 'castles' were not fortifications at all and were more likely than not to be domestic dwellings dating from the second half of the first millennium AD.

Most travellers, perhaps fortified by a visit to the village tearoom and after admiring the gate lodge to Meggernie Castle, instead cross the bridge and strike out for Loch Tay. The narrow single

track road winds and climbs steeply through some magnificent
Highland Perthshire scenery and is not for the timid driver. There
are few trees here, just miles of heather, rough grass and bracken,
with the hills above and a lonely burn below. Descending from a
height of around 1800 feet the road passes Lochan na Lairige and
the Lawers Dam both of which are towered over to the west by
Meall nan Tarmachan, one of a whole ridge of mountains generally
known as the Tarmachans. These peaks, together with the visually
less impressive Ben Lawers on the east, divide Glen Lyon from
Lochtayside. The car park at the Ben Lawers Visitor Centre, a full
eight miles from Bridge of Balgie, is the recognised starting point
for an assault on the mountain, though there are of course other
routes, while the displays at the centre itself allow one to explore
the area in a less energetic way.

Loch Tay, one of the finest freshwater lochs of Scotland,
gradually comes into view during the descent to the A827, the
main road between Kenmore and Killin along the north side of
the loch. Fourteen and a half miles in length and in places a mile
wide it cuts the shape of an italic 's' across the terrain of Highland
Perthshire. Unlike its siblings on either side, Earn and Rannoch,
serpentine Loch Tay cannot be seen in its entirety from ground
level and indeed in some of the middle stretches it is impossible
to see either end. It lacks the engaging femininity of Loch Earn,
due in part to its sheer size and also to the mainly treeless hills
which give it a harder edge. Neither does it have the intimacy of
Loch Rannoch's north side, its masculine character being compounded by a certain aloofness which keeps the road either high
above or behind a barrier of fields.

The ancient area of Breadalbane, meaning in Gaelic 'the upland
of Alba', lies all around Loch Tay and extends further to the west
to take in glens Dochart, Lochay and Orchy and the towns of
Crianlarich and Tyndrum. Most of Breadalbane used to lie in the
old county of Perthshire but when the western parishes were
transferred to Stirling District in 1975 the new Perth and Kinross
District was left with only the eastern rump. Even a sizeable portion
of Loch Tay itself now comes within the jurisdiction of Stirling.

But long before the existence of county and district councils
Breadalbane was governed by the Campbells, and even though
this once powerful family has vanished from the area the name of
Campbell is still inextricably linked with it. The clan originated in

Argyll in the west of Scotland, the senior line and clan chiefs still bearing the Duke of Argyll title. A cadet branch settled in Glen Orchy and during the fifteenth century made the first of their inroads into the Breadalbane heartlands. By grants of land, tactical marriage and ordinary purchase the Campbells gradually infiltrated the length of Lochtayside until Sir Colin Campbell, 6th of Glenorchy, was able to build his castle of Balloch at the eastern end. When asked why he chose to site his home at the very edge of his territories he hinted darkly that it would not be at the edge for very long.

In fact there was to be very little gain in territory towards the east, the advance coming instead in the form of a peerage and this took place under unusual circumstances. John Campbell, son of Sir John, 10th of Glenorchy, was sent by the government in 1669 to quell a severe outbreak of disorder in Caithness. This he carried out successfully and during his sojourn in the north struck up a friendship with the impoverished Earl of Caithness. In time the young Campbell became the earl's principal creditor and in return the earl, who was without family, agreed that Campbell should inherit all his titles and estates. This duly happened in 1677 when, amid an outcry over Campbell's methods, he was duly invested with the title Earl of Caithness. Very quickly a rival claimant came forward and Campbell was forced to send an army of over 700 Breadalbane men to the far north to argue his case. A pitched battle was fought against the Sinclairs who were defeated, so the story goes, by the simple stratagem of allowing them to capture a consignment of whisky before the battle started. In 1681, however, the authorities accepted the right of the Sinclair claimant and Campbell was compensated for his loss by being created Earl of Breadalbane.

In 1842, at a time when the 2nd Marquis hosted, at his recently completed Taymouth Castle, one of the most glittering balls of the nineteenth century in honour of the young Queen Victoria, the family was probably at the zenith of its fortunes. Troubles there had been and many more lay ahead, but what was remarkable was that many of them were predicted by a Highland seer known as the Lady of Lawers. The village of Lawers, where she once lived, stood by the water's edge on the north-west shore of the loch and indeed its ruins are still well-preserved. The Lawers estate was in the possession of another branch of the Campbells and it is assumed that the Lady was the wife of one of the lairds, although there is no documentary proof of her existence. The sayings attributed to her were passed down the generations in Gaelic and it is believed that only one remains to be fulfilled. One which referred to the area in general foretold the time when the jaw of the sheep would drive the plough from the ground, and this certainly took place under the rule of the 2nd Marquis who, by means of the infamous Breadalbane clearances, replaced many of his tenants with sheep. (It is intriguing to speculate that the marquis might have been persuaded by the Lady's prophecies that the clearances were inevitable.) She also predicted the fall of the Campbells with apparently great accuracy although at the time of Victoria's visit in 1842, when their vast estates stretched for almost exactly 100 miles across Scotland, this must have seemed almost incredible. But 80 years later, in 1922, the process of breaking up the estates began and was completed in 1949, shortly after the appearance of an announcement in the *Perthshire Advertiser* that the remaining estate of Kinnell, near Killin, was to be sold. The last Campbell, according to the Lady, 'would pass over Glenogle with a grey pony leaving nothing behind' and this indeed is how the 9th Earl, having sold up, was seen to leave. The 10th Earl now lives in London and apart from the name has no further connection with Breadalbane.

From Lawers the A827 proceeds south-west towards the small town of Killin and from here the proposed route doubles back by the much more attractive South Loch Tay Road. It is a stunningly beautiful journey from one end to the other, along an almost empty road, with many superb views up and down the loch and across to Ben Lawers. Having passed the hamlet of Ardeonaig we cross back into Perth and Kinross and continue through a number of small settlements; Ardtalnaig, for one, with its wild roses and ruined houses and somewhere nearby, according to legend, the grave of the mythical Banquo's brother; Acharn for another with some of the finest waterfalls in the county. The few signs of habitation are in marked contrast to the once flourishing population of Lochtayside. Perhaps the most telling symbol of days long gone are the abandoned shielings (shown on Ordnance Survey maps at many points around the loch and high above the roads), all that remains of an ancient agricultural custom in which the farming folk and their cattle, after the long hard winter, moved for three or four months to the fresher summer pastures of higher up. Here the cattle would regain their strength (many were so weak after the winter that they had to be carried to their grazings) and fatten, ready for sale at the autumn trysts, and the women and children would spin and make butter and cheese, some for their own consumption, some to pay the rent and the remainder destined for sale at the next fair. The change in under two centuries from a working and agricultural economy to one based on leisure and tourism is symbolised by the popular water sports complex of Croft na Caber (not a pseudo-Gaelic place-name as some think) and the crannog reconstruction offshore, near the eastern end of the loch.

Kenmore lies at the extreme east end of Loch Tay and could claim with justification to be Perthshire's loveliest village. Much of this is due to its location on a little peninsula at the water's edge, sandwiched between the sandy beach of the loch on one side and the young Tay issuing from it at the other. Another pleasing feature is the planned layout of the houses, facing each other across the wide main street, with the church at one end, the gates to Taymouth Castle opposite, and in the middle the dominating presence of the Kenmore Hotel, reputed to be Scotland's oldest inn. The inn was built in 1572 as the first step in transferring the centre of parish life from the now forgotten village of Inchadney to Kenmore, purely for the convenience of the Campbell laird. The church followed shortly after but was rebuilt in 1760, the year the cottages were erected, while the construction of the bridge in 1774 marked the completion of the nucleus of the present village. The interior of the church, in contrast to the white exterior walls, is unusually dark which probably explains the presence of a noteworthy modern engraved glass window which lets in more light than would stained glass. Here also is a memorial to William Gillies, a minister of the parish and author of the superbly researched history of the area, *In famed Breadalbane*. In the churchyard outside can be seen the grave of 'the infant son of the Maharajah Duleep Singh, late ruler of the Sikh nation, Punjab, India'. The Maharajah, who seems to have been a frequent visitor to the area, was a figure somewhat bewildered by the tempestuous politics of his time. He lost his throne to the British at the age of five, was subsequently brought up as a Christian in a British family and later, as a favourite of Queen Victoria, was presented with an estate in Suffolk. In his later years he renounced Christianity and even attempted a revolution against British rule but was nevertheless still forgiven by the Queen. Perhaps he found a measure of peace in rural Perthshire for there can be few lovelier spots than the shores of Loch Tay, either on a summer's morning, with dinghies bobbing, halyards clinking and the loch a sparkling brilliance, or in the fading light of evening when the village and waters are suffused with a warm glow of contentment.

But this image of peace and goodwill is misleading as two great castles, both home to the rapacious Campbells, once stood to the east and west of Kenmore. The earlier one was sited on the Isle of Loch Tay, a former crannog which takes its alternative name, Sybilla's Island, from the young queen of Alexander I who died and was buried there in 1122. In her honour Alexander founded a monastery on the island which in turn became a nunnery and then, following their move from Finlarig at the west end of the loch, a Campbell stronghold. In the sixteenth century the Campbells moved a few miles further east and built the castle of Balloch which the fourth Earl demolished in 1799 to make way for the much larger and grander Taymouth Castle. Since the departure of the Campbells this huge and aesthetically overpowering edifice has functioned as an hotel, a hospital for Polish troops and a Home Office Civil Defence School. It can be seen in the distance from the Kenmore to Aberfeldy road where, now slowly decaying, it stands as a fitting memorial, as the Victorians would say, to the fleetingness of power, status and wealth.

From the north side of the Kenmore bridge it is possible to skirt round the woods of Drummond Hill and rejoin the B846 near the Coshieville Hotel. Instead of turning off for Glen Lyon we continue climbing northwards, past the stark outline of Garth Castle, until looming behind the immediate hills we begin to glimpse the great ridge of Schiehallion. Turning left onto the Schiehallion Road we sweep past Loch Kinardochy and with the northern slopes of that great mountain on the left cross into Rannoch.

Neither the speed and comfort of a car nor the few but well surfaced roads can suppress the sense of barely tamed wilderness that is Rannoch, for the area has only been a part of civilised Scotland since the mid-eighteenth century. Before this time it was beyond any law or jurisdiction, either by Lowland sheriff or Highland landowner, and inhabited by outlaws and desperate men who knew they were reasonably safe from capture. The area was the subject in 1755 of a detailed report by one James Small, a factor appointed by the government to administer the estates after their forfeiture by Robertson of Struan, and the following extract gives some idea of their condition. 'Ranoch, with respect to theft, is...universally well known...For as Ranoch lay in the center of the Highlands, with wide extended hills and scarce a single man in it but either stole or connieved at theft, it was the common randevous of all theeves and stolen cattle.' If this were not bad enough the people of Rannoch also ran a profitable sideline in that early form of insurance known as blackmail and, according to the Old Statistical Account of Fortingall parish, many of the population from Stirling to Coupar Angus apparently paid up to prevent their property from being plundered. In the autumn months the blackmailers, numbering at one time around 300, would gather together to drink whisky and settle their accounts. As the author states, probably without any exaggeration, 'it would have required a regiment to have brought a thief from that country'.

The same author also describes the almost unbelievable poverty and backwardness of Rannoch in the mid-eighteenth century, and indeed it is difficult to accept that living conditions then could have improved much since early mediaeval times. Roads and bridges did not exist. Homes were simple huts which could only be entered by crawling on all fours and in which it was impossible to stand upright. Few had beds, most of the population lying in their clothes and wrapped in a blanket on fern- or heather-strewn earth (the above Mr Small suggested in one of his reports that this particular discomfort 'fitts them for the hardships of their theevish expeditions'!). Food for the poorest could consist of nothing but boiled cattle blood and meal, day in and day out.

The Macgregors of Rannoch were mainly though not entirely responsible for the area's lawless reputation. One of the most tragic of Scottish clans the *Griogaraich* suffered the horrific cruelties of 'ethnic cleansing' long before it was practised in twentieth century Germany and Yugoslavia. In simple terms, their lack of a strong chief and dilatoriness about acquiring a proper title to their estates resulted in them having no land to call their own. Without such a homebase they were forced to prey on others which in turn resulted in further prosecution and a downward spiral towards near extinction. In 1603 James VI took the ultimate step of proscribing the very name of Macgregor, an act which was only repealed in 1774 and which gave an added poignancy to their clan sobriquet, *Clann a'Cheo*, the Children of the Mist. As the *Chronicle of Perth* laconically put it, describing the proceedings of the 'justice court' in Perth on 10 May 1624, 'only 3 hangit, McGregoris'. Most barbaric of all was the cash payment made by the Privy Council for Macgregor heads.

The turning point for Rannoch came after Culloden when the government finally imposed its authority on the region. Following the construction of new roads and bridges and the establishment of the village of Kinloch Rannoch, all under the supervision of James Small, the region was able to participate in the improvements which were sweeping the country during the later years of that century. Another man to share much of the credit with Small was Dugald Buchanan who arrived in Rannoch in the mid-1740s, probably as a SSPCK preacher, and at the time of his death in 1763 had become a much loved teacher, minister and poet. To the great annoyance of his parishioners the villagers of his native Balquhidder claimed the body for burial while the former had to be content with erecting a red granite memorial in the centre of Kinloch Rannoch.

This, then, is the background to an appreciation of Rannoch. The ghosts of caterans and the struggling poor still haunt a landscape in which a mantle of undeniable beauty has been laid over an essentially lonely and remote wilderness. The paper-thin veneer of civilisation in the shape of narrow roads and small inhabited outposts looks exactly that. Scratch it away and things will look little different. For Rannoch, in spite of occupying the virtual centre of Scotland, has no through traffic and as a result is too remote to be economically viable. Should the long discussed extension to link Rannoch Station with the main A82 ever materialise then the region could well be transformed. Until then, however, it is destined to remain economically barren, taunted on either side by the steady stream of transport endlessly plying the main commercial and tourist routes between the north and south.

From a vantage point of over 1000 feet the Schiehallion Road looks across a broad heathery landscape towards the distant mountains of Badenoch before ultimately descending through woods into Kinloch Rannoch. Kinloch, meaning 'head of the loch', is a curious misnomer as the village is at the foot, lying between the eastern end of the loch and the huge rocky mass of Craig Varr high above. The dark grey stone of the buildings, which always contrive to look ill at ease under a bright sky, and the remote situation might suggest an introverted community but this would

The pleasant village of Kinloch Rannoch and at its heart the memorial to the Gaelic poet, Dugald Buchanan. The photo is taken from the bridge over what the Ordnance Survey calls the River Tummel and what locals used to call Dubhaig — the dark stream. Some traditionalists still maintain that the Tummel properly starts several miles to the east where it exits from the loch of the same name.

be far from the truth. In fact an open and welcoming square lies at the heart of the village and there are several hotels and shops to cater for the needs of residents and tourists alike. Indeed, of the many wonders of Perthshire nothing has surprised me more than finding a copy of the same day's *Frankfurter Allgemeine* at lunchtime in one of the village stores. Even so, the village is necessarily quiet with only the walkers on their way to Scotland's west coast passing right through while those who arrive by car and who keep right on to the end of the road — about 15 miles further on — have no alternative but to come back. Oddly enough the public lavatories have been built on one of the best sites in the village. Overlooking the river and its bridge, they also enjoy a pleasant outlook over Schiehallion, here seen at its conical best, and over the next-door garden with its colourful display of summer flowers.

From the village square a short stretch of road leads to the loch side and the long view across the waters to the mountains of the west. These, including the distinctive and distant peaks of Buachaille Etive Mor and the Black Mount, mark the western boundary of

243

Rannoch Moor. The wide expanse of moorland, still several miles away, is echoed in the landscape around the loch. The mountains stand well back and give the loch an unexpected open and fresh appearance, bordered not by the slopes characteristic of other Perthshire lochs but by fields and low-lying woodland. A road circumnavigates the loch, the faster side, as seems *de rigeur* in Perthshire, being along the north shore although there is little need, in terms of destination and volume of traffic, for having a fast road at all. It runs very close to the waterside and in places, such as Killichonan, one can park the car and make the most of the little sandy beaches.

The hamlet of Bridge of Ericht lies near the western end of the loch at a point where it is swelled by the outflow from Loch Ericht. The southern portion of this loch lies in Perthshire with the remainder in Inverness-shire. Such is the complicated nature of the watershed in these parts that while the loch ultimately drains into the Tay basin the headwaters of the River Truim, which for several miles run closely parallel to it, end up in the Spey. Loch Ericht, in spite of its remoteness, has not escaped being pressed into service as an important cog in the hydro-electric power schemes of Highland Perthshire. It is dammed at the southern end and, taking in water via a system of tunnels and aqueducts not just from Loch Garry but from the famous fishing waters of the Spey as well, is probably damned at the other. Curiously, the raising of the water level of Loch Ericht echoes an ancient legend about a lochside parish by the name of Feadail which suddenly subsided and was lost for ever beneath its icy waters. A story such as this would usually be dismissed as purely mythical but then again, the loch does lie along a fault line and one does wonder.

The hydro-electric industry has been one of the great unsung successes of Perthshire, providing many millions of units of power each year by one of the safest and least polluting methods of energy generation. Even so, in spite of its environmental correctness, it still meets only a comparatively small proportion of Scotland's electricity requirements. The Tummel-Garry Scheme originated before World War II and was completed at the war's end with the help of German prisoners of war. The various water resources of its massive catchment area of over 700 square miles were harnessed into one single system by the construction of a number of dams and many miles of wide-diametered tunnels through the hard

Perthshire rock. Great care was taken to limit damage to the landscape; several power stations were built underground while the remainder, such as the 1930s Tummel Power Station, have generally been built in an architecturally sympathetic way. I hope that one day some of them will be listed as being worthy of preservation.

The head of Loch Rannoch marks the eastern edge of Rannoch Moor. The road continues for a further five miles to Rannoch Station, following the River Gaur for some of the way through an increasingly bleak and desolate landscape. It is at its best, perhaps, after a rain storm when the spent clouds, in the aftermath of battle, mirror the chaos of the landscape. There are no clear-cut divisions into hill and glen, field and water, heather and grass, just a monotonous mixture of fairly level bogland, dotted with lochans, tufts of vegetation, patches of forest and scattered boulders left by glaciers of the ice age. Over all of this the lonely winds of Rannoch blow.

There are usually a surprising number of cars at the station, left by walkers who either trek to the next station up the line at Corrour and return by train, or who head due west along the signposted path to Loch Laidon and Glencoe. But the biggest surprise, of course, is that there should be a station here at all, for it only serves a road which in turn only seems to serve the station. The railway line was built in the 1890s by a team of 5000 Irish navvies and today, known as the West Highland Line, connects Glasgow with Fort William and Mallaig. This was another astonishing feat of engineering which had already defeated the likes of Telford who had wanted to build a road across the moor. In places long viaducts were built and in others, when no firm ground at all could be detected, the railway was floated on a layer of turf, brushwood and thousands of tons of ash. At one point the enterprise ran out of money and was only completed when a director of the West Highland Railway provided the funds from his own personal fortune. In gratitude for saving their jobs a likeness of this noble fellow was carved by the navvies on a boulder at the end of the platform at Rannoch Station. The undertaking nearly claimed the lives of a number of men, including Robert McAlpine (later Sir Robert of the well-known construction company), who at the planning stages set out in January 1889 to investigate a section of the proposed route. Clad in city clothes with only umbrellas for shelter they got well and truly lost and were discovered just a matter of hours before the moor was engulfed in a snow storm.

A summer morning at Rannoch Station, one of the remotest parts of Perth and Kinross. Surrounded by bare hills, wide views, profound silence and an overwhelming sense of solitude, it is nevertheless still possible to catch an overnight sleeper from here straight to London Euston. At the north end of the platform is the carved likeness of J H Renton whose financial help ensured the completion of the railway across the moor.

From this western extremity of Perthshire we return to civilisation, this time travelling along the south side of Loch Rannoch. The road takes us past the provocatively named Georgetown, built after the '45, through remnants of the ancient Caledonian pine forest, past Rannoch School and back to Kinloch Rannoch. A mile or so to the east of the village is Dunalastair Water, a little loch created by the hydro-electric dam at the far end. It takes its name from the Dunalastair estate, or Mount Alexander to use the anglicised form, which for many years had been the home of the Robertsons of Struan, chiefs of Clan Donnachaidh. Legend has it that 'the children of Duncan' became Robertsons immediately after Bannockburn when Robert the Bruce, in gratitude for the clan's loyalty, promoted them to the rank of honorary 'sons of Robert'. A more likely reason is that the use of surnames, which had hitherto in broad terms been very fluid, began to crystallise at the time of Robert, the 4th chief, whose descendants thus became Robertsons. The clan held lands all over Atholl and even at one stage on both sides of Loch Tay too, but the area around Struan at the mouth of Glen Errochty is their heartland. The Robertsons were perhaps the most reluctant of all Highland chiefs to abandon their traditional role. They remained as fiercely independent as greater powers would allow, and where other chiefs had abandoned their people to the mercy of sheep did everything in their power to protect their own from the harsh world of southern economics.

One of the best known figures in the long annals of the clan was Alexander Robertson of Struan, the 13th chief and widely known as the Poet Chief. He often wrote on pastoral themes but was not beyond producing a certain amount of ribald verse which, in the eyes of the more staid critics, was sufficient cause to consign him to the ranks of poetic infamy — 'a disgusting mixture of profligacy and religion' was one comment of 1824. This seems a little unfair as English poets such as Herrick could combine their talents in this direction with an ecclesiastical living and still enjoy a high reputation. The Poet Chief, however, is better known for his staunch support of the Jacobite cause. He was active in the uprising of 1689 when barely out of his teens and in defeat had his estates confiscated. They were restored in due course but were again taken from him after his participation in the '15. In 1745, as an old man of approaching 80, he witnessed the Battle of Prestonpans and as one of the spoils of victory was given the carriage, coat and chain of General Sir John Cope and persuaded to return home. He arrived at Dunalastair in great style, his clansmen actually carrying the carriage the last few miles from Tummel Bridge where the road ended. Yet again his beloved estates were forfeited and he lived out his remaining years at nearby Carie, where he died in 1749.

There is a choice of routes from Dunalastair Water. The B847 heads north towards Trinafour and then turns eastwards into Glen Errochty, eventually linking up with the A9 at Calvine. This road in its early stages offers some fine side views of Schiehallion with its long ridge sloping down to the east. The Glen Errochty section is pleasant but unspectacular. In contrast the more attractive B846 continues due east towards Killiecrankie, following the Tummel most of the way, and it is this route that we shall take. Tummel Bridge lies on this road at the Rannoch-Atholl boundary and takes its name from the older of the two bridges here, a high-arched stone structure built by General Wade in 1733. The more modern one, which seems to have been thrown across with the minimum of thought and expenditure, now carries all the traffic. Here there are two power stations, two electricity substations and pylons seemingly radiating in all directions, all of which make the village one of the focal points in the hydro-electric network. Thankfully the woods around the village hide much of it.

Loch Tummel, very different in character from its sister Rannoch, is almost a microcosm of what we like to regard as typical Highland scenery. A mere seven miles in length it is surrounded by high forested hills while in places at water level the loch laps the edges of rich green fields. Magisterial Schiehallion keeps a watchful eye over all. The main road steadily climbs through the silver birch and bracken of the northern slopes and although some of the views are particularly lovely it is worth driving on to the Queen's View at the far end before stopping. From the viewing platform, which seems to hover high over the water, the vista across the loch and mountains is one which remains long in the memory. If any view in Perthshire could be said to characterise Scotland then this would have to be it. There are, however, two things to bear in mind. Firstly, because of the Clunie Dam at the eastern end, the water level is higher than it once was and therefore the view is not the same as the one so much enjoyed by the queen. Whichever queen that was for, secondly, no-one actually knows which royal personage is commemorated here. The obvious choice, Victoria, believed that the viewpoint was named after her even though, as she herself realised, the designation predated her first visit there. A plaque at the spot suggests that it was named after the wife of Robert the Bruce, but again this seems unlikely as fine views and the beauty of landscape were generally unappreciated prior to the eighteenth century. This is another of Perthshire's little mysteries.

A further four miles along this pleasantly winding and wooded road and we arrive at the modern bridge high over the River Garry. The dark waters far below come from the loch of the same name near the Inverness-shire border and have been shadowed virtually the whole way by both the modern A9 and the Inverness-Euston railway line. Instead of joining the new A9 at the Garry Bridge we turn right onto the old road, now the B8019, and head south on a little detour into Pitlochry.

On the northern edge of the town is a sign indicating the Loch Faskally boat station where rowing boats can be hired for a relaxing hour or two. The loch was created in 1950 when the

The Queen's View, looking westwards along Loch Tummel towards Schiehallion. Queen Victoria recorded in 1866 a particularly unsuccessful attempt to enjoy a cup of tea at this spot. The fire would not burn, nor the kettle boil, and when John Brown finally resorted to begging a can of hot water trom a nearby house it was too cold on his return to make a good brew. The queen, as they say, was not amused.

hydro-electric dam was built across the Tummel and the glen upstream was flooded. It is just the right size for small craft and the tree-lined banks add a pleasant touch of intimacy, the only drawback being the thunder of traffic crossing the A9 bridge overhead. Away from the bridge, however, the noise quickly evaporates into a watery peacefulness where the slow dipping of blades is usually the only sound to be heard. For the more energetically inclined there are a number of woodland walks radiating from the boat station.

The dam itself is one of the most popular attractions in Pitlochry and is only a short walk from the town centre. There is a walkway across the top where one can admire not only the huge volume of water being held back but also the wider setting of the town as a whole with Ben-y-Vrackie to the north and the open slopes of the Braes o Tulliemet to the south. On the far side is a visitor centre and the well-known fish ladder. Over 900 feet in length and consisting of 34 stepped pools, each connected by a pipe, the

The Pitlochry dam, completed in 1950, towers over the River Tummel. On the left in the foreground can be seen a section of the fish ladder which allows salmon to bypass these massive concrete walls.

ladder is a means of allowing salmon to bypass the dam on their way to their spawning waters further upstream. Several other dams have similar ladders but this is the best known. There is also an observation chamber where one can usually see one or two of the 5400 salmon which on average pass through every year between the months of April and October.

Pitlochry's other major attraction is a further five minute walk along the river bank from the fish ladder. This is the Pitlochry Festival Theatre, a modern building of glass and grey brick which enjoys splendid views over the river and the hills beyond and which is worthy of its appellation 'Scotland's theatre in the hills'. It was first opened in 1951, just a year after the dam, but in contrast to this solidly built concrete structure, consisted merely of two large tents. The smaller one contained the auditorium with everything else, including the stage, dressing rooms and restaurant, being squeezed into the other. The tents were replaced in 1953 by a semi-permanent building (now the curling rink), which retained echoes of canvas and tent poles in its design, and in 1979 by the present structure. The season runs from May to October of each year and, instead of presenting a run of six plays consecutively, a different play is performed on each night of the week. Hard work for the performers perhaps, but it does allow visitors to 'stay six days and see six plays'.

The town's long main street slopes gently down towards its southern end. The creeper-clad Fishers Hotel acts as the centre-piece while the rest of the street is architecturally enlivened by a single surviving Victorian arcade and by the angles of many dormer windows and gable ends. It is a lively little town of grey stone and bright shop windows, full of visitors trailing between the numerous hotels and the wool, coffee and gift shops. The residents meanwhile tend to shelter from this tourist onslaught in the Victorian villas behind the main streets. Pitlochry is a comparatively new town, owing its growth originally to the construction of the new Wade road in 1727 but primarily to the development of tourism a century later, and consequently has no buildings of any great age. Enjoy it as an interesting and characterful country town and as a centre for exploring Highland Perthshire.

Much older is the village of Moulin, formerly the main settlement in the immediate area, which straddles the A924 high above Pitlochry. The resiting of the new military road away from the village was the main cause of the village's decline. Nevertheless it can still boast a fine church, reputed to be the oldest foundation in Atholl, and beside it in the churchyard an eighteenth century Dutch bell. Through the village centre flows a merrily gurgling burn and nearby stands the welcoming L-shaped seventeenth century inn, a truly charming place to stop for a little refreshment.

From Pitlochry we turn north again and, continuing on the B8019 past the Garry Bridge, enter the Pass of Killiecrankie. This impressive gorge is owned by the National Trust for Scotland and with its array of wildlife and vegetation has deservedly been declared a Site of Special Scientific Interest. The visitor centre contains some interesting displays of local flora and fauna as well as the Battle of Killiecrankie, while outside there are several walks to be enjoyed, up and down the hillside and through the trees whose colours in the autumn are quite magnificent. Down near the river can be seen the site of the famous Soldier's Leap where one Donald McBean, a redcoat, jumped a clear 18 feet across the raging waters to escape the pursuing Jacobites. Many others were not quite so lucky and drowned at the same spot. A modern day parallel can be seen in the autumn of each year when returning

The main buildings of Moulin are the old coaching inn and the church, the latter supposedly the oldest foundation in Atholl although the present building dates from 1875. Behind the church is the village square with a circular bench around the trunk of a beautifully shady tree.

salmon fling themselves out of this same boiling cauldron of water, tails flapping madly for that extra half inch of distance, in an attempt to get further upstream to the waters of their birth. Some make it, some not, and a few beach themselves on the rocks in the attempt. The rocks here, and indeed by many waterfalls on salmon rivers, used to be a source of free and effortless food; a book of 1802 describes how local residents would leave baskets at the spot and wait for the fish to jump in — would that salmon fishing were always that easy!

On the other side of Killiecrankie, a small and pleasant village, the great battle of 1689 took place. In this first clash of the long drawn out Jacobite campaigns the government forces were defeated by John Graham of Claverhouse although he himself was shot at the culmination of the battle. The spot where he supposedly fell is marked by a standing stone (probably of much greater antiquity) in a field just to the east of the road. He was buried a few miles away in the parish church of Old Blair which is well-hidden behind Blair Castle. It can be found by following, for about a mile, the road signposted to Old Blair from the southern end of the present village of Blair Atholl. The tiny St Bride's Kirk is roofless though the walls are well-preserved and it is here in a vault, beneath two padlocked metal doors, that the bones of the great Jacobite hero now lie. His armour was later removed from the tomb and is now preserved at Blair Castle.

Old Blair lies near the junction of three ancient routes to the north. The narrow road at the gate to the churchyard is named Minigaig Street and is the start of the centuries old path, the Minigaig, which ran from Atholl along Glen Bruar to Badenoch and which fell into comparative disuse after Wade forced the road over Drumochter. It was not completely abandoned, however, as drovers travelled it as recently as the early years of this present century, no doubt a legacy of the period when the tolls at Dalnacardoch on the Wade road made the Minigaig preferable. It passes over some high and wild country and reaching a height of 2745 feet can in places be dangerously exposed to the elements. In the winter it is impassable. Running close to the Minigaig but taking a more westerly line into Badenoch is the even older Comyn's Road. Near St Bride's is the car park for those hardy souls who tackle the long trek along Glen Tilt to Deeside. The glen is steep-sided and narrow, bounded to the south-east by the slopes of Beinn a'Ghlo and unlike the Minigaig reasonably sheltered. It used to be heavily populated 200 years ago but with most of the people now gone the remaining settlements seem even more remote. One such place is the lodge at Fealar which, at an altitude of around 1800 feet and situated a good mile off the beaten track and only three miles from the Aberdeenshire border, is one of the most isolated houses in Perthshire.

It would be reasonable to assume that Blair Atholl, situated on the main route north and dominated by the famous castle close by, should be the ancient and historic centre of the region. It is in fact a reasonably recent settlement, dating from the first half of the nineteenth century when Wade's road was deflected away from its original course through Old Blair, and as such can be a bit of a disappointment. The grey stone buildings are pleasant enough, and even have a vaguely aristocratic air about them, but the long ribbon design of the village, strung out along the boundary walls of the castle grounds, has denied it a heart. 'Blair' signifies a plain, the presence of which is well disguised by the high ridge of hills immediately behind the village. A glance at an Ordnance

Blair Castle is one of the top tourist attractions in Perth and Kinross. Summer visitors, as well as admiring the interior rooms, can stretch out on the wide lawns and watch the strutting peacocks and the play of shadows on the white castle walls. It is perhaps too easy in these peaceful surroundings to overlook the castle's turbulent past.

Survey map, however, will reassure the doubters that Blair Atholl does indeed lie in the middle of a level area of ground where the Tilt meets the Garry.

In the centre of this plain was built Blair Castle, today one of the most popular tourist attractions in Perthshire. It is approached via a long avenue of lime trees which leads off the main road, and while at the far end the car park charges may be a little steep you get a better class of bird strutting between the cars. No mere pigeons begging for scraps here, but ducal peacocks demanding them. The castle with its white sprawling walls has an architectural integrity which belies its long and violent history. It has been occupied by enemy forces on a number of occasions, besieged by the rightful occupant in 1746 and radically altered several times over the centuries. Traditionally dating from the thirteenth century it has been in the ownership of the Murray family, later the Dukes of Atholl, since 1629. The biggest change in its appearance was carried out by the 2nd Duke who removed the battlements and demoted it to the status of a large mansion known at one stage as Athole House. Such was the difference that the Reverend Chauncey

Hare Townshend, who in 1840 wrote with great humour of his travels in Scotland, stated, 'I believe it was once a Castle; but...it hath been stuccoed and whitewashed into the similitude of a hospital'. The castellations were restored in 1870 at around the time the entrance hall was built. With its high wood-panelled walls, adorned with rifles, swords and other militaria, this is the one room (of the many other impressively furnished ones) that visitors tend to remember.

The progenitor of all Murrays is believed to have been a Flemish knight by the name of Freskin, who was possibly one of David I's twelfth century imports. He was granted lands in Moray and in time the territorial designation of his descendants, 'de Moravia', evolved into the surname of today. By the sixteenth century the Murrays of Tullibardine were accepted as the senior line and from this point they rapidly climbed the social hierarchy from landed gentry to the highest rank in the peerage. They became Earls of Tullibardine in 1606 and through a judicious marriage inherited the Atholl estates and earldom in 1629. The 2nd (Murray) Earl of Atholl was created the 1st Marquis in 1676 and the 2nd Marquis the 1st Duke in 1703. For a brief period in that century they also enjoyed full regal powers though not on the British mainland. In 1736 they inherited the sovereignty of the Isle of Man and had the right to summon their own parliaments and issue their own coinage. Although the 3rd Duke sold his sovereignty to the Crown in 1765 the three-legged heraldic device of the island still appears in the Atholl coat of arms. The last symbol of regal power survives in the shape of the Atholl Highlanders, the only legally permitted weapon-bearing private army in the country which was raised in its present form in 1839 and whose colours were presented by Queen Victoria during her visit of 1845. One of the more recent ceremonial functions for which they turned out was the funeral of the 10th Duke. This tall, gentle-giant of a man, affectionately known as Wee Iain, died in 1996 and the great wave of sadness which swept across Highland Perthshire took by surprise those who thought that the common man of Scotland had no further regard for the aristocracy. Even in Perth the news of his death was whispered in unusually reverential tones. The duke returned the affection by leaving the bulk of his estates and Blair Castle not to his successor (a very distant cousin) but to a charitable trust.

The road for the north in fact leads virtually due west out of Blair Atholl and after three miles arrives at Bruar. This is one of the lesser known settlements of Perthshire and yet one could very easily spend half a day here enjoying walks, good shopping, food and an excellent museum. The magnificent waterfalls were the original claim to fame and were visited and described by several literary travellers of the eighteenth century. In 1787 Burns himself spent a couple of days with the Duke and Duchess of Atholl and during his stay found himself less than satisfied with the barren appearance of the hillside through which the Bruar and its falls tumbled. As a thank-you to his hosts and as a way of making his point he penned the well known *Humble petition of Bruar Water to the noble Duke of Athole* in which, speaking as the river, he suggested that the planting of trees would greatly improve the area. Within ten years the duke had planted the hillside with 120,000 larch and Scots pines and today the two-mile walk up to the falls and back again on the opposite side is a refreshing combination of sunlight, shade, forest green and the pleasant sounds of birdsong and rushing water.

The large carpark at the start of the walk caters rather more for the Clan Donnachaidh Museum and the enormous House of Bruar shopping complex. The museum is devoted to the history and memorabilia of the Robertson clan and was the first purpose-built museum of its kind in Scotland. At the time of writing there are plans afoot to take this a stage further and create a clan museum for the whole of Highland Perthshire which would bring together all or most of the local clans in a brotherly linking which seems somewhat at odds with their earlier histories. The museum is now dwarfed by the very recently built House of Bruar whose illuminated round tower is a welcome sign of life on the long and lonely stretches of the A9 at night. Inside is an elegantly laid out and upmarket shopping mall selling clothes, glassware, china and food and it is a sign of the times that this is probably now the most popular attraction at this spot.

A mile beyond Bruar and still on the B8079 are the tiny settlements of Calvine and Struan, situated at the mouth of Glen Errochty. The most unusual feature here is the knot of bridges crossing the Garry. The original stone structure of the 1760s was in turn surmounted a century later by a railway bridge beside which, in the 1890s, a further metal bridge was added to allow a doubling of the track. Nowhere else, as far as I am aware, do we find three bridges so close together and all crossing the same river.

From Calvine the only practicable route north is via the A9 along Glen Garry. Wade was the first to see the strategic potential of this glen as a better way through the Highlands than the age-old hill paths already mentioned. This was presumably because at its greatest altitude, 1500 feet at Drumochter, it is still a thousand feet below the highest point of the Minigaig. The completion of the military road between Perth and Inverness in 1729, a remarkable feat given the terrain, was marked by the erection of the Wade Stone which can still be seen — if you look carefully — beside the A9 (southbound) between Dalnacardoch and Dalnaspidal. The well-known Drumochter summit marks the county boundary and many heavy vehicles even on the new and impressively-engineered A9 struggle to cope with the long climb, as do trains on the railway line close by. Two hills face each other across the border, the Sow of Atholl on the Perthshire side and the slightly smaller Boar of Badenoch opposite.

The other route to the north is along Glenshee to Deeside. To explore this area we have to return to Pitlochry and take the A924 across Moulin Moor, through Glen Brerachan to Kirkmichael. The climb out of Moulin is steep and very quickly the pastures that were soft and green beside the Tummel are smothered by the dark heather which has such a tight grip on the higher land. The road then falls away into lonely Glen Brerachan, an ancient route between Atholl and Angus where in around 1392 a party of Highlanders defeated the men of Angus in fierce battle. The former, led by a chief of Clan Donnachaidh and by a son of the Wolf of Badenoch, were returning from the 'Raid of Angus' with stolen cattle when the latter, having regrouped, mounted a last and ultimately ineffectual attempt at snatching victory. The Gaelic place-names in the immediate vicinity still resound the Highland triumph.

At Straloch, midway between Moulin and Kirkmichael, the hills form a high-rimmed basin and there being no further progress possible towards the north the road abandons its assault and turns instead towards the south. A track, however, continues along Gleann Fearnach, where the population was cleared last century to make way for sheep, and after about 15 miles through the bleak grouse moors of Atholl arrives at Fealar. A further four miles from

Straloch, passing the Kindrogan Field Centre and the row of cottages that is Enochdhu, is the village of Kirkmichael.

A small village at the heart of a large parish, Kirkmichael is situated at a crossroads on the old drove road network and was once famed for its cattle markets. Drovers who had come by the Cairnwell pass, instead of continuing down Glenshee towards Blairgowrie would strike across the hills from the Spittal and meet up with their counterparts who had come down Gleann Fearnach. Several days would be spent here before the drovers continued their slow journeys towards Crieff or Falkirk. But man and beast have long since gone and Kirkmichael today is a quiet village of whitewashed buildings divided by the River Ardle, whose fast-flowing waters give it a touch of life. The A924 continues for another eight miles through the wide and gentle landscape of Strathardle, past little Ballintuim with its sign of another era advertising the Telegraph Office, past Blackcraig Castle with its wonderful nineteenth century bridge and bridgehouse high above the river, to Bridge of Cally where the Ardle combines with the Black Water to form the River Ericht.

Immediately south of Kirkmichael the B950, a surprisingly wide and fast road, turns eastwards and connects with the A93, the Royal Route to Deeside through Glenshee. The glen marks the eastern boundary of Atholl and is different in character from the heartlands. Unlike the openness and richness of the landscape further west the glen is darker, the countryside seemingly poorer and the steeper mountains on either side more threatening. Glenshee translates as 'the fairy glen' and the inhabitants, with their innate belief in the reality of such beings, would have linked the grim landscape and the strong elemental forces of nature with the doings of the supernatural. The population is today sparse, confined in the main to the areas of rough pasturage on either side of the river. The few houses and the hotel at Spittal form the only settlement in the long 32-mile stretch between Bridge of Cally and Braemar. This is in contrast to the situation several centuries ago when Glenshee, judging by all the archaeological evidence, was heavily populated.

The Spittal of Glenshee lies at the head of Glenshee proper and at the point where two burns flowing down either side of Ben Gulabin unite to form the Shee Water. Its very name is still strongly suggestive of the traveller's refuge which, in one of the

NEGOTIATING THE TOP BEND OF THE DEVIL'S ELBOW, GLENSHEE, THE HIGHEST PUBLIC ROAD IN BRITAIN, ALTITUDE 2000 FEET. STEEPEST GRADIENT 1 IN 3.

Was this the first bus to be fitted with climbing ropes and crampons? Photographed at the correct angle, the distant hill on the left should actually appear higher than the one on the right. Sadly, the Devil's Elbow, just to the south of the Glenshee ski slopes, is no more (Courtesy of Perth & Kinross Libraries).

most inhospitable parts of Scotland, it once was. There has certainly been a settlement here for many centuries though the Spittal Inn's claim to a foundation date of AD 961 has to be questionable. In the summer the Spittal has a somewhat dowdy appearance and only comes into its own during the ski-ing season. When the snows come the quiet Glenshee Woollens shop changes its sign and metamorphoses into Cairdsport, a busy ski hire business. Similarly the tourist cars and coaches which in the summer file past on their way to Deeside are replaced by a steady stream of skiers queuing their way from crack of dawn and earlier towards the slopes. At the end of the day the slow convoy of cars and coaches returns past the lights of the Spittal, warm and welcoming across the icy snows, to the towns and villages of the Lowlands.

The Spittal suffers some of the worst weather in the county. Old accounts of parish life tell of how the inhabitants not infrequently found themselves trapped inside their homes by snow drifts the height of the door and more. The only recourse in this situation, which avoided having to shovel snow into the house to get outside, was to send a child outside by way of the chimney with instructions to dig his way back in. It has been said that the chimneys in this area were deliberately made wider than usual for this very reason. There are also stories of farmers feeding the deer with hay in the worst of the weather and of how, when anyone was late in performing this duty, the deer would issue a reminder in the form of a sharp knock on the door with their antlers.

From the Spittal a wide new road turns to the north-east and begins the long hard climb up Gleann Beag to the ski slopes. In the course of five miles the height above sea level doubles from 1100 feet at the Spittal to 2200 feet at the Cairnwell pass. The biggest hazard on the old road was the notorious Devil's Elbow, a steeply climbing double hairpin bend which in snow and ice tested the bravery and skills of every driver. It may have acquired a worse reputation than it actually deserved as many postcard publishers of, say, fifty years ago, by clever picture editing, steepened considerably the true gradient. Some vehicles, in fact, in clinging to the roadway seemed to be defying the very law of gravity itself. At the bottom of the Elbow stood a well which was regularly used by cursing coach drivers who found steam from overheated radiators pouring down their central aisles, frequently to the hilarity of children on school skiing trips. The new road has bypassed the Devil's Elbow and in doing so has edited out a memorable paragraph in the history of Scottish motoring. The crest of the hill, lying in a dip between The Cairnwell on the west and Glas Maol on the east, is the natural watershed between the Tay and the Dee and here, as ears pop and engines labour, the driver is met with the 'Welcome to Aberdeenshire' signs and beyond, the ski slopes, chairlifts and tows. County boundaries even in modern times can be a bone of contention. In 1988 Tayside Regional Council argued that as they bore the expense of keeping the A93 open in winter then they should be entitled to a share of the sporting revenues. But Grampian Regional Council quickly rebuffed this take-over bid and today the new authority of Aberdeenshire maintains its hold over a ski resort which still bears a Perthshire name.

The A93 at The Cairnwell is not only the most northerly road in Perth and Kinross but the highest public road in the United Kingdom and a fitting place to conclude an armchair exploration of the two counties. Stand here, then, with your back to Aberdeenshire, and look with the mind's eye over the area which lies before you: the heather-clad hills of Atholl, the peaks of Breadalbane and the rounded tops of the Sidlaws and Ochils; the great rivers draining the Highlands and the long narrow lochs harnessed for their power; the ancient clans in the Highland glens, the broad fields of the Lowland straths and the trade and commerce of the still lovely towns. Remember too the battles which have been fought here, between Jacobite and Hanoverian, Gaelic and English, clan and capitalism, landlord and tenant. And remember finally the good things, the poetry and songs of Willie Soutar and Lady Nairne, the music of Niel Gow, the trees and gardens, the castles and stately homes, the fishing and walking, the festivals, the wildlife, the whisky and above all the beauty of the landscape. This, in all its rich variety, is Perth and Kinross. *Slàinte!*

SELECT BIBLIOGRAPHY

Newspapers

Blairgowrie Advertiser
Courier and Advertiser
Kinross-shire Advertiser
Perthshire Advertiser
Perthshire Advertiser Centenary Number, 12 August 1929
Perthshire Constitutional
Perthshire Courier
Strathearn Herald

Periodicals

Atholl and Breadalbane Community Comment
Auchterarder and District Community News Magazine
Coupar Angus Newsletter
Discovery and Excavation in Scotland
Journal of the Perthshire Society of Natural Science
Kinross Community Council Newsletter
Proceedings of the Society of Antiquaries of Scotland
Scots Magazine
Scottish Field

Books

Aitken, John. *Making passage to Perth.* 1980.
British Geological Survey. *The Grampian Highlands.* 4th ed., 1995.
British Geological Survey. *The Midland Valley of Scotland.* 3rd
    ed., 1985.
Butler, D. *The ancient church and parish of Abernethy.* 1897.
Carnie, R. H. *Publishing in Perth before 1807.* 1960.
Census statistics (various volumes, 1755–1991).
Comrie Women's Rural Institute. *Comrie: our village.* 1966.
Cooke, Anthony (ed.) *Stanley: its history and development.* 1977.
Cooper, John Ashley. *The great salmon rivers of Scotland.* 1980.
Crawford, O. G. S. *Topography of Roman Scotland.* 1949.
Cunningham, A. D. *A history of Rannoch.* 1984.

Day, J. P. *Clackmannan and Kinross*. 1915.

Dempster, W. J. *Patrick Matthew and natural selection*. 1983.

Devine, T. M. & Mitchison, R. *People and society in Scotland, 1760–1830*. 1988.

Dewar, Annie. *Logierait church and parish*. 1989.

Dickson, A. & Treble, J. H. *People and society in Scotland, 1914–1990*. 1992.

Dingwall, Christopher H. *Ardler: a village history*. 1985.

Durie, Alastair J. *The Scottish linen industry in the eighteenth century*. 1979.

Easson, D. E. *Charters of the abbey of Coupar Angus*. 1947.

Fasti Ecclesiae Scoticanae (various volumes).

Fawcett, Richard. *A history of St John's Kirk, Perth*. 1987.

Findlay, W. H. *Heritage of Perth*. 1984.

Fleming, Maurice. *The ghost o Mause and other tales...of east Perthshire*. 1995.

Forrester, David. *Logiealmond: the place and the people*. 1944.

Fothergill, Rhoda. *The Inches of Perth*. ca 1980.

Fraser, W. H. & Morris, R. J. *People and society in Scotland, 1830–1914*. 1990.

Gerber, Pat. *The search for the Stone of Destiny*. 1992.

Gibson, Colin. *Bonnie Glenshee*. ca 1960.

Gillies, W. A. *In famed Breadalbane*. 1938.

Graham-Campbell, David. *Perth: the fair city*. 1994.

Groome, Francis H. (ed.) *Ordnance gazetteer of Scotland*. 1893 edition.

Haldane, A. R. B. *The drove roads of Scotland*. 1952.

Harding, Albert W. *Pullars of Perth*. 1991.

Harvie-Brown, J. A. *A fauna of the Tay basin and Strathmore*. 1906.

Henderson, Edward. *The history of Lochoreshire*. 1988.

Heward, Edmund. *Lord Mansfield*. 1979.

Hodge, J. M. *Raspberry growing in Scotland*. 1921.

House, Jack. *Pride of Perth: the story of Arthur Bell and Sons*. 1976.

Howse, Derek. *Nevil Maskelyne: the seaman's astronomer*. 1989.

Hunter, Thomas. *Woods, forests and estates of Perthshire*. 1883.

Jack, J. W. *Glenfarg and district: past and present*. ca 1920.

Kennedy, James. *Folklore and reminiscences of Strathtay and Grandtully*. 1927.

Kerr, John. *Highland highways: old roads in Atholl*. 1991.

Kerr, John. *Life in the Atholl glens*. 1993.

Leitch, Roger (ed.) *The book of Sandy Stewart*. 1988.

Lenman, Bruce. *The Jacobite risings in Britain, 1689–1746*. New ed., 1995

Liddell, Colin. *Pitlochry: heritage of a Highland district*. 1993.

Linklater, Eric & Andro. *The Black Watch*. 1977.

Lynch, Michael (et al.) *The Scottish medieval town*. 1988.

Macdonald, John A. R. *The history of Blairgowrie*. 1899.

McGibbon, David & Ross, Thomas. *The castellated and domestic architecture of Scotland*. 5 vols. 1887–1892.

Mackay, A. E. G. *History of Fife and Kinross*. 1896.

Mackay, N. D. *Aberfeldy: past and present*. 1954.

McKerracher, Archie. *Perthshire in history and legend*. 1988.

Macnair, Peter. *Perthshire*. 1912.

McNeill, Peter & Nicholson, Ranald. *An historical atlas of Scotland*. 1975.

Marshall, Thomas Hay. *The history of Perth*. 1849.

Melville, Lawrence. *Errol: its legends, lands and people*. 1935.

Melville, Lawrence. *The fair land of Gowrie*. 1939.

Miller, T. D. *Tales of a Highland parish (Glenshee)*. 1929.

Moncreiff, The Hon. Rhoderick and Alison (eds). *The annals of Kinross-shire*. 1990.

Moncreiffe, Sir Iain of that Ilk. *The Highland clans*. 2nd ed., 1982.

Munro, David. *Loch Leven and the River Leven: a landscape transformed*. 1994.

National Trust for Scotland. *Ben Lawers and its alpine flowers*. 1964.

New statistical account of Scotland: vol 9, Fife and Kinross. 1845.

New statistical account of Scotland: vol 10, Perth. 1845.

Ogilvy, Graham. *The River Tay and its people*. 1993.

Paterson, Wilma & Behan, Prof. Peter. *Salmon and women: the feminine angle*. 1990.

Peacock, David. *Perth: its annals and its archives*. 1849.

Pennant, Thomas. *A tour in Scotland, 1769 and 1772*.

Penny, George. *Traditions of Perth*. 1836.

Perth Pamphlets (volumes of newscuttings in the A. K. Bell Library, Perth).

Porteous, Alexander. *Annals of St Fillans*. 1912.

Porteous, Alexander. *The history of Crieff*. 1912.

Ramsay, A. A. W. *The arrow of Glenlyon*. 1930.

Reid, Alexander G. *The annals of Auchterarder and memorials of Strathearn*. 1899.

Robertson, J. *General view of agriculture in the county of Perth.* 1799.

Rogerson, Robert. *Quality of life in Great Britain.* 1990 and 1997 editions.

Royal Commission on the Ancient and Historical Monuments and Constructions of Scotland. *Counties of Fife, Kinross and Clackmannan.* 1933.

Royal Commission on the Ancient and Historical Monuments of Scotland. *North-east Perth: an archaeological landscape.* 1990.

Royal Commission on the Ancient and Historical Monuments of Scotland. *South-east Perth: an archaeological landscape.* 1994.

Seath, J. W. & R. E. *Dunbarney: a parish with a past.* 2nd ed., 1991.

Sinclair, Duncan McD. *By Tummel and Loch Rannoch: your ABC guide.* 1989.

Smart, Edward. *History of Perth Academy.* 1932.

Smith, Roger. *The great flood.* 1993.

Smout, T. C. *A history of the Scottish people, 1560–1830.* 1969.

Smyth, Alfred P. *Warlords and holy men: Scotland AD 80–1000.* 1984.

Statistical account of Scotland, 1791–1799: vol 11, south and east Perthshire, Kinross-shire. Reprinted 1976

Statistical account of Scotland, 1791–1799: vol 12, north and west Perthshire. Reprinted 1977.

Stavert, Marion L. *Perth: a short history.* 2nd ed., 1991.

Stewart, Alexander. *A Highland parish or, the history of Fortingall.* 1928.

Stewart, Elizabeth. *Dunkeld: an ancient city.* 1926.

Sunday Mail. *Discover Scotland: the Sunday Mail guide to Scotland's countryside.* Issued in weekly parts, 1989–1990.

Taylor, D. B. (ed.) *Third statistical account of Scotland: vol 27, the counties of Perth and Kinross.* 1979.

Tranter, Nigel. *The fortified house in Scotland: vol 2, central Scotland.* 1963.

Tranter, Nigel. *The Queen's Scotland: the heartland.* 1971.

Tullibardine, Marchioness of. *A military history of Perthshire, 1660–1902.* 1908.

Urquhart, J. D. *Historical sketches of Scone.* 1883.

Walker, Bruce & Ritchie, Graham. *Exploring Scotland's heritage: Fife and Tayside.* 1987.

Walker, Nancy. *A historical guide to the county of Kinross.* 1980.

Walker, Nancy. *Kinross House and its associations.* 1990.

Wallace, Lorne. *A village of crossroads and characters* [Dunning]. 1991.

Wheater, Hilary. *Aberfeldy to Glenlyon.* 1981.

Wheater, Hilary. *Kenmore and Loch Tay.* 1982.
Withers, C. W. J. *Gaelic Scotland: the transformation of a culture region.* 1988.

Other sources

Numerous biographies, clan and family histories, guide books, official reports, local plans, Ordnance Survey maps, and the writings in various sources of two of Perthshire's greatest historians, R. S. Fittis and the late J. E. (Eddie) Macmillan.

INDEX

Aberdalgie 140
Aberfeldy 15, 25, 28–29, 60, 66, 170, 224–229
Abernethy 39, 140, 153–154
Abernethy, Bill 69
Aberuchill Castle 129
Acharn 238
Adam, Robert 161, 170, 175
Adam, William (architect) 131, 170, 226
Adam, William (jurist) 170–171
agriculture 26, 34, 47–48, 51, 54, 63–67, 103, 114, 124, 131, 162, 238–239
Aldie, House of 172
Almondbank 180, 182–183
Alyth 2, 25, 39, 59, 102, 106–108
Amulree 39, 195–197
Appin of Dull 28, 232
Archer, William 58
Ardler 116–117
Ardoch, Roman fort at 36–38, 143–144
Ardtalnaig 194, 238
Arkwright, Richard 213
Arthurian legends 104–105, 190
Atholl 38, 49, 224–225, 246, 253–258, 261
Atholl, Dukes of 14, 46, 145, 198, 200, 204, 206–208, 213, 219, 254–256
Atholl, Katharine, Duchess of 50–51, 108, 201
Atholl and Breadalbane Community Comment 230–231
Atholl estates 14, 182, 224, 255
Atholl Highlanders 255
Auchterarder 25, 41, 45, 62, 144–147

Baird, General Sir David 131–132, 136
Balado 174
Balfour, Robert (Master of Burleigh) 178–179
Ballantine, Georgina 32–33
Ballintuim 258
Balloch Castle 237, 240
Bankfoot 3, 25, 136, 188, 213
Barlass, Kate 43
barytes 6, 29, 230
Bean, Alan 135
Begg, Robert Burns 177
Beinn a'Ghlo 253
Beinn Ghlas 9
Bell and Sons, Arthur 19, 71–72, 75
Bell, Arthur Kinmond 71

Bell, Bessie 188–189
Bell, Joseph 172
Ben Gulabin 258
Ben Lawers 8–9, 11–12, 16, 33, 236, 238
Ben Lui 28
Ben Vorlich 9, 144
Benarty Hill 159, 165
Bertha 37–38
Birnam 3, 28, 202–203
Bishop Hill 159, 167–168
Black Watch 50, 99, 226–228, 232
Black Water 113, 258
Black Wood of Rannoch 13, 246
Blackford 45, 73, 144–145
Blair Atholl 46, 225, 232, 253–254, 256
Blair Castle 44, 46, 199, 253–255
Blair family 119
Blairadam 170–171
Blairgowrie 15, 59, 63, 102, 108–113, 119, 123, 229, 258
Braco 25, 143–144
Branklyn Garden 9
Breadalbane 49, 224, 230, 236–237, 261
Breadalbane, Earls and Marquises of 22, 195–196, 214, 237–238
Breadalbane estates 224, 238
brickworks 121
Bridge of Earn 25, 62, 140, 152–153
Bruar 7, 256
Bruce, Michael 167–169, 213
Bruce, Sir William 176–177
Buchan, Alexander 168–169
Buchan, John 182
Buchanan, Dugald 242–243
Buchanty 135, 186, 190
Burleigh Castle 178–179
Burns, Robert 19, 172, 177, 229, 256

Cairnwell, The 258, 260
Caithness Glass *see* glass making
Caledonian Forest 12–13, 246
Cambusmichael 216–217
Cameron, Sir Neil (Lord Cameron of Balhousie) 55
Campbell clan 234, 236–238, 240
Campbell of Glenlyon, Robert 232, 235
Campbell of Inverawe, Major Duncan 228
Campbell-Bannerman, Sir Henry 105–106
Campsie Linn 29, 68
Cargill, Donald 112–113
Carlin Maggie 174

Carpow, Roman fort at 38
Carse of Gowrie 9, 11, 48, 58, 116–124
Castle Huntly 119
Castle Menzies 226, 231
Christianity, introduction of 38–39, 149, 165
Clan Donnachaidh Museum 7, 256
Clearances 49, 195–196, 238, 247, 257
Cleaven Dyke 211
Cleish 157, 159, 171
Cleish Hills 159, 162, 172, 176
climate 20, 89, 259–260
Clunie 210–211
Cluny House Gardens 14, 226
Collace Quarry 118
Comrie 2, 3, 66, 88, 129–131, 141
Comyn's Road 253
cotton industry 69, 213
Coupar Angus 41, 68, 102, 113–116, 241
Covenanters 44
Craig Rossie 147, 155
crannogs 35–36, 177, 197, 210, 239–240
Creag na Caillich 34
Crichton, James (Admirable Crichton) 57, 210
Crieff 3, 11, 15, 21, 45, 62, 64, 72–73, 88, 125, 132–134, 137, 141, 146, 195, 258
Croft-na-Caber 36, 239
Cromwell, Oliver 91–92, 94, 222
Crook of Devon 159, 162, 174
Cultybraggan, prisoner of war camp at 130
Currie, Sir Donald 206, 233–234

Darwin, Charles 57–58
David I 41, 92, 205, 255
deforestation 13–14, 34
Deil's Cauldron 130
depopulation 196, 253, 258
Devil's Elbow 259–260
Dewar and Sons, John 72, 150
Dewar, Lord 9
Dickson, James 18
Disruption of 1843 143, 146
Donnachaidh, Clan 246, 256–257
Douglas, Catherine 43
Douglas, David 16–17, 19
Douglas, Willie 166
Douglas fir 14, 16
Douglas-Home, Sir Alec (14th Earl of Home) 51
Dron Hill 155
droving 64–65, 142, 195–196, 253, 258
Drummond Castle 138, 141, 216
Drummond family 136, 141, 215–216
Drummond Fish Farm 129
Drumochter 224, 253, 257
Duleep Singh, Maharajah 239
Dull 41, 196, 225, 231–232
Dunalastair 246–247
Duncan, Rev Richard 137

Dundas, Henry (1st Viscount Melville) 130–131
Dundurn 128
Dunkeld 3, 11, 14, 28, 38, 41, 43–44, 60, 198–199, 203–208, 222, 225
Dunning 45, 66, 147–151
Dunsinane Hill 9–10, 38, 117–118, 203, 223
Dupplin Cross 40, 151
Dupplin estate 150–151

Earthquake House 4
earthquakes 3–4
economy 47, 63–78, 229–230, 242
Edradour Distillery 72
education 53–62, 89, 131, 167
emigration see migration
employment 63–78, 121–123, 161, 183
Encyclopaedia Perthensis 78
Episcopalianism 44, 61, 112, 141–142, 170, 205
Errol 121–123
Erskine, Rev Ebenezer 170

Fair maid of Perth, The 70, 76, 81, 98, 100, 155
Fairbairn, Sir Nicholas 50
fairies 7, 258
fairs 66, 108
Fendoch, Roman fort at 37, 189
ferries 198–199, 218
Fingalian legends 190, 193, 235
fishing 23, 30–33, 68, 164–165, 235, 252
flood defences 27
floods 24–26, 85, 90
forestry 14–15
Forneth 209–210
Fortevoit 38–40, 150–151
Fortevoit, 1st Lord 150
Fortingall 14, 59, 232–235, 241
Fortriu 38–39
Fothrif 157
Fotla 38
Fowlis Wester 134

Gairney Bridge 167–168, 170
Gannochy Trust 71, 86
Garth Castle 232, 240
Gask House 138–139
Gask Ridge watchtowers 37, 137–138
Geddes, Sir Patrick 57
General Accident Fire and Life Assurance Corporation 52, 74–75
geology 5, 12, 121
Georgetown 59, 246
Gilmerton 3, 134
Gladstone, William Ewart 61
glass making 74
Gleann Fearnach 257–258

Glen Brerachan 257
Glen Errochty 246–247, 256
Glen Garry 257
Glen Lednock 130
Glen Lyon 39, 230, 232–236, 240
Glen Quaich 195–197
Glen Tilt 21, 253
Glenalmond 28, 180, 194–195, 197
Glenalmond College 60–62, 185–186,
    191–192
Glendevon 125, 156
Glendoick Gardens 19
Gleneagles Hotel 146–147, 150
Gleneagles Spring Waters 144
Glenfarg 66, 155, 167
Glenshee 113, 143, 257–259
Glenturret Distillery 72–73, 134
Gloag, Ann 75
Gloag, Helen (Empress of Morocco) 143
Gloag and Son, Matthew 72
gold 5–6
Gow, Nathaniel 138, 199
Gow, Niel 198–199, 261
Gowrie 38
Gowrie, Earls of *see* Ruthven family
Gowrie Conspiracy 44, 97, 182, 219
Graham of Balgowan, Thomas 183–185,
    189–190
Graham of Claverhouse, John 44, 112,
    208, 252–253
Grandtully 28, 225–226
Gray, Mary 188–189
Gray family 119
Gray of Kinfauns, Lord 9, 119

Haldane family 146–147
Harrietfield 180, 186–187
Hay family 41, 116, 119–121
Heartland Radio 230–231
Henderson, Hamish 111–112
Hercules the Bear 156
Hermitage 14, 200–202
Highland Boundary Fault 2–3, 5, 15, 102,
    180, 188
history of Perthshire 34–52
Highland Spring Ltd 73, 144
Hooker, Sir William 16, 202
Huntingtower Castle 181–182
Hutton, Prof Charles 7
hydro-electricity 127, 235, 244–245, 248–
    249, 261

ice age 10–12
Inchaffray Abbey 41, 136
Inchtuthil, Roman fortress at 37–38, 211
Innerpeffray 136–137
Inver 198–200
Invergowrie 1, 54, 89, 121, 123

Jacobite uprisings 44–46, 91–92, 98, 100,
    133, 136, 138–139, 141, 149, 179, 195,
    208, 212, 216, 227–228, 247, 251–252,
    254, 261
    aftermath 46–47, 49, 242
James I 42, 53

Kay Gyroplane 55
Kenmore 30, 196, 232, 239–240
Kennaway, James 147
Kenneth MacAlpin 39–40, 150–151, 205, 222
Kettins 116, 124
Kilgraston School 62, 151
Killiecrankie 44, 247, 251
Killiecrankie, Battle of 44, 208, 251–252
Kinfauns Castle 119
Kinkell parish 137
Kinkell Bridge 137
Kinloch, George 117
Kinloch Rannoch 242–243, 246
Kinnaird family 121, 123
Kinnesswood 162, 167–169
Kinnoull Hill 9, 22, 29, 96, 101, 117, 140
Kinross 25, 157, 159, 161, 166, 168, 172,
    174–177
Kinross Advertiser 158
Kinross House 176–177
Kinross-shire 157–179, 233
Kinrossie 117
Kirk, Rev Robert 7
Kirkmichael 113, 257–258
Knox, John 43, 90–91, 93, 222
land ownership 47, 144–145

language 43, 47, 49, 60, 112, 139–140,
    229, 261
Lansdowne, Marquis of 212
Lawers 131, 237–238
Lawers House 131
Lawers, Lady of 237–238
lead mining 5
Ledlanet Nights 178
Little Glenshee 188
local government reorganisation 1, 41,
    128, 158
Loch Earn 9, 125–128, 210–211, 236
Loch Ericht 5, 244
Loch Faskally 248–249
Loch Freuchie 197
Loch Leven 149, 157, 159–160, 162–169,
    176–177
Loch of the Lowes 22, 209
Loch Rannoch 8, 13, 15, 224, 230, 236,
    242–246, 248
Loch Tay 5, 8, 28, 33, 35–36, 126–127,
    180, 194, 224, 232, 236–240, 246
Loch Tummel 8, 197, 243, 248–249
Locus Breadalbane 229–230

Logiealmond 134, 180, 184–190, 198
Logierait 28, 224–225
Longforgan 1, 19, 39, 89
Lynedoch, Lord see Graham of
    Balgowan, Thomas

Mac Fisheries 67
Macbeth 10, 166, 202
McEwen, John 145
Macgregor clan 235, 241–242
Macintosh, Charles 198–200, 203
Macintyre, Duncan Ban 46
Mackenzie, Alexander 206
Mackenzie, Rev William 3
Mackintosh, Charles Rennie 233
Maclaren, Ian *see* Watson, John
MacLaren, James 233
MacLean, Dougie 207
Macnab clan 127
Macpherson, James 47, 190–191
Malcolm Canmore 10, 40, 146, 154, 203, 215
Mansfield, Earls of 208, 219–221
Mar, Earl of 45
Mary, Queen of Scots 166, 176
Maskelyne, Nevil 7–8
Massacre of Glencoe 235
Matthew, Patrick 57–58
Mause, ghost of 113
Meigle 102–106
Meikleour 14–15, 29, 102, 211–212
Menzies clan 41, 231
Menzies, Archibald 16
Mercer family 99–100, 172, 212
Methven Castle 135
migration 2, 34, 48, 127, 196
Millais, Sir John Everett 96–97, 202
Miller, James 146, 150
Millhaugh Bridge 188
Milnathort 25, 157, 159, 175, 177–178
Minigaig pass 46, 253, 257
Mitchison, Naomi 147
Monart glass *see* glass making
Moncreiffe Hill 29, 140, 152–153, 155
Moncreiffe of that Ilk, Sir Iain 141
Montrose, Marquis of 44
Morison family 77–78
Moulin 225, 251–252, 257
Murray, Sir David (Lord Scone and
    Viscount Stormont) 219
Murray, Lord George 45–46
Murray, William (1st Earl of Mansfield)
    172, 220–221
Murrays of Tullibardine 182, 255
Murthly Castle 214, 226
Muthill 45, 137, 141–142, 149, 216

Neish clan 127
Neish Island 126–127

Nicoll, Robert 213
Nine Maidens 154–155

Ochil Hills 5, 25, 155–157, 159, 162, 172,
    210, 261
Ochtertyre House 131
Old Blair 252–253
Oliphant, Carolina (Lady Nairne) 138–139, 261
Oliphant family 41, 138–139
ospreys 22–23, 209
Ossian 190–193

pearl fishing 69
Perth 3, 9, 11, 19, 24–25, 29, 41, 43,
    45–46, 49–50, 66, 69–72, 75, 79–101,
    125, 140, 152, 172, 181, 188, 195, 212,
    218–219, 221, 242
    A K Bell Library 71, 81, 86
    Aerodrome 55
    Battle of the Clans 100–101
    Bell's Sports Centre 71, 85–86
    Branklyn Garden 16, 18
    Bridgend 27, 95–96
    bull sales 65
    capital of Scotland 42, 52–53
    Cherrybank Gardens 19
    City Hall 82–83, 99
    city walls 90
    Civic Trust 56, 94, 99
    County Buildings 97
    Cromwell's citadel 44, 91, 100
    Dewar's Rinks 84–85
    Fair Maid's House 98
    Fairfield 87–88
    Fergusson Gallery 48, 85
    Festival of the Arts 86–87
    harbour 27, 29–30
    High Street 77, 80–82, 93, 99, 218
    Inches 24–26, 44, 85, 88, 95–96,
        99–101, 155, 218
    Leisure Pool 84
    monasteries 41, 43, 90
    Moncreiffe Island 101
    Museum and Art Gallery 25, 33, 83,
        85, 99
    New Town 49, 56, 95
    Perth Bridge 26–27, 44, 49, 80, 90
        95–97, 181, 218
    Perth in Bloom 88
    Queen's Bridge 25, 97, 99
    royal burgh 41, 221
    St John's Centre 82
    St John's Kirk 26, 43, 83, 90–92, 96,
        99–100
    St Paul's Church 98
    schools 55–59, 96, 220
    Tay Street 27, 80, 87, 93, 97–98, 101
    Theatre 24, 71, 87

Town Lade 27, 180–181
university 53–54
Perth and Kinross Council area x, 1
Perth and Kinross District 1, 89, 116, 128, 158, 236
Perth, 3rd Duke of 46, 133, 138
Perthshire (former county) 1, 42, 116, 123, 128, 236
Perthshire Advertiser 1, 79, 88, 213, 238
Perthshire Canal 125–126
Perthshire Tourist Board ix, 76, 116
Picts 21, 36, 38–40, 103–104, 128, 134–135, 151, 154, 221
Pitcairngreen 183–184
Pitkeathly Wells 151–152
Pitlochry 6, 22, 25, 59, 72, 202, 224–225, 230, 248–251
plant life 10, 12, 108
politics 50–51
Pontius Pilate 234
population 1, 101, 108–109, 160, 222
Potter, Beatrix 199–200, 202–203
Pow of Inchaffray 135–136
Pullar and Son, John 49, 70

quality of life survey 89
Queen's View 248–249

Rachel House 177
Raid of Angus 257
railways 29–30, 49, 67, 71, 76–77, 95, 119, 123, 202, 245–246, 248
Ramsays of Bamff 107–108
Rannoch 21, 49, 60, 197, 224, 240–247
Rannoch Moor 10, 224, 244–245
Rannoch School 62, 246
Rannoch Station 242, 245
Rattray 108–109, 111–113
reed beds 122–123
Reformation 43, 90–92, 115, 205, 219, 222
Renton, John and Dorothy 17
River Almond 27–28, 37, 69, 136, 180–181, 186, 188, 190, 194, 212
River Ardle 113, 258
River Braan 14, 28, 197–198, 200–202
River Devon 156, 173
River Earn 11, 26, 28, 37, 125–126, 128–132, 135–137, 140, 144
River Ericht 28, 102, 108–109, 112–113, 258
River Garry 28, 248, 251, 254, 256
River Isla 28, 37, 102, 209
River Lyon 28, 232, 234
River Tay 11, 13, 22, 24–33, 37–38, 44, 67–69, 99, 118–119, 122, 125, 140, 154–155, 180–181, 198, 203–204, 208, 212–214, 216, 218–219, 221, 225–226, 234, 239, 260

River Tummel 13, 28, 225, 243, 247, 249–250, 257
roads, military 141–142, 198
roads, Roman 216
roads, Wade 45–46, 192–195, 226, 251, 253, 257
Robertson, Alexander (Dundonnachie) 204
Robertson of Struan, Alexander 46, 138, 240, 247
Robertsons of Struan 246–247
Roman Catholicism 44, 205, 215
Romans 20, 36–38, 93, 130, 137–138, 143–144, 169, 189, 211, 218, 234
Rossie Priory 121
royal burghs 41, 146
Royal Naval Aircraft Workshops 182–183
Ruggles-Brise, Lady Dorothea 200
Rumbling Bridge (Kinross-shire) 159, 172–174
Rumbling Bridge (Perthshire) 198
Ruskin, John 96
Ruthven family 181–182, 219

St Adamnan 222, 232, 235
St Columba 38, 205, 222, 232
St Donevald 154
St Fillans 126–128
St Fink 154–155
St Johnstone FC 83–84
St Madoes 39, 120
St Margaret 40, 215
St Ninian 39
St Serf 149, 165
salmon 21, 23, 30, 67, 217–218, 250, 252
salmon fishing *see* fishing
salmon netting 23, 67–68
Sandeman family 70–71
Schiehallion 6–8, 11, 224, 240, 243, 247–249
Scone 11, 16–17, 35, 38, 40–42, 45, 55, 93, 216, 219, 221–222
Scone Palace 16, 121, 189, 218–220, 222–223
Scotlandwell 160, 167, 169
Scots, early history of 39, 128, 221
Scots Language Resource Centre 140
Scott, Sir Walter 70, 76–77, 81, 98, 100, 155, 170–171, 191
Scottish Campaign for Public Angling 32
Scottish Crop Research Institute 54
Secession Church 168, 170
Sheriffmuir, Battle of 45, 195
sheriffs 41, 146, 157, 240
shielings 238–239
Sidlaws 5, 102, 117–119, 123, 210, 261
ski-ing 20, 259–260
slate 5

Sma Glen 37, 134, 180, 185, 189–195
Small, James 240–242
Society in Scotland for Propagating
    Christian Knowledge 47, 59, 197, 242
soft fruit industry 63–64, 110–111
Sommersett, James 221
Soutar, William 81, 140, 261
Souter, Brian 75
souterrains 35
Sow of Atholl 257
Spittal of Glenshee 21, 258–260
Stagecoach 75–76
standing stones 34, 252
Stanley 29, 213, 218
Stanley Mill 213–214, 216–217
Stewart, Alexander (Wolf of Badenoch)
    206, 232, 257
Stewart, George Drummond 215
Stewart, Dr Margaret 94
Stewart, Sir William Drummond 214–215
Stewart of Garth, General David 190,
    228, 232
Stobhall 215–216
Stone of Destiny 221–223
Stone, Jerome 190–191
Stormont 180, 208–215, 219
Stormontfield 216–218
Strathallan School 62, 151
Strathardle 258
Strathbraan 28, 180, 188, 195, 198
Strathearn 37–38, 45, 102, 125–156
Strathmore 15, 37, 102–117, 124
Strathtay 28, 226
Struan 246, 256
Stuc a' Chroin 9, 144
suffragettes 49, 129

Tarmachans 9, 236
Tay Access Group 32
Tay Foundation 68
Taymouth Castle 214, 219, 237,
    239–240
Tayside Regional Council 1, 14, 26, 60,
    118, 260

textile industry 69–70, 106, 109–110, 149,
    161–162, 213
Thief of Glenalmond 194–195
Thomson, Ian 144
Tibbermore, Battle of 44
Todd and Duncan 161
tourism 29, 47, 49, 51, 76–77, 109, 160,
    195, 202, 229–230, 239, 251, 254
Towser 72
travellers 110–112
trees 12–14, 203, 234, 256
Tullibardine Distillery 144
Tummel Bridge 232, 247

United Auctions 65
University of the Highlands and Islands
    54
University of St Andrews 53–54, 95, 232
Vane Farm 165, 169

Vasart glass see glass making
Victoria, Queen 76, 202, 237–239,
    248–249, 255
Vikings 39, 154

Wade, General George 192–193, 231,
    247, 253, 257
Wade Stone 257
Wallace Road 155
Walls, Maggie 148–149
Watson, John (Ian Maclaren) 186–188
Waulkmill 218
Weem 225, 231
Wester Balgedie 167
whisky industry 52, 70–72, 144, 178
White, Dr Francis Buchanan 19
wildlife 20–23, 165, 209, 251, 260
witches 100, 134, 148–149, 174
wolves 20–21
Wordsworth, William 191–192
Wyntoun, Andrew of 166

Yellow London Lady 8
Ysart family 74